DATE DUE

NOV 1 8 2006		
AUG 1 2 2009		
APR 0 8 2010		

Demco

The

gy

ng

vis

Published in 2005 by:
Nelson Thornes Ltd
Delta Place
27 Bath Road
CHELTENHAM
GL53 7TH
United Kingdom

05 06 07 08 09 / 10 9 8 7 6 5 4 3 2 1

A catalogue record for this book is available from the British Library

ISBN 0 7487 9037 3

Page make-up by Florence Production Ltd

Printed and bound in Spain by GraphyCems

Contents

•••••• Preface   v

•••••• Acknowledgements   vi

•••••• Chapter 1   The Learner and the Teacher   1

Defining learning and teaching
Visions of the learner
Visions of the teacher
A model of reflectivity for this book
Reflectivity and craft-knowledge
Conclusions and personal reflections

•••••• Chapter 2   Cognitive Development and Learning   17

Piagetian theory
Vygotskian theory
The modular challenge to constructivist theories
Conclusions and personal reflections

•••••• Chapter 3   Intelligence and Academic Ability   41

Intelligence and academic ability
Intelligence as a social construct
The importance of beliefs about intelligence
IQ testing
General intelligence and multiple intelligences
Sternberg's triarchic theory of intelligence
Developing intelligence and educational ability
Conclusions and personal reflections

•••••• Chapter 4   Styles of Thinking, Learning and Studying   71

Defining terms: cognitive style, learning strategy and learning style
What makes a good system for classifying learning styles?
Cognitive styles
Field dependence
Multidimensional systems of learning styles
Comparing the systems
Learning strategies
Conclusions and personal reflections

•••••• Chapter 5   Thinking Skills   95

What are thinking skills?
The rationale underlying current work on developing thinking
Programmes for the development of thinking skills
Thinking skills in higher education
Conclusions and personal reflections

•••••• **Chapter 6   Motivation**   117

The significance of motivation
Maslow's hierarchy of needs
Self-determination theory
Attribution theory
Self-efficacy
Goal orientation theory
The effect of expectations on motivation
Conclusions and personal reflections

•••••• **Chapter 7   Emotional Factors in Learning**   137

Learning and relationships
Research into relationships and education
Peer relationships
Emotional intelligence
Conclusions and personal reflections

•••••• **Chapter 8   ICT and Learning**   163

Explanations of some basic terms
Evidence for the effectiveness of ILT in enhancing learning
Factors affecting the uptake of ICT and ILT
Benefits of ILT: the constructivist understanding
Benefits of ILT: the social constructivist understanding
Individual differences in ILT use
Conclusions and personal reflections

•••••• **Chapter 9   Teacher Stress**   179

The legal context
Defining teacher stress: where psychology meets politics
The experience of teacher stress
Causal factors in teacher stress
A transactional picture
Managing teacher stress
Conclusions and personal reflections

•••••• **Chapter 10   Education Research**   203

The historical context
The aims and purpose of education research
Epistemological foundations
Qualitative and quantitative methods
Major research methods
Multiple studies: review and meta-analysis
Criticisms and limitations of education research
Conclusions and personal reflections

•••••• **References**   224

•••••• **Index**   243

Preface

This is a textbook of modern educational psychology and its application in enhancing the quality of classroom teaching. Each chapter focuses on one factor affecting the quality of learning and explains how a range of theories and up-to-date research can be applied in the classroom. Cognitive factors, including cognitive development, intelligence, learning styles and thinking skills are covered in detail, and additional influences, including motivational and emotional factors. The final three chapters are concerned with professional issues and address the effective use of information learning technology, teacher stress and the conduct and application of educational research.

There is no shortage of useful textbooks on the psychology of education, but this book is a little different, based on a distinctive philosophy. I deliberately set out to avoid writing a general introduction to psychology angled towards teachers; nor did I want to produce a tool kit of strategies for the application of psychology. This is not to say that such books cannot be very helpful, but they have been done well before and I had a different vision. The aim of this book is to enhance teachers' professional understanding of their work by putting across a detailed understanding of some 'real' psychology. By 'real' I mean the sort of ideas that are used by modern psychologists and which underlie education policy.

As both a practising teacher and chartered psychologist, I have been struck by how much psychology can be used in teaching but how often it is not. In *The Psychology of Effective Learning and Teaching* I have sought to identify a range of ideas that form the focus of exciting current research, but which also have clear applications in the real world of the classroom. I believe that identifying and working with this interface between real education and cutting-edge psychology is the key to developing professional practice in teaching.

This book is aimed at all training and qualified teachers. I have aimed to be clear enough to be comprehensible to those new to psychology, teaching or both, but at the same time challenging and up-to-date enough to be of interest to the experienced practitioner, particularly those undertaking higher degrees in education. I hope you find it useful and, as I did when I began to delve into the literature on psychology of education, I hope you discover a whole new range of professional practices and interests.

Matt Jarvis

Acknowledgements

Photo credits

Nassif Jeremie/Corbis Sygma (p. 51)
Cheri Stahl/Robert Sternberg/Yale University (p. 57)
Gary Wolstenholm/Photographers Direct (p. 78)

Dedication

To the memory of Peter Jarvis

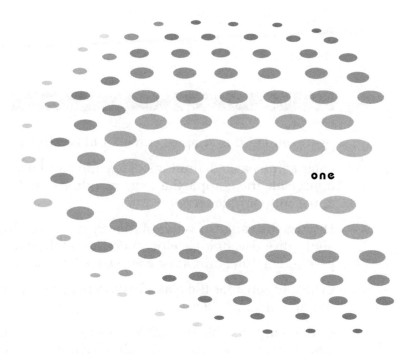

one

The Learner
and the
Teacher

The Learner and the Teacher

learning objectives

By the end of this chapter you should be able to:

• Offer some basic definitions of learning and teaching and appreciate the complexities surrounding defining these apparently simple terms.

• Discuss the range of views of the learner according to alternative psychological perspectives, including the cognitive, psychodynamic, humanistic and social constructionist.

• Critically consider the classification of teachers as executive, therapeutic and liberationist.

• Understand the role of craft-knowledge in teaching and appreciate the political dimensions of linking teaching to the crafts.

• Describe and evaluate the notion of teaching as a reflective profession with particular reference to the work of Schon and the work of Jennings and Kennedy, and appreciate the model of reflectivity offered in this book.

• Be familiar with the findings of research into perceptions among learners and teachers of what makes an effective teacher.

Defining learning and teaching

Given that we all learn, it is unsurprising that we all have an intuitive idea of what learning is. However, when we pause and try to define learning in depth, we cannot help but be struck by the awesome breadth and complexity of the concept. Classic psychological definitions of learning, free from the context of education include 'the mechanism by which organisms adapt to their environment' and 'the process by which relatively permanent changes occur in behavioural potential as a result of experience' (J. R. Anderson, 1995; cited in Gross, 2000, p. 145). However, while these simple definitions capture the essential elements of learning that it involves change to the individual through experience, to the educator they raise more questions than they answer: What are the mechanisms by which we learn? Does learning take place within an individual or is it an interpersonal process? Should we think of it as a set of cognitive mechanisms or rather as an emotional, social and motivational experience? Does everyone learn or learn most effectively the same way? What should be the focus of learning, facts or skills? Is the capacity of the individual to learn fixed or variable according to their experience? The aim of this book is to tackle these and other issues.

Arriving at a simple definition of teaching can be equally problematic. McIntyre (2000, p. 3) offers the elegantly simple 'acting so as to facilitate learning'. This type of definition is helpful in reminding us that the 'bottom line' as to whether an educational practice is 'correct' is not defined by the use or non-use of any particular technique or strategy, but rather by its impact on the learner. There are of course numerous views as to what actions best serve the aim of facilitating learning, predicated largely on the alternative visions of learning outlined above. As well as methodological debates over the relative effectiveness of different teaching activities, we are beset with ideological debates over the function of the teacher. For example, should the teacher be an agent of social stability, transmitting cultural norms of world understanding, or rather an agent of social change, subverting the status quo? The aim of this chapter is to introduce some of the ways psychologists and educationalists have conceived of the learner and the teacher.

Visions of the learner

Psychology differs from other contemporary sciences in that it is not a unified body of knowledge and understanding but instead depends on a number of alternative theoretical perspectives or *paradigms*. Each psychological paradigm has the potential to offer a different vision of the nature of the learner, and it can be instructive to step back from the obvious shared attributes of those individuals engaged in learning and consider the variety of ways in which as teachers and psychologists we think about the people we work with. This chapter outlines four paradigms particularly important to education, and we can see how each has influenced educational theory and practice.

Cognitive psychology: the learner as information processor

Cognitive psychology has been the dominant paradigm in both academic psychology and education for over three decades. Cognitive psychologists are concerned with mental processes such as perception, attention, memory, language and thinking. There are important individual differences in cognition that can have a profound effect on learning. The notion of *intelligence* reflects the cultural belief that cognitive ability is quantifiable and that as individuals we have a varying amount of such ability. There are now a range of theories of intelligence, some of which challenge the cultural norm of intelligence as a fixed quantitative and measurable psychological entity, explored in depth in Chapter 3. A once radical approach to cognitive ability, rapidly growing in influence at the time of writing, concerns the extent to which thinking skills can be learnt during formal education. This idea, which runs counter to traditional ideas of intelligence, is currently being explored in a number of programmes (discussed in Chapter 5). Recent years have seen a growing acceptance that, irrespective of quantitative differences in cognitive ability, individual learners are characterised by qualitative differences, or *learning styles*. People with different learning styles process information differently, leading them to orient towards particular subjects, modes of presentation and teaching styles. Learning styles are discussed in detail in Chapter 4.

Cognitive developmental psychology has taught us about the ways cognition develops throughout the lifespan. Most significantly it has elucidated developments in children's thinking from birth to adolescence. In contrast to the emphasis of 'pure' cognitive psychologists on organisation of learning material, the cognitive development theories of Jean Piaget and Lev Vygotsky (Chapter 2) emphasise the role of active learning in which the learner makes full use of their information-processing capabilities by actively engaging with learning material rather than passively receiving it. These differences in emphasis underlie some important debates regarding effective teaching strategies.

Psychodynamic psychology and the emotional learner

The dominant representation of learning is of an intellectual process, best understood in terms of cognitive psychology. However, learning and teaching can also be intensely emotional experiences, and the acknowledgement of this has led to an alternative approach to education, dominated by *psychodynamic* thinking. The psychodynamic approach to psychology derives from classical psychoanalytic theory, in particular the work of Sigmund Freud and the object relations theorists (Jarvis, 2004a). Psychodynamic psychology focuses on emotion rather than cognition and emphasises the importance of relation-ships, early experiences, subjective experience and the unconscious mind.

There are several ways in which psychodynamic principles can be helpful in understanding learning and teaching. Both learners and teachers bring with them a unique developmental history to every learning situation. Thus when a student experiences a powerful irrational response to a situation such as meeting a new teacher or studying a new topic, we can often understand this using the tools of psychoanalytic theory (Wittenberg *et al.*, 1983; Coren, 1997). For example, a child with a loving mother and harsh father may *transfer* the qualities of these relationships on to teachers and thus respond well to female teachers but badly to male teachers. Teachers are far from immune to such irrational responses, whether to learners, colleagues or institutions. The aim of psychoanalytic practice is *insight*, and it can prove extremely helpful for teachers to recognise such responses and to understand them in terms of their developmental history. *Educational therapy* involves the application of psychodynamic therapeutic techniques to helping learners who have emotionally based problems with learning. Psychodynamic thinking and the emotional influences on learning are explored in detail in Chapter 7.

Humanistic psychology: the learner and human potential

Humanistic psychology is perhaps more a philosophical and ideological position than a psychological paradigm in the same way as cognitive and psychodynamic psychology (Hayes, personal communication). Humanistic psychologists emphasise human freedom of choice, potential and innate 'goodness'. The movement emerged as a reaction to the psychology of the early twentieth century, which was dominated by the crude and mechanistic *behaviourism*, which revolved around conditioning experiments on animals, and the complex and speculative Freudian psychoanalysis. To humanistic psychologists, other approaches to psychology take an unduly negative view of human nature. Instead the learner is seen as striving for personal achievement, motivated to become the best person they can (Rogers, 1961).

Humanistic psychology has been more directly influential in American education than in the UK. However, humanistic theory has proved important in the development of psychologists' understanding of motivation and relationships, and it underlies some of the most popular approaches to counselling used in education. Perhaps more importantly, humanistic principles are important in the view education professionals take of learners. A positive view of human nature and human potential can underlie good teacher–learner relationships and high expectations of achievement, both reliable indicators of educational effectiveness (Chapters 6 and 7).

The socially constructed learner

To many psychologists, sociologists, cultural theorists and educationalists, we now live in a *postmodern* era. A detailed exposition of postmodernism is outside the scope of this book, but put simply, postmodernists have challenged the unquestioning acceptance of the existence of 'facts' and the objectivity of 'grand narratives' such as science (Lyotard, 1984). Instead of acceptance of facts, psychologists influenced by postmodernism, broadly known as *social constructionists*, encourage us to look for the influence of social, political and historical influences on the development of popular ideas. Such ideas can then be reframed not as facts but as 'social constructs'.

Using the tools of social constructionism, it can be instructive to think of the ways in which current political and social agendas affect our view of education. Current discourses around education in the public domain see learners very much in terms of their achievements in public examinations. This in turn leads us to judge educational techniques and institutions in terms of their effectiveness, defined in terms of examination achievements. There is always a temptation to adopt such popular discourses uncritically, but a social constructionist perspective encourages us to take a step back and see this view of learners not as an immutable fact but rather as having been socially constructed for political benefit; for example, putting emphasis on the easily measurable in order to facilitate achievement of national targets.

One branch of social constructionism, known as *critical psychology*, has focused particular attention on deconstructing psychological concepts. Critical psychology has proved useful to educationalists by challenging the origins of many of the ideas we work with. For example, teachers and psychologists influenced by social constructionism might see *intelligence* or *ability* (Chapter 3) as having been constructed for political purposes, for example to maintain the class system or to restrict immigration (p. 44). *Gender*, the term referring to the psychological rather than biological aspects of sex, can similarly be seen as existing in order to maintain the social dominance of men by positioning women as nurturing and submissive. Social constructionists (e.g. Burman, 1994) have been damning of psychological theories such as *attachment theory* (p. 142) which have positioned women in particular social roles.

Thinking in this way about psychological concepts such as intelligence, gender and attachment poses us with a challenge. Intellectually stimulating as it can be to deconstruct cherished psychological constructs, is social constructionism useful to psychologists and teachers dedicated to achieving practical benefits for learners? The answer seems to be yes, provided we can think past the obvious and avoid the throwing out of practically valuable babies with socio-political bathwater. Potentially abusive constructs like attachment and intelligence still have important practical applications. To take the example of intelligence, it should be possible to simultaneously maintain deep concerns about the traditional view of intelligence as a single, unchangeable and measurable psychological entity on the basis that this can be used to discriminate against working-class learners, and at the same time to make use of contemporary theories of intelligence to design programmes of study that make optimum use of learners' mental abilities. Drawing on the psychoanalytic practice of Wilfred Bion (1962), we can describe this simultaneous awareness of practical applications and socio-political implications by the metaphor of *binocular vision*. For the critically minded practitioner it may be that this type of binocular vision is essential, although of course it may be implicit rather than conscious. As a practitioner it can be something of a luxury to think purely in critical psychological terms as this inevitably means to de-emphasise the practical value of pedagogical tools. It may also encourage the development of cynicism.

Visions of the teacher

Teaching has existed as an occupation for over 2000 years, but during that time and across a range of societies the teacher has assumed a range of forms and been seen as serving a range of functions. In the twentieth-first century there are still important debates concerning the nature and purpose of the teacher. Teaching can, for example, be defined in terms of its ideological position. Dating back to Socrates there has been a tradition of teaching as a subversive activity, in which the role of the teacher has been to show learners how to question the status quo. This tradition was encapsulated for many by Postman and Weingartner's (1971) concept of the 'crap-detector'. Unsurprisingly, government policy has never supported the notion of subversive teaching, and as McIntyre (2000) reminds us, Socrates was put to death for the crime of 'corrupting youth'.

Fenstermacher and Soltis' classification of teachers

Fenstermacher and Soltis (1992) have made the influential distinction between teachers as executives, therapists and liberationists. The *executive* model of the teacher sees the teacher as orienting their skills and knowledge to achieve optimum learning. They thus place most emphasis on planning lessons so as to deliver knowledge in the most efficient manner. By contrast, the *therapist* model sees teachers as primarily responsible for the psychologically healthy development of learners and thus sees pastoral care as a higher priority. The *liberationist* model is more concerned with helping the learner become independent and freethinking. This is achieved by an emphasis on teaching thinking and learning skills.

Although the therapist model has clear roots in the psychodynamic tradition of education, and executive and liberationist models can be viewed in terms of different cognitive traditions, it would be a mistake to link these models too closely with the major psychological paradigms. Personality and ideology are probably at least as important in a teaching model as are teachers' implicit psychological paradigm. The highly empathic educator is thus likely to orient towards a therapist model and the conformist is likely to orient towards the currently dominant social representation of education and adopt a more executive position.

Useful as Fenstermacher and Soltis' model can be for teachers seeking insight into their educational beliefs and practices, it is worth remembering that all teaching involves an eclectic fusion of executive, therapist and libera-tionist roles, and that what the model describes is degrees of emphasis rather than three distinct camps of practitioners. A further limitation of the model is that it assumes a lack of awareness on the part of teachers of the interactions between effective delivery, emotionally healthy learners and effective learning strategies and attitudes. It is well established that emotionally well-adjusted learners have greater capacity to attend to and retain information and that developing higher thinking skills leads to better recall of information. Thus an effective teacher, even where their explicit goals are framed in terms of the development of knowledge and achievement of qualifications (an executive), will implicitly attend to the emotional needs and thinking and learning skills of learners. Similarly, a (therapist) teacher whose explicit emphasis is on the fulfilment and adjustment of their charges will probably acknowledge the advantages to both fulfilment and adjustment conveyed by achieving a higher level of qualification.

Craft-knowledge and teaching

The term 'craft-knowledge' refers to the 'capacity for fluent, insightful, only half-conscious intuitive judgement . . . which is most characteristic of the highly experienced and expert teacher' (McIntyre, 2000). In other words, it is the almost indefinable weaving together of the skills exercised during effective pedagogy, such that the teacher can respond instantaneously and produc-tively to the multiple needs and constantly changing scenarios of the classroom. The term 'craft' serves as an analogy, comparing this process to that employed by expert craftsmen. While there is little doubt that teachers employ craft-knowledge, the term has a political dimension; if teaching is a craft in the same way as say carpentry, can teaching simultaneously be said to be a profession? I return to this question after discussing the notion of the teacher as reflective professional.

The teacher as reflective professional

A broad vision widely espoused by educationalists has been of the teacher as a 'reflective professional'. The term has become so widely and inconsistently used that it has to some extent been devalued. Nonetheless, it captures effectively the essence of teaching as having professional status and the teacher as an active participant in individual professional development and as a contributor to wider pedagogical development. There are now a number of different understandings of reflectivity, but they share the belief that a profes-sional such as a teacher or psychologist can develop by thinking about their practice, understand it better and refine it using these insights.

Schon's approach

The most influential view of reflective practice comes from Schon (1983, 1987). Schon has proposed a complex model of professional expertise by drawing on cognitive and social constructionist theory. Based on social constructionist awareness, Schon proposed that professions entered a crisis by the 1980s due to the growing awareness of the limitations of *technical rationality*, the dominant belief that professional ability could be understood simply in terms of mastering a set of skills. Based on a cognitive understanding of automatic processing of information (Allport, 1980; Tharp and Gallimore, 1991) Schon developed the term 'knowledge in action' to describe the ability of the experienced professional to respond automatically to a situation without diverting attentional resources and distraction. Rather than subscribing to technical rationality, Schon suggested that professional expertise could be better understood in terms of 'professional artistry', whereby experienced professionals make use of knowledge in action.

To Schon the reflective professional is distinguished by the capacity to consciously bring to bear a subjective awareness of their knowledge in action. This means that actions that would otherwise be implicit and automatic become explicit and can be reflected upon individually and shared in a process of professional discourse. Much of this reflection occurs simultaneously with the action, thus the reflective professional is constantly analysing and modifying their practice. This is called *reflection in action*. This is not, as has sometimes been suggested, to devalue the automatic processing involved in responding to situations in the form of craft-knowledge, but rather to suggest that conscious reflection upon these automatic processes is an effective tool of professional development.

Schon's ideas have been enormously influential in educational academia. The concept of reflectivity has enormous *heuristic* value (i.e. as a cognitive tool to aid thinking about a topic) among those seeking to look at development of pedagogy. Among practitioners the term 'reflective practice' has also proved something of a rallying cry for those seeking to improve the professional status of teachers and been linked closely with Schon. However, there are limitations to Schon's view of reflective practice. His emphasis on constant reflection in action minimises the importance of other reflective processes, such as retrospective analysis of practice in the form of logs (Bain *et al.*, 2002; Kerry and Wilding, 2004) and emotional self-awareness as emphasised by psychodynamic practitioners (Wittenberg *et al.* 1983).

There are, in addition, *epistemological* difficulties with Schon's work, i.e. with his philosophy of knowledge. Usher *et al.* (1997) suggest a logical inconsistency between reflection in action as a *feature* of professional practice and deliberate attempts to *apply* Schon's model by demonstrating reflectivity. Those influenced by Schon can only try to apply the model and, by definition, this cannot be to achieve Schon's ideal. In addition, Schon's liberal mix of cognitive and social constructionist principles is epistemologically messy, fusing theoretical ideas based on largely incompatible views of the nature of knowledge and human understanding. Cognitive psychology is part of a *positivist* tradition, which sees knowledge in the form of facts to be discovered, whereas the postmodern epistemology of social constructionism rejects such facts. In the light of this incompatibility there is a question as to whether a theory combining cognitive and social constructionist principles can be said to hang together logically.

Alternative views of reflectivity

The reflective practitioner can draw on several sources of information, and one important emphasis in more recent work of reflective practice has been on elucidating these sources. Zeichner and Tabachnick (2001), cited in Kerry and Wilding (2004), have suggested four perspectives from which to understand reflective practice in education. These are shown in Box 1.1.

Zeichner and Tabachnick's classification has the advantage of breadth, encompassing a role for planning, application of research and consideration of the individual needs of the learner. It also serves as a useful template for the education professional wishing to develop their capacity for reflection after action. However, appealingly simple and comprehensive as this classification system appears, there are potential limitations. On one hand, its very breadth takes away precision from the term *reflectivity*. Is the teacher who prepares elaborate lessons with careful consideration of both content and mode of delivery demonstrating reflectivity or simply effective planning? Can the teacher who pays particular attention to catering for the needs of a learner with an unusual learning style or learning difficulty be said to be *reflective* or rather sensitive and considerate? Certainly this broad definition of reflectivity moves away from Schon's use of the term, particularly as most 'reflection' in this broad sense takes place outside the classroom and cannot be seen in terms of reflection in action. The acknowledgement of the socio-political backdrop to education certainly suggests a *thoughtful* professional, but not necessarily one engaged in reflection on refining their practice.

Box 1.1

Zeichner and Tabachnick's classification of reflective practice

- *The academic perspective*: concerned primarily with reflection on subject matter.
- *The social efficiency perspective*: concerned with reading and applying education research.
- *The developmentalist perspective*: concerned with reflecting on the needs of learners.
- *The social reconstructionist perspective*: concerned with reflecting on the broader socio-political context of education.

On the other hand, comprehensive as this classification at first appears, it is not complete. A critical aspect of reflectivity not addressed by Zeichner and Tabachnick concerns personal insight – the psychodynamic domain of reflectivity. Drawing on Schon's model of the reflective practitioner and on psychoanalytic theory, Jennings and Kennedy (1996) suggest that the failure to reflect on professional practice can be a defensive response to change. Thus whenever teachers are faced with changes in systems – precisely when reflection is most valuable – the temptation is to *act* rather than reflect in order to escape the demands of thinking. This sort of *defensive unthinking* can also arise in response to other forms of stress, such as in dealing with learners in the aftermath of 'unthinkable' personal tragedy (Iszatt and Colmer, 1996) or sexual abuse (Trowell *et al.*, 1996). A feature of all psychodynamic practice is *self-awareness* in the sense of monitoring emotional responses to individuals, clients, institutions and systems (Jennings and Kennedy, 1996). From this perspective, perhaps the most important thing to reflect on is oneself. Jennings (1996) suggests that an important practical application of their approach lies in providing 'thinking space' in which teachers and other education professionals can reflect on their emotional responses to their learners, colleagues, managers and systems. This can be achieved through mentoring, supervision and the planned integration of personal and professional development.

11

A model of reflectivity for this book

I suggest that adopting a reflective attitude to reading can enhance the useful-ness of a textbook like this. This is not to propose a grand overarching framework with which to understand reflectivity in the sense of Schon's work. Its aim is simply to help the reader apply the psychological theory and research presented here to their own practice – what we might term 'reflec-tion in reading'. Throughout this book there are periodic 'reflection point' boxes. Broadly, reflection points aim to encourage three types of reflection in reading:

- reflection on the relationship between theory and/or research and professional practice;
- reflection on personal responses to psychological theory and/or research findings;
- reflection on personal characteristics as identified by psychological theory and/or research.

The relationship between theory and practice

This book is concerned with psychological theory and research. This can often be a source of frustration rather than inspiration to busy practitioners, to whom the insights of psychologists can appear as overly academic, jargon-ridden and divorced from the realities of life in the classroom. However, if we value the notion of reflective practice, one of its important aspects involves considering one's practice in the light of theoretical views on teaching and learning, and of research findings. It is worth taking a step back and considering the purpose of theory and research. A *theory* is an explanation for a psychological phenomenon. *Research* involves gathering and analysing data. Traditionally, scientists have sought to establish which theory is correct and to discard alternatives, based on research evidence. However, psychology is a multi-faceted discipline, and very often we find that alternative theories seek to explain different aspects of a phenomenon. They can thus be complementary rather than competing. Chapter 2 examines theories of cognitive development and Chapter 7 looks at theories of emotional development. No contemporary psychologist would suggest that it is our place to choose whether attachment theory or Piagetian theory provides the definitive explanation for child development.

One aspect of reflection on psychological theory and research concerns the extent to which psychological theories and research findings fit in with the experiences the teacher has in their everyday practice. For example, does our experience support Piaget's idea of an innate motivation to learn (p. 19) or Wittenberg's view of the learner as powerfully emotional and influenced by their developmental history (p. 141)? This principle is perhaps the bedrock underlying the professional application of theory and research to educational practice. Without this awareness one can be left with a choice between non-reflective teaching, relying on accumulated craft skills (not to suggest that this equates to poor practice in itself) and a rigid following of a particular school of thought without consideration of the circumstances in which it is being applied – this *is* likely to lead to poor practice.

Personal responses to theory and research

Our individual responses to ideas presented in psychological theory and research can be affected by cognitive, emotional and socio-political factors. Our individual information-processing style and learning strategies may affect the extent to which we can make use of ideas. For example, social constructivist theory (Chapter 2) uses highly abstract concepts such as the *zone of proximal development* and the *intermental developmental zone*. To some practitioners these concepts serve as valuable heuristics (i.e. tools of thinking), which illuminate the nature of productive interaction between teacher and learner. To others they will be so abstract as to be meaningless. This is not to say there is a correct attitude for teachers to adopt towards such ideas, rather the opposite – there will inevitably be a range of views and it can be a mistake to seek a consensus.

We also respond to psychological concepts on an emotional level. For example, we may respond defensively when our academic self-concept is threatened by difficulty in understanding complex theoretical ideas or our professional self-concept is threatened by challenging new theory or data. This can lead us to reject potentially useful psychological material. We may also experience personal threat in response to theory or research that interacts with our own developmental history. For example, those with unhappy experiences of childhood relationships may respond defensively by rejecting psychodynamic approaches to explaining the learner–teacher relationship (Chapter 7), because these theories place considerable emphasis on early relationships. More seriously, such a defensive attitude may predispose the teacher to reject entirely the importance of emotional and developmental influences on learners, and so cater only for the cognitive aspects of learning.

A third factor affecting our responses to psychological material is its interaction with our personal politics. Many psychological concepts, theories and research findings are far from politically neutral, and it should come as no surprise that the highly politically aware teaching profession responds to them accordingly. An example of a contentious topic is intelligence. Intelligence has powerful political connotations because historically it has been used for repressive political purposes, such as restricting immigration, bolstering the class system and even justifying genocide. Those with even a vague awareness of these facts tend to respond negatively to discussions of learners' intelligence or academic ability. This is unfortunate, firstly because there are good reasons not to be threatened by unpalatable ideas like a genetic component to intelligence and, more importantly, because there are extremely useful applications of modern views of intelligence (discussed in Chapter 3).

Insight into personal characteristics

The teaching profession is unusual in that all practitioners have at some point experienced being a client. One effect of studying education and psychological theory and research is to gain insight, not only into one's practice but also into one's own educational development. Reading a book like this can involve a number of 'aha' moments as one's own experiences of education are suddenly illuminated. For example, we all have a profile of multiple intelligences and higher thinking skills; we have our own learning styles and strategies, and have been influenced by a host of social, emotional and motivational variables. In everyday adult life, even working in education, we may not have many opportunities to reflect on these personal characteristics and their effects on our practice. In studying the psychology of teaching and learning, personal and professional development go hand in hand as we reflect on the ways our individual characteristics interact with professional practice. To take the example of studying learning styles, a teacher may come to realise that they are a verbal learner rather than a visual learner – verbal learners are in a minority – and that they have underused the visual strategies which would be highly useful for the majority of learners (Chapters 3 and 4).

Reflectivity and craft-knowledge

Popular as it has been, the notion of reflectivity does have it critics. It is probably fair to say that the enthusiasm of education professionals for the idea of reflectivity is largely due to its palatability to teachers in what D. H. Hargreaves (1997) has termed the 'post-professional era', in which the erosion of teachers' autonomy has been widely interpreted as a diminution of their professional status. It was much in the spirit of post-professionalism that Chris Woodhead (1999), former chief inspector of schools, attacked the 'cult of the reflective practitioner', and suggested that teachers should seek professional development from those with more advanced craft skills, *not* through the study of theory or research. This approach is to promote teaching as craft *as opposed to* a reflective profession, raising the question of whether teaching can be simultaneously a craft and a profession.

Treating teaching as a craft *can* demote it from being a profession, depending on the intention of the person applying the label (Kerry and Wilding, 2004). Teaching, like skilled artisanship, combines the qualities of an art and a science, hence the analogy of craft-knowledge is an effective heuristic to describe what teachers do. Yet when used politically to diminish the status of teachers, the term 'craft' can be used to compare teaching to something that anyone can do with a few simple rules, thus 'expertise' in teaching becomes linked in discourse to the content of a DIY leaflet (Kerry, personal communication). One way to resolve this is to separate the analogy of craft-knowledge from the socio-economic connotations of 'the crafts'. The craft-knowledge construct can be abused to attack the professional status of teaching, but it is not abusive in itself. This is an example of the benefit of adopting *binocular vision* (p. 6) when considering a term with a socio-political dimension.

Setting aside as far as possible the political dimensions of his controversial statement, Woodhead did raise a serious issue: Is the reflective professional demonstrably superior to the teacher who relies on highly developed craft-knowledge rather than reflectivity? By and large, although research has shown distinct differences between expert and novice teachers (Sternberg and Horvath, 1995), these differences could equally be explained in terms of reflectivity or craft-knowledge. Because of the very breadth of the activities and characteristics encompassed by the term 'reflective' and because of the ubiquity of craft-knowledge, it is quite impossible to separate and compare reflective teachers and 'crafty' teachers. Given this lack of direct testability, the question of the usefulness of reflectivity falls rather to whether

practitioners find it helpful, to which the answer is a self-evident yes.
A sensible position may therefore be to support the idea of teaching as a
reflective profession while not denigrating teachers' craft-knowledge.

Conclusions and personal reflections

Irrespective of the first image of the classroom or lecture theatre that
comes to mind when we think about teachers and learners, both the
teacher and the learner can be viewed in a number of surprisingly different
ways. Learners can be viewed primarily as cognitive beings, emotional
beings, as vessels of human potential or in terms of the social and political
context in which they exist. Teachers can be seen as executives, therapists or
liberators, according to their ideology and practice, or in terms of being
craftsmen and women or reflective professionals depending on the status
accorded to them.

It is healthy and inevitable that individual teachers will be drawn
towards particular visions of the learner and the teacher, depending on
personality, political persuasion and experience. However, I would counsel
against becoming too entrenched in particular debates simply because, while
these are important distinctions in principle, most practising professionals
are pragmatists and adopt an eclectic attitude, consciously or unconsciously
applying different principles in different situations. It is also healthy that many
readers will be drawn to the political dimensions of education and
psychology. I would reiterate, however, that this is only productive if we can
maintain binocular vision, seeing the political context without losing sight of
the needs of the learner.

Self-assessment questions

1. Critically compare the view of learning taken by cognitive and
   psychodynamic theories.

2. What implications does social constructionism have for psychology
   and education?

3. Define binocular vision and give examples of its application in
   considering the socio-political dimensions of psychology and
   education.

4. Critically discuss the concept of reflectivity. To what extent is
   teaching a reflective profession?

Further reading

•••••• Jennings, C. and Kennedy, E. (1996) *The Reflective Professional in Education.*
Jessica Kingsley, London.

•••••• Kerry, T. and Wilding, M. (2004) *Effective Classroom Teacher*. Longman, London.

•••••• McIntyre, D. (2000) The nature of classroom teaching expertise. In: *The Psychology of Teaching and Learning in the Primary School* (ed. Whitebread, D.). Routledge Falmer, London.

•••••• Schon, D. A. (1987) *Educating the Reflective Practitioner*. Jossey Bass Wiley, San Francisco.

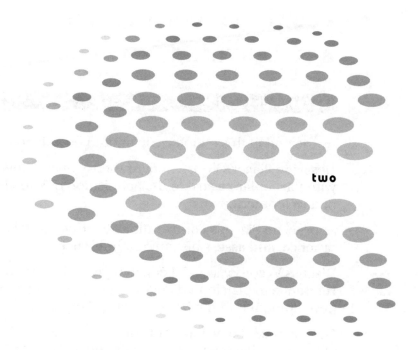

two

Cognitive Development and Learning

Cognitive Development and Learning

By the end of this chapter you should be able to:

- Describe Piaget's constructivist theory of cognitive development with particular regard to the acquisition of knowledge and stages of development.

- Appreciate Piaget's contributions to educational thinking and practice, and assess his current influence.

- Discuss Vygotsky's social constructivist theory, with particular reference to distributed cognition, the zone of proximal development and the importance of language.

- Outline recent developments of social constructivist theory with particular reference to scaffolding and intermental developmental zones.

- Understand applications of social constructivism, including scaffolding, whole-class interactive teaching, cooperative group work and peer tutoring.

- Be aware of the existence of contemporary modular approaches to cognitive development and appreciate the challenges they pose to constructivist theories.

Some of the most important contributions psychology has made to education come in the form of cognitive development theory, a broad approach dealing with the processes by which we acquire knowledge and understanding of the world, and the ways in which the nature of our mental processes changes with age. The best-known contributor to this field has been Jean Piaget, the Swiss philosopher, sociologist and psychologist. Piaget's importance in education cannot be overstated, and many of the ideas we take for granted in modern education derive from his work, including the matching of conceptual difficulty of work to the age and ability of the learner and the role of active engagement on the part of the learner in effective learning. Many contemporary educational strategies such as instrumental enrichment and cognitive acceleration (Chapter 5) are direct descendants of his ideas.

Important as Piaget has been in the development of educational thinking, his current influence has been largely superseded by that of his Russian contemporary, Lev Vygotsky, and so most of this chapter is given over to a review of Vygotsky's ideas and their applications. Vygotsky's emphasis was on the interpersonal basis of learning and the role of expert instruction. His influence is seen on current practice, for example in whole-class interactive teaching, scaffolding, cooperative group work and peer tutoring. Collectively, Piagetian and Vygotskian approaches to learning are known as *constructivist*, because they emphasise the active processes by which learners construct their understanding of the world. Vygotskian approaches are distinguished from Piagetian by calling them *social constructivist* approaches, denoting their emphasis on social processes.

Piagetian theory

Piaget researched and wrote on the subject of children's cognitive development from the 1920s until the 1980s. Perhaps Piaget's greatest insight was his understanding that the ways in which children think are not less sophisticated than those of adults simply because they have less knowledge, but that they think in a qualitatively different manner. Piaget was interested in how children think and how children and adults learn. Some commentators have found it helpful to distinguish between Piaget's theory of learning and what is effectively his separate, yet closely related, theory of child development.

Piaget's theory of learning

Agency and the lone scientist

The concept that perhaps distinguishes Piaget's view of learning and cognitive development from alternative approaches is *agency*. To Piaget 'agency' referred to the human motivation to actively pursue knowledge; in other words, to be the agents of our own learning. Piaget noted that even very young children are very inquisitive about their own abilities and about the details of the world. Learning and cognitive development are thus active processes in which we explore the world and construct a mental representation of reality based on what we discover in our explorations. The sophistication of our mental representation of the world increases with age as we explore in a more sophisticated manner, building on our existing understandings to create successively more advanced mental representations.

A somewhat misunderstood aspect of Piaget's view of the child as motivated to learn by discovery concerns the role of other people. On a theoretical level, the Piagetian child functions as a 'lone scientist', individually exploring the world and individually assimilating new information and accommodating to new experience. However, it is a common error to extrapolate from this understanding of individual learning processes to a belief that there is no role for other people in the Piagetian view of learning or even that children learn best in isolation. In fact, in the context of education, Piaget placed considerable emphasis on the role of social interaction as a source of experience and information, even though his theoretical understanding of learning was very much on the mental processes by which the individual adapts to these experiences.

Schemas and adaptation

Schemas are mental structures, each of which contains all the information the individual has relating to one aspect of the world. We have schemas for people, objects, actions and more abstract concepts. Piaget believed that we are born with a few innate schemas, which enable us to interact with others. During the first year of life we construct other schemas. When our existing schemas are capable of explaining what we can perceive around us, we are said to be in a state of *equilibrium*. But whenever we meet a new situation that cannot be explained by our existing schemas, we experience the unpleasant sensation of *disequilibrium* or *perturbation*. We are driven to improve our understanding of the world in order to escape disequilibrium. Every time we overcome disequilibrium we become better adapted to our environment. Therefore learning is not only a discovery of the world but an *adaptation* to it. Piaget identified two processes by which equilibration takes place, *assimilation* and *accommodation*. Piaget described the mechanisms of assimilation and accommodation somewhat inconsistently in different texts (von Glasersfeld, 1996). Put simply, we either understand new information in the light of our existing knowledge (i.e. we assimilate it) or we take a radical new idea on board (i.e. we accommodate to it).

Reflection point

Piaget proposes a motivational aspect to learning, suggesting that we are all driven to fill the gaps in our knowledge. In your experience, to what extent is this the case and what factors might influence individual motivation to learn?

Cognitive development

Operations

As well as knowledge of things we will encounter in the world, we also need to understand the rules by which the world operates. Piaget called these rules *operations* and, critically, he suggested that the reason for qualitative change in reasoning during development is the development of operations. The very young child does not have operations at all, and they are thus said to be *preoperational*. The first operations to appear are *concrete*. This means that children can understand the rules governing something provided they can see it. Later, rules governing abstract concepts are understood. The rest of Piaget's theory is largely dependent on this idea of operations. The logical errors that Piaget identified in children's thinking take place because of the limited operations available to them. Table 2.1 summarises the development of operations across Piaget's stages of development.

Table 2.1 **Piaget's stages of logical development**

Approximate age	Stage	Status of operations	Status of logic
0–2 years	Sensorimotor	No symbolic thought or operations	Prelogical
2–7 years	Preoperational	Symbolic thought but no operations	Semilogical
7–11 years	Concrete operational	Operations can deal with physical objects	Logical
> 11 years	Formal operational	Operations can deal with abstract concepts	Fully logical

The sensorimotor stage

The sensorimotor stage lasts for approximately the first two years of life. Piaget believed that our main focus at this point is on physical sensation and on learning to coordinate our bodies. We learn by trial and error to associate actions and their effects. At around eight months the child develops an understanding of the permanence of objects. By the second year of life infants are quite mobile, and so are well equipped to actively explore their environment. They are extremely curious and often experiment with actions to discover their effects. For most of the sensorimotor stage, the child is profoundly egocentric; not only does it not see the perspective of others, but it does not recognise the boundaries between itself and others. Thus other people are experienced as extensions of the infant's body. By the end of the sensorimotor stage, the infant is aware of other people as separate beings, has a grasp of language and can think using symbols such as words.

The preoperational stage

By the end of the second year, the child has sufficient grasp of language for its thinking to be based around symbolic thought rather than physical sensation. However, it has not developed sufficiently to grasp logical rules or operations, hence the term *preoperational*, and it deals with the world very much as it appears rather than as it is. The child can thus be described as *semilogical*. Preoperational children are characterised by *centration*. This means that they can focus only on one aspect of a situation at a time. Because of this they are highly egocentric and animistic and they have difficulty with conservation tasks.

Egocentrism

The term 'egocentrism' refers to the child's difficulty in perceiving the world from any viewpoint other than its own. This difficulty applies across physical and abstract concepts. Piaget and Inhelder (1956) famously demonstrated egocentrism in the physical world with their 'three mountains' procedure. Each model mountain had a different marker on the top, a cross, a house or a covering of snow. A doll was positioned to the side of the three mountains. Children were sat in front of the scene and shown pictures of the scene from different viewpoints. Their task was to select the picture that best matched what the doll could 'see'. Piaget and Inhelder noted that children aged less than seven years old had difficulty with this task, and tended to choose the picture of the scene from their own point of view.

Animism

Piaget reported that children aged 2–4 years typically attribute lifelike characteristics to inanimate objects. They may, for example, worry about hurting or offending their toys, or indeed they may punish their toys when they are 'naughty'. This phenomenon of animism is closely related to egocentrism, because it takes place when children judge all objects to have the same feelings and motives as themselves. By about four years, Piaget believed that children have a clear understanding of which objects around them are alive and which are not.

Conservation

Conservation refers to the understanding that objects remain the same in quantity even when their appearance changes. Piaget reported that young children had difficulty with tasks of conservation. He demonstrated this in a number of situations, two of which are particularly well known. In his number conservation procedure Piaget found that if two rows of counters are laid out side by side, with the same number of counters spaced apart at the same distance children correctly spotted that there were the same number of counters in each row. Similarly, Piaget found that if children see two glasses together with liquid coming up to the same height in each, they correctly spot the fact that they contain the same amount of liquid. But if liquid was poured from a short, wide glass to a taller, thinner container, young children typically believed there was now more liquid in the taller container. This is a failure of liquid conservation.

Class inclusion

Children need to understand the important operation of *class inclusion* – some classes of object fall within others. For example, cats are animals. Animals are the larger or *superordinate* class and cats are the smaller or *subordinate* class. Piaget found that preoperational children found it hard to think clearly about the two classes at the same time, so they could not consistently identify subordinate and superordinate classes.

The concrete operational stage

In the concrete operational stage, the child's mind is mature enough to use logical thought or operations, although children can only apply logic to objects and situations that are present and physical, hence *concrete* operational. Children lose their tendency for animism at this stage. They become rather less egocentric, although they do not lose the tendency altogether, and they can succeed at conservation and class inclusion tasks. However, concrete operational children have great difficulty carrying out logical tasks without the physical objects in front of them.

The formal operational stage

In the formal operational stage, children become capable of formal reasoning, i.e. they can follow the form of an argument without being distracted by its content. This means they can correctly answer syllogisms like this one from P. K. Smith *et al.* (1998): 'All green birds have two heads. I have a green bird called Charlie. How many heads does Charlie have?' The correct answer is two, but before a child becomes capable of formal reasoning, they are more likely to become distracted by the content and point out that birds do not really have two heads. Formal operational thinkers can also think about abstract concepts and devise and test hypotheses. Piaget took this to mean that children had entered a new stage of adult logic, where abstract reasoning was possible. As well as systematic abstract reasoning, formal operational thinking permits the development of a system of values and ideals, and an appreciation of philosophical issues.

The current status of Piaget's ideas

Piaget's fundamental ideas that children are motivated to learn and that their reasoning changes qualitatively with age have survived the test of time. Indeed they have become so universal as to enter the realm of common sense. Children are certainly curious from a young age, and can therefore be described as agents of their own learning. The idea of the schema as the basic unit of knowledge is widely accepted by psychologists, although there is little direct evidence of assimilation and accommodation as two separate processes. However, there have been many challenges to the details of Piaget's theory. One problem for Piaget's view of learning is posed by contemporary studies revealing that motivation to learn *increases* once we have some understanding of a subject (Andreani, 1995). This does not fit with Piaget's idea of agency, which suggests that we are motivated to learn by our discomfort at *not* understanding something. Agency remains a credible idea with many proponents, but it is a controversial one.

The details of Piaget's stage theory are also open to challenge. In the 1970s a group of researchers at Edinburgh University demonstrated that so-called preoperational children were capable of performing tasks of conservation (McGarrigle and Donaldson, 1974) and decentring (Hughes, 1975), once the tasks were presented to them in a manner that made 'human sense' (Donaldson, 1978). This suggests that in fact there may be little basis for a distinction between preoperational and concrete operational thinking. Recently, however, Wilberg (2002) has provided stronger support for such a distinction in a study of children's understanding of nationality. A total of 106 German children aged 4–6 years were classified as preoperational or concrete operational based on their responses to class inclusion questions. They were then asked a series of questions about Germany and being German. Responses to class inclusion questions but not age predicted the sophistication of the answers about Germany and German nationality. Recent reviews, e.g. Subbotsky (2000) have concluded that, in line with Piaget's theory, animism in young children is a robust phenomenon, although there is evidence that even young children can reliably distinguish between animate and inanimate objects under particular circumstances such as when questioned about their regenerative properties after injury.

The distinction between concrete and formal reasoning has generally been upheld consistently by research. However, there appears to be a problem in Piaget's belief that all adolescents achieve formal reasoning. In a longitudinal study – a study where participants are followed up over a long period – Bradmetz (1999) studied the cognitive development of 62 children from age seven years until age 15 years, regularly giving them a battery of tests, including the Inhelder and Piaget science task, designed to measure formal thinking. By 15 only one of the young people proved capable of formal thinking, less than 2%. This suggests that, as well as underestimating the reasoning abilities of young children, Piaget somewhat overestimated the abilities of adolescents. It seems he exaggerated the extent of the developments in reasoning that take place during childhood.

Applying Piagetian ideas to education

Piaget's theories have been most influential in primary education, although the principles of his learning theory are applicable across all sectors. Piaget's research was generally not aimed directly at education, although in one of his later publications (Piaget, 1970), he made clear his support for the newer child-centred methods. Following the 1967 Plowden report, which advocated a shift away from traditional didactic teaching in favour of more child-centred methods of primary education, and Piaget's 1970 book on education, teachers began to put Piaget's ideas into practice in the classroom on a grand scale. Two of the main ways we can apply Piaget's ideas to education are by adapting to children's understanding of the world and by facilitating discovery learning.

Adapting to the child's understanding of the world

As children lack adult logic, teachers need to adapt to their ways of thinking rather than expect children to adapt to them. Thus teachers should expect a degree of egocentrism in younger children. Margaret Donaldson (1978) recites an amusing account by the novelist Laurie Lee of his first day at school, which was spoiled by a misunderstanding between himself and his teacher (Box 2.1).

To the child, the word 'present' meant a gift not a time, and the young Laurie Lee was unable to decentre and think about what the teacher might have meant. Interestingly, the teacher also displayed a form of egocentrism by not appreciating the egocentric perspective of the child. This tendency for adult egocentrism results not so much from cognitive immaturity as lack of concentration. Although such lapses are absolutely inevitable when teaching large numbers of young children, they can cause distress.

It is also important to create tasks and situations that are appropriate for children at their particular stage of development. Piaget was a stern critic of educational practices that involved overburdening younger children with tasks that exceeded their level of development. An example of this is teaching young children mathematical tasks. Piaget suggested that preoperational children who did not understand conservation or class inclusion but who could do sums were merely learning a meaningless skill in isolation and could not understand what they were doing.

The National Curriculum reflects Piaget's stages; one of its key aims is that children should encounter ideas when they are ready to cope with them. We would not for example give children still in the concrete operational stage tasks that require skills of abstract reasoning. Such tasks would become appropriate only after the children had achieved formal operations. This means that the primary curriculum, which ends with Piaget's concrete operational stage at age 11, should contain little or no material that requires formal reasoning. Key Stage 3, covering ages 11–14, also contains relatively little formal reasoning, reflecting research showing Piaget was optimistic and that few children achieve formal reasoning before their mid-teens.

25

Box 2.1

An example of egocentrism in the classroom

I spent the first day picking holes in paper and went home in a smouldering temper.
'What's the matter love? Didn't he like it at school then?'
'They never gave me the present.'
'Present. What present?'
'They said they'd give me a present.'
'Well now, I'm sure they didn't.'
'They did! They said: "You're Laurie Lee, aren't you. Just you sit there for the present." I sat there all day but I never got it.'

Source: Donaldson (1978)

A criticism of the National Curriculum is that, limited by its Piagetian understanding, it provides insufficient challenge for the most able learners.

Facilitating discovery learning

According to Piaget, children need to construct their understanding of the world rather than passively accepting it from others. This is an active process, and could not be achieved in the traditional classroom situation where information was delivered didactically. Children learn best by *discovery*. The role of the teacher influenced by Piaget is thus to facilitate learning situations in which children can find things out for themselves and so construct their understanding. Of course, effective discovery learning does not mean simply leaving children to their own devices. Rather the teacher presents children with tasks specifically designed to create disequilibrium and thus create the motivation for them to discover things for themselves. A wide variety of such tasks need to be given so the child can construct their knowledge of all necessary aspects of the world. In nursery and primary school, materials like water, sand, bricks and crayons help children to build physical and hence mental constructions. Later, projects and science practicals help children explore the nature of their world.

Two points have caused considerable confusion. Recall the term 'lone scientist'. Be clear that although Piaget saw the construction of knowledge as an individual psychological process, he was not an advocate of children learning in isolation. Discovery can take place in pairs and groups, and what other children are doing can serve as a valuable source of information. Be clear as well that to Piaget the most effective discovery resulted not merely from casual exploration but problem-solving. Providing sand and water to play with but without hinting at goals to achieve is not really in keeping with the spirit of Piagetian theory (Siegler and Crowley, 1996).

Piagetian theory also has implications for how teachers interact with learners during learning. To Piaget, the aim of education is to develop children's thinking rather than just to increase their level of knowledge. This means that, when learners are trying to work things out, what is important is their *reasoning* rather than the correctness of the final answer. It is therefore important that teachers encourage children for producing answers that are technically wrong but well thought out. Current work into developing learners' thinking skills is founded on this Piagetian principle (Chapter 5).

Discussion of Piaget's contributions

The ideas that it is beneficial for learners to take an active role in their learning and that education should develop sophistication of thinking as well as a body of knowledge are currently widely accepted nowadays. They remain perhaps Piaget's great legacies in educational practice. However, a large body of outcome studies conducted in the 1970s that compared the effectiveness of didactic and discovery learning found no consistent advantage for either approach. There are several possible explanations for this. One important factor was probably the rather inadequate understanding of Piagetian theory that underlay much of the application of his ideas. Much so-called Piagetian teaching was poorly informed and consequently badly planned, sometimes consisting of little more than leaving children to their own devices and failing to provide the stimulating challenges that would motivate children to actively discover and learn. Another likely factor in the failure to demonstrate the effectiveness of discovery learning was the underutilisation of social inter-action. Much of the emphasis in more recent research has been on the role of interaction with peers and tutors. This is better understood from the social constructivist approach of Lev Vygotsky, our next topic.

Vygotskian theory

Lev Vygotsky was a contemporary of Piaget in Piaget's early days, though Vygotsky died young in 1934. His work was first published in the West in the 1960s, since when it has grown hugely in influence, especially in the past two decades (Wertsch and Tulviste, 1996). Vygotsky agreed with Piaget on many key points; for example, that cognitive development takes place in stages charac-terised by different styles of thinking. He disagreed, however, with Piaget's view of the child as 'lone scientist' and instead placed his emphasis on social interaction during learning and the culture in which the child grows up. Consequently, his approach is sometimes known as *social constructivist* theory.

Culture, mediation and tools

Vygotsky's work developed in the context of early twentieth-century Russian post-revolution academia and, influenced by Karl Marx, he placed tremen-dous emphasis on the role played by culture in the child's development. His view, very much in line with that of contemporary cultural psychology, was of the individual developing within, and profoundly influenced by, a social, cultural and historical context (Cole, 1996). Like Piaget, Vygotsky saw the child as an active agent of their own learning, but he emphasised the extent to which learning is *mediated* by the child's culture. Mediation is a key concept in Vygotskian theory, referring collectively to the ways in which culture interacts with individual development. Vygotsky's work is subject to subtly different interpretations when it comes to the nature of mediation. Kozulin (1998) provides a helpful way of thinking about mediation, identifying three categories of mediator:

- Psychological tools
- Technical tools
- Other individuals.

Tools, also known as *artefacts*, thus fall into two categories. *Psychological tools* are higher mental functions. To Vygotsky, children are born with basic cognitive functions such as perception and focused attention. However, they lack higher mental functions such as thinking and problem-solving. These higher mental functions are seen as the psychological tools of the culture in which the individual lives. Psychological tools are transmitted to children by older members of the culture in the course of guided learning experiences, such as lessons in school, and include the ability to use language, art and mathematics. Experiences with other people gradually become internalised to form the child's individual mental representation of the world. The sharing of guided learning with other members of the same cultural group allows each individual to share a world view with their peers. The implication is that people in different cultures will have quite different sets of tools, hence different ways of thinking. The second category of tool is *technical*. Technical tools are external material objects and affect the ways a child can interact with their environment. The computer is a good example of a technical tool currently transforming many cultures.

Social interaction and the zone of proximal development

In keeping with his Marxist roots, and in contrast to Piaget, who emphasised how much a child can learn by exploring its environment, Vygotsky placed his own emphasis on the fact that children can develop a quicker and more advanced understanding during interaction with other people, such as adults or more experienced peers. For example, according to Vygotsky, children could never develop formal operational thinking without the help of others. Piaget's view was rather that formal operational thinking develops when the child is sufficiently mature and has made sufficient discoveries to construct a mental representation that can cope with formal reasoning. These discoveries would probably involve experiences of interacting with others but the interactions themselves are not central to formal reasoning.

Vygotsky conceived of learning as taking place between a learner and a more advanced peer or adult instructor. He conceived of knowledge as existing initially on an *intermental plane* (i.e. between two people) and only then on an *intramental plane* (i.e. in the mind of the individual). The difference between what a child can understand on its own and what it can potentially understand through interaction with others is called the *zone of proximal development* (ZPD). Whereas Piaget believed that the limiting factor in what a child could learn at any time was its stage of development, Vygotsky believed that the crucial factor was the availability of other 'experts' who could instruct the child. Unlike Piaget, Vygotsky emphasised instruction from others in how to do things in order for the child to achieve its potential.

The role of language

Compared to Piaget, Vygotsky placed far more emphasis on the importance of language in cognitive development. For Piaget, language simply appeared when the child had reached a sufficiently advanced stage of development. The child's grasp of language depended on its current level of cognitive development. For Vygotsky, however, language developed from social interactions with others and was a very important psychological tool. At first the sole function of language is communication, and language and thought develop separately. Later the child internalises language and learns to use it as a tool of thinking. In the preoperational stage, as children learn to use language to solve problems, they speak aloud while solving problems; this is called egocentric speech. The child engaged in egocentric speech is also engaged in learning to regulate the actions of others, e.g. through requests, but crucially they are also learning to be regulated by others. This is why young children receiving instructions will repeat them back, sometimes many times. Later, speech becomes internalised and thus silent. This internalisation allows the child to mentally manipulate ideas and to follow instruction from others. The child who, rather than obeying instructions, simply repeats them back may be a source of stress to parents, but from a Vygotskian perspective they are well on the way to internalising the instructions, whereupon they will understand and (perhaps) obey them.

The current status of Vygotsky's theory

Vygotsky appears to have been correct in saying that Piaget underestimated the importance of social interaction with more experienced people during learning. Many studies have demonstrated that children receiving help from other people pick up skills that they probably could not have mastered alone. In one such study, Roazzi and Bryant (1998) gave children aged four and five years the task of working out how many sweets there were in a box on a set of weighing scales. In one condition children worked alone and in another they had the help of an older child who was not allowed to explicitly tell them the solution. In the assisted condition the older children clearly went through the process of giving successively less explicit prompts until the younger children worked out how to perform the task. Most children in this condition mastered the task while those working alone did not. This supports strongly the existence of a gap between understanding and potential understanding that we might call the ZPD.

Support for the existence of the ZPD is fairly unequivocal, but this does not necessarily validate other aspects of Vygotsky's theory, such as the transition of knowledge from the intermental to the intramental. A study by C. Howe *et al.* (1996) suggests that although children benefit from working together in discovery tasks, they can still form rather different mental representations of the task. A total of 113 children aged 8–12 years took part in group tasks concerned with understanding the movement of objects down an incline. Their understanding of the science was assessed before and afterwards. Vygotskian theory predicts that the children would develop a shared understanding of the mechanisms involved in movement down an incline. In fact, although the children's understanding increased following the task, their understandings remained individualised and did not converge on a single, advanced understanding. Although such results give support to the efficacy of group work, which is usually understood in a Vygotskian framework, on a theoretical level they actually find in favour of Piaget, whose theory predicts individual construction of understanding, rather than Vygotsky.

Vygotsky's idea that children initially think aloud then internalise speech and use it to think silently remains the subject of research and is very much open to question. Vygotsky's theory would seem to predict that younger children would understand material better having read it aloud whereas there would be no such benefit in older children. Prior and Welling (2001) tested this idea by taking Canadian children aged 5–8 years and giving them passages to read followed by comprehension tasks. In one condition they read aloud and in another they read silently. In fact, the 7–8-year-olds benefited from reading aloud whereas the 5–6-year-olds did not. This runs counter to the Vygotskian view.

A rather more controversial aspect of Vygotsky's theory was the idea that because psychological tools are specific to different cultures, cultures without formal schooling do not develop abstract thinking. Effectively this is saying that some cultures are better at thinking than others, an assumption that is at best ethnocentric and at worst racist. Contemporary social constructivists influenced by Vygotsky bypass this issue somewhat by speaking of cultures as having different 'toolkits' (Wertsch, 1991), i.e. qualitatively different sets of tools rather than having more or fewer tools than one another.

Later developments in social constructivist thinking

Vygotsky's theory has provided a tremendous starting point for contemporary theorists, not least because so many of his ideas, in spite of their usefulness, are rather underdeveloped. Although there have been numerous theoretical developments in social constructivist theory, a detailed review is not possible here. However, two important concepts are briefly reviewed because of their applicability to education. *Scaffolding* describes the strategies used to assist learners across the ZPD. *Intermental development zones* have been suggested as a theoretical alternative to Vygotsky's ZPD.

Scaffolding

The term 'scaffolding' was introduced by Jerome Bruner and colleagues (e.g. Wood *et al.*, 1976) as a metaphor to describe the interactions by which a learner is assisted through the ZPD. As the child progresses through a ZPD,

Table 2.2   **An example of crossing the ZPD**

Level of help	Nature of prompt	Example
5	Demonstration	Mother assembles two blocks
4	Preparation for child	Mother positions blocks for child to push together
3	Indication of materials	Mother points to blocks
2	Specific verbal instructions	Mother says 'get four big blocks'
1	General prompts	Mother says 'now you make something'

Source: Adapted from Wood (1991)

the amount of instruction, or scaffolding, from experts will reduce. At first, explicit and detailed instructions are needed but later on, prompts are sufficient to help the child progress. Table 2.2 shows an example of the transition through the ZPD (Wood, 1991). Here a mother is helping a four year-old put together wooden blocks.

There have been several attempts to refine the notion of scaffolding. Wood (1998) introduced the notions of *contingency* and *uncertainty* to understanding scaffolding. The term contingency denotes the fact that interactions on the part of the teacher are contingent (i.e. dependent) on the success of the learner at each point. Where the learner fails, the level of teacher intervention increases; as they succeed, the level of intervention decreases. This means that at any point the control over learning depends on the learner's achievements; the better the achievement, the more control the learner acquires over the task. In a recent longitudinal study, Conner and Cross (2003) followed up 45 mother–baby dyads, observing scaffolding in joint problem-solving tasks at 16, 26, 44 and 54 months. A clear pattern emerged in which the mothers used successively less intervention as age increased and moved from non-contingent intervention with toddlers (i.e. their help was not dependent on the success or failure of the children) to more contingent scaffolding. Wood also emphasised the importance of uncertainty in scaffolding. Uncertainty, i.e. lack of clarity over the features of a task, demotivates learners. An important aspect of effective scaffolding is therefore to reduce uncertainty and to ensure that the learner is focused on the task itself, not peripheral aspects of the situation such as what they are meant to be doing or how to use equipment.

Studies comparing scaffolded and non-scaffolded learning episodes have demonstrated that active involvement on the part of a teacher in interacting and providing appropriate assistance is reliably associated with improvement in outcome. For example, Day and Cordon (1993) compared learning in American third-graders when engaged in a variety of tasks with and without scaffolding. As expected, achievement was greater in the scaffolded condition. Interestingly, an additional finding was that achievement motivation, verbal IQ and impulsivity were less predictive of outcome in the scaffolded condition. This is critical for educationalists as it suggests that teaching that involves effective scaffolding can counter the negative impact of low verbal IQ, low achievement motivation and high impulsivity, offering a diverse range of learners a more level playing field.

Intermental developmental zones

Recall that Vygotsky conceived of the ZPD as the gap between current and potential understanding, and this understanding exists initially on an inter-mental plane between the learner and the teacher. Amalgamating these ideas, Mercer (2000) has proposed that we should think of teaching and learning in terms of intermental development zones (IDZs) rather than zones of proximal development, which are more appropriate for understanding the processes of learner *assessment*. To Mercer, teaching is a process of *interthinking*, the creation of the intermental plane. For every learning task, there is not so much a gap in understanding but a shared communicative space in which teacher and learner collaborate. The key to effective teaching is therefore the mainten-ance of teacher–learner dialogue in which the learner's understanding is constantly kept at a level just beyond their prior understanding.

Reflection point

Ideas like the zone of proximal development and intermental developmental zones are advanced concepts that serve as *heuristics* or mental tools to help us understand a situation rather than describing an observable phenomenon. How useful do you consider such heuristic devices in psychological theory?

Implications of social constructivist theory for education

To a rather greater extent than Piaget, Vygotsky was interested in applying his ideas to education. Perhaps Vygotsky's most fundamental idea is that learning is linked closely to social interaction. From a Vygotskian perspective, the key to successful learning is to maximise the opportunities for meaningful inter-action between a learner and another individual who takes the role of teacher during learning experiences. There are several mechanisms by which this can happen. Teachers, and learning support assistants in particular, can work with individuals, assisting in problem-solving. They can also interact with more than one learner collectively in whole-class interactive teaching. Peers also provide a source of social interaction during cooperative group work and peer-tutoring exercises.

Whole-class interactive teaching: the role of triadic dialogue

While social constructivist theory proposes an active role for the teacher, including whole-class teaching, this is not simply to advocate a return to a didactic 'chalk and talk' approach. The feature of successful whole-class interactive teaching is the maximisation of the time each learner spends interacting with his or her teacher. In an influential meta-analysis of international research into the factors affecting educational effectiveness, Scheerens (1992) concluded that time spent in whole-class interactive teaching was one of the most robust factors associated with effectiveness, probably because of the degree of teacher–learner interaction it facilitates.

The classic interaction in whole-class interactive teaching takes the form of *triadic dialogue*. As suggested by the term 'triadic', such interactions have three elements: teacher initiation, learner response and teacher feedback. Essentially the teacher is asking a question or posing an issue, to which learners comment or answer, and the teacher completes the episode by providing feedback on the learner response. Triadic dialogue provides an efficient means of cultural transmission in which the teacher can get across to the learner precisely what they are required to know. However, adopting a critical psychological perspective, some commentators (e.g. G. Wells, 1994, 1999) have pointed out that triadic dialogue can be seen as a system of social control, which disempowers learners wishing to develop independent lines of thinking. Wells suggests that, in his focus on dyadic cultural transmission, Vygotsky has underemphasised the role of the wider cultural context in which interaction takes place. Note, however, that this suggestion has been firmly rebutted by other commentators (e.g. Davydov, 1995).

The Talk Lessons programme: establishing a common discourse of learning

One common problem in teacher–learner interaction highlighted by social constructivist theory lies in establishing a shared understanding of what is meant to take place during learning activities and why. In other words, as long as learners and teachers are operating on different principles of a lesson's purpose and what activities help to achieve that purpose, it is not surprising that they disagree on what constitutes acceptable activity. Mercer (2000) has proposed a radical approach to tackle this problem and to optimise teacher–learner interaction. Based on his concept of the intermental development zone, Mercer has implemented a programme called Talk Lessons, intended to establish a shared understanding between learners and teachers of the purpose and conventions of lessons. In particular, Talk Lessons aims to help learners realise what verbal interactions are helpful in aiding learning. The lesson format is interactive, with learners contributing to the discussion, creating a shared rather than transmitted understanding. Box 2.2 shows an example of the outcome from such a session.

There are perhaps two major reasons why the Talk Lessons programme can be effective. Firstly, it makes ground rules explicit, particularly helpful for learners with a poor understanding of the complexity of context-specific social conventions. Secondly, it can lead to a sense of shared ownership of rules, which are recognised as there to help rather than restrict the activities of learners.

Box 2.2

Outcomes from a Talk Lessons session

Our talking rules

- We share our ideas and listen to each other.
- We talk one at a time.
- We respect each other's opinions.
- We give reasons to explain our ideas.
- If we disagree we ask why.
- We try to agree in the end.

Source: Mercer (2000)

Cooperative learning: group work and reciprocal teaching

From a Vygotskian perspective, peers as well as teachers can be important influences on cognitive development. *Cooperative group work*, when used as an alternative to individual discovery learning, appears to speed up children's development. Bear in mind that Piaget was an advocate of cooperative group work and that it is not inextricably linked to a social constructivist approach. Indeed we have already reviewed the work of Christine Howe and colleagues (C. Howe *et al.*, 1996; see p. 30), which suggests that group work facilitates individual learning without necessarily achieving a *shared* understanding. Nonetheless, because of the degree of social interaction involved in group work, it is most commonly understood from a social constructivist perspective.

One approach to group work explicitly based on a social constructivist understanding is the *reciprocal teaching* approach, developed by Brown and Palincsar (1989) to facilitate the learning of reading. In Brown and Palincsar's approach, learners operate in groups of 2–7. The task is reading; each learner takes on the rotating role of 'teacher' for one paragraph. All group members read the paragraph silently. The teacher then offers a summary and asks a question, which the rest of the group attempt to answer. The teacher then sums up and clarifies their thinking, and the group moves on to the next paragraph, another member assuming the mantle of teacher. Reciprocal teaching pushes each individual to think rapidly and creatively in order to be able to instruct his or her peers. It also encourages intensive and highly focused interaction involving scaffolding as each learner, having only recently made the relevant advance themselves, is in a good position to see the difficulties faced by peers (Foot *et al.*, 1990).

Research has supported the effectiveness of cooperative group work. In particular, it seems that children enjoy group interaction and this leads to increased motivation. In one study, Nichols (1996) followed the progress of

American high-school geometry students across an 18-week semester. A control group underwent traditional teaching, one experimental group underwent nine weeks of traditional teaching followed by nine weeks of group problem-solving, and the other experimental group underwent nine weeks of group problem-solving and nine of traditional teaching. Motivation was assessed by multiple measures at various points in the semester. Motivation was lowest in the control group and increased sharply in the experimental groups during the group work phase. This suggests that group work is effective at promoting motivation.

One strategy that has been commonly used in recent years, following the increased recognition of the importance of interaction in learning, involves arranging classroom furniture to structure learners into groups. However, research has shown clearly that seating alone does not lead to effective interaction. In a study of junior-school children, Galton and Williamson (1992) noted that although children sat in groups 60% of the time, they only spent 5% of their time in cooperative learning exercises. They suggest that sitting children in groups designed to interact and then giving them individual tasks constitutes a mixed message, confusing children about the extent to which they should be interacting. The message from these studies is clear: groups can only work effectively if engaged in a group task. Some researchers have gone further, suggesting that effective groups are not only engaged in a clear task but also have a structure in which every learner has clear roles. Gillies (2003) followed the progress of American high-school children studying science, maths and English in either unstructured or structured groups for three terms. All groups consisted of four mixed-ability learners, two boys and two girls. The structured groups had a formal division of labour, whereas the unstructured groups worked on a more ad hoc basis. The structured groups made more progress, supporting the effectiveness of group structure. Kutnick and Manson (2000) have summarised findings of group work research and have offered recommendations (Box 2.3).

Box 2.3

Recommendations for group work

- Groups of different sizes work best for particular tasks. For example, pairs work best for problem-solving and larger groups deal better with practical applications.
- Tasks must be appropriate and unambiguous.
- Groups should be of mixed ability.
- Although learners, especially children, may express a preference for single-sex groups, the quality of interaction is typically better in mixed groups.

Source: Kutnick and Manson (2000)

Peer tutoring

A related strategy involving structured interaction between learners is peer tutoring, in which a more advanced learner takes on the tutor role in order to assist a less experienced or able peer. This replicates the type of interaction that characterises siblings, in which younger children can be observed to develop more rapidly than their older brothers and sisters because of the availability of scaffolding from a more advanced child (Dunn and Munn, 1985). Peer tutoring has been applied to a huge range of age groups, from primary school children to adults in higher education. The nature of peers has varied considerably in different programmes, ranging from more experienced learners of the same age to considerably older learners. Johnson-Pynn and Nisbet (2002) demonstrated that even preschool children can serve as peer tutors. Twenty-eight pairs of 3–5-year-old children worked on a task involving building houses from blocks. In each dyad, one child was experienced in this task and the other was a novice. Without adult prompting, children as young as three years demonstrated skills to their novice peers, offered them verbal encouragement and directed them towards parts of the construction. In short, they turned out to be effective tutors. Among older children, training in peer-tutoring skills has been found to be of benefit (Nath and Ross, 2001).

Overall, research has found positive effects of peer tutoring. A recent meta-analysis of studies of peer tutoring in primary schools by Rohrbeck *et al.* (2003) found that the average tutee made significantly greater progress than controls. Interestingly, the size of the effect was greater for younger children, for those in poverty and for minority ethnic groups, suggesting that this type of learning is an effective levelling strategy for tackling inequality. But looking at individual attempts to organise peer tutoring, it seems there is considerable variance in their success. Tudge *et al.* (1996) have drawn the following conclusions about peer tutoring:

- Simply pairing up two learners of different ability or experience does not necessarily lead to effective tutoring. In addition, the goal needs to be clearly understood and tutor and tutee must have the necessary skills to understand the problem and communicate effectively.
- Providing a problem to solve is necessary but not sufficient for effective peer tutoring. Other interventions such as verbal encouragement may be needed to induce collaboration.
- Co-workers provide both distractions and help. On balance, working with a peer tutor is more beneficial than working alone.

The modular challenge to constructivist theories

A common feature of the approaches of Piaget and Vygotsky is that they are *domain-general* in nature. Both Piagetians and social constructivists see all the

changes in mental abilities that take place during a child's cognitive development as happening because of the same underlying developmental process.
A domain is an aspect of cognitive development, such as language (particularly important to Vygotsky) or physical understanding of the world
(particularly important to Piaget). Thus, for Piaget, the child's increasing
ability to conserve, their declining egocentrism and their loss of animism are
all results of a general increase in cognitive ability that comes as the child
builds successive layers of understanding through exploration of the world.

In recent years, however, another approach has been gaining in popularity. This is the *domain-specific* approach, which sees different mental
abilities as developing independently of one another. A *module* accounts for
each domain of cognitive development. A module is a structure in the brain
designed to handle particular types of information; for example, there is a
module for language. According to modular theorists, language develops
independent of other cognitive functions. Some modular theorists such as
Jerry Fodor (1983) have suggested that cognitive development can be
accounted for entirely by the maturation of different modules. To Fodor we
are all born with modules adapted to processing the kind of information that
has proved necessary in our evolutionary past. There is thus little or no role
in cognitive development for curiosity, as emphasised by Piaget, or social
interaction, as emphasised by Vygotsky. This is not to suggest that children do
not need experiences for cognitive development. However, it does suggest that
what a child can learn at any particular time is limited by the maturity of the
relevant modules rather than by variations in the child's environment.

Fodor's theory has the advantage that it neatly explains why some people
can be so advanced in some aspects of cognitive development and not in
others. Domain-general theorists such as Piaget and Vygotsky would find it
difficult to explain why some children with autism can have very good development in certain skills, such as mathematics, but very poor development of
language and social skills. There is also a less well-known condition called
Williams syndrome, characterised by low general IQ but very rich language
and social skills. To modular theorists, these conditions are much easier to
explain: autism is associated with poor development of the modules responsible for language and social interaction, whereas Williams syndrome is
associated with good development of these modules and poor development
of others.

There are limitations to Fodor's theory, in that it does not easily explain
the effects of experience on individual cognitive development. Karmiloff-
Smith (1996) has suggested a less rigid modular theory of cognitive
development known as the *progressive modularisation* approach. To
Karmiloff-Smith the child is born with domain-relevant biases in the brain
which preferentially, but not exclusively, respond to certain types of information. Here she differs from Fodor's domain-specific approach as well as from
Piaget's domain-general approach. These biases give the child a good start in

processing different stimuli in the world. The child then modifies its initial understanding by building successively more complex understandings of the world through experience, much as Piaget suggested. In a sense, Karmiloff-Smith's account of cognitive development can be seen as a compromise between the ideas of Fodor and Piaget. Because Karmiloff-Smith believes that modules are progressively formed over developmental time, with domain specificity emerging as a function of both the initial biases and experience, her theory can explain the dramatic individual differences in particular mental abilities shown by particular clinical groups such as children with autism or with Williams syndrome.

The modular approach to cognitive development poses important challenges to the constructivist theories that have dominated education for the past three decades. Modular development neatly explains a range of psychological conditions that teachers are likely to encounter, including dyslexia and autistic tendencies. Outside the clinical domain, the normal variations in learners' skills can also be neatly explained by modularity. Chapter 3 explores this in depth by looking at Howard Gardner's theory of multiple intelligences. Cognitive and learning styles are also most easily accounted for by modular approaches, explored in Chapter 4.

At the time of writing, there are exciting debates between developmental psychologists who favour domain-specific theories and developmental psychologists who favour domain-general theories. Essentially, both approaches can be used to explain any finding in cognitive development (Goswami, 1998), although some facts are more neatly explained by one or the other. As we have seen, multiple intelligences require a modular basis to at least some aspects of cognitive development, but cognitive acceleration (Chapter 5) is predicated on the assumption of domain-general development. Fortunately, domain-general and domain-specific development are not entirely mutually exclusive (Goswami, 1998). It is entirely possible that there is a domain-general process of development as Piaget and Vygotsky said, but that in addition certain specific abilities do develop independently of generalised development at particular points as particular modules mature.

Reflection point

Modular theory is growing in influence. To what extent does it invalidate existing theories? How do you feel as a practitioner when one theory that has influenced your practice is challenged by another?

Conclusions and personal reflections

Many of the most profound insights into the processes of learning come from cognitive development theory. The classic work of Jean Piaget changed forever the way we think of learning, in particular children's learning.

Although contemporary research has cast doubt on some of Piaget's findings on children's reasoning, the principles of qualitative change in reasoning with age and the importance of active and motivated learning are extremely important in education. Perhaps the greatest weakness of Piaget's approach has been the view of the learner as 'lone scientist'. Although this term has been widely misinterpreted, and Piaget did not suggest that learning should take place in isolation, it is now widely agreed that learning is very much a social process in which a learner takes on understanding from a more experienced tutor.

This social understanding of learning owes much to Vygotsky, and much of the most influential contemporary educational theory and practice are derived from his social constructivist theory. Whole-class interactive teaching, cooperative group work and peer tutoring all depend on the social constructivist principle of maximising focused interaction between a learner and a more expert other. Unlike teaching predicated on Piagetian principles, the effectiveness of these techniques is widely supported by research. Although the strongest force for cognitive development in education is currently social constructivism, the study of cognitive development in psychology has been strongly influenced by the modular approach, which sees development as domain-specific rather than as a single generalised process. This approach is well suited to explaining multiple intelligences, learning styles and conditions like autism, which are characterised by distinctive profiles of different mental abilities. It seems likely that both modular and social constructivist approaches will remain important in understanding learning.

Self-assessment questions

1. Critically discuss Piaget's research into children's reasoning in the light of contemporary research.

2. How useful has the Piagetian understanding of learning and cognitive development been in the context of education?

3. What do you consider to be the main features of social constructivist theory? Consider Vygotsky's theory and recent developments.

4. Discuss how social constructivist theory has influenced educational practice. To what extent are social constructivist principles supported by education research?

5. Critically compare social constructivist and modular approaches to cognitive development. What are their different implications for education?

Further reading

•••••• Daniels, H. (2001) *Vygotsky and Pedagogy*. Routledge Falmer, London.

•••••• Goswami, U. (1998) *Cognition in Children*. Psychology Press, Hove, W. Sussex.

•••••• Karmiloff-Smith, A. (1998) Development itself is the key to understanding developmental disorders. *Trends in Cognitive Science*, **2**, 389–398.

•••••• Meadows, S. (1993) *The Child as Thinker*. Routledge, London.

•••••• Salomon, G. (1993) (ed) *Distributed Cognitions: Psychological and Educational Considerations*. Cambridge University Press, New York.

•••••• Smith, L. (1996) (ed.) *Critical Readings on Piaget*. Routledge, London.

•••••• Vygotsky, L. S. (1978) *Mind in Society*. Harvard University Press, Cambridge MA.

•••••• Wood, D. (1998) *How Children Learn*. Blackwell, London.

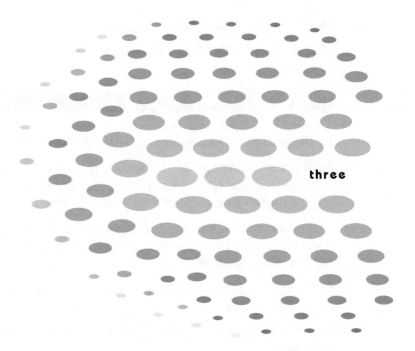

three

Intelligence and Academic Ability

Intelligence and Academic Ability

By the end of this chapter you should be able to:

- Appreciate the range of views surrounding the nature of intelligence and their implications for the ways teachers and psychologists think about academic ability.

- Understand the idea that intelligence can be viewed as a social construct, and be familiar with cultural variations in conceptions of intelligence.

- Be aware of the importance of learners' understanding of the nature of intelligence.

- Define IQ, describe its testing and assess its usefulness in education.

- Critically compare the concepts of general cognitive ability and multiple intelligences, and understand their applications to education.

- Describe Sternberg's triarchic theory of intelligence and apply it to improving educational practice by devising active learning tasks.

- Understand the current status of the nature–nurture debate concerning the origins of intelligence and its implications for education.

- Discuss approaches to boosting intelligence, including preschool intervention programmes and hothousing.

- Describe and evaluate research into grouping by academic ability.

- Be familiar with the concept of giftedness and some of the issues surrounding gifted learners.

Most of us place great value on our intelligence. However, there is surprisingly little consensus about what we are really speaking of when we use the word. The traditional British and American view of intelligence is of a real, single, measurable, inborn and unchangeable entity that determines our material success. If this view of intelligence were beyond question, then it would probably not be a very helpful concept in education. However, all the elements of this popular view of intelligence are open to challenge, and much of this chapter concerns these challenges. The most basic challenge comes from psychologists from social constructionist schools, who have challenged the tenet that intelligence is a real entity, pointing to the historical factors underlying our understanding of the term and the wide variations across cultures in the ways it is used. This is important because different ways of thinking about intelligence are associated with differences in success in education.

If intelligence is a measurable entity, then we need to consider carefully how it is tested. One amusingly circular definition of intelligence is that it is the thing that IQ tests measure. If that were all intelligence is, then why bother to measure it? Certainly intelligence quotient (IQ) is less predictive of achievement than other factors such as motivation. However, IQ tests do have some legitimate if limited uses in education. Even if we accept that intelligence is both real and useful, there remain important questions to answer. Should we think of intelligence as a single quality or a set of mental abilities? In fact, strong arguments can be made for both these positions, and actually they may not be as irreconcilable as they first appear. Similarly, the once bitter nature–nurture debate surrounding the origins of intelligence can now be largely reconciled, and the interaction between genes and environment can be understood and usefully applied to education.

43

Intelligence and academic ability

The terms 'intelligence' and 'ability' are not synonymous. As we shall see in this chapter, there are a variety of views concerning the nature of intelligence, but whatever perspective we take on intelligence, it is a technical term open to precise if not consistent definition. By contrast, when we use the word 'ability' we are talking pragmatically about what we believe a learner can achieve, based principally on their current achievements. Our understanding of the nature of intelligence will profoundly influence our understanding of learners' academic ability, and one excellent reason for studying the nature of intelligence is to give teachers a more sophisticated understanding of their students' ability.

Intelligence as a social construct

Insights from critical psychology

Perhaps the most fundamental question we have to address regarding intelligence is whether it is a real psychological entity or merely a *social construct*, i.e. a concept developed in a particular historical context to satisfy a political purpose rather than to describe a reality. As we saw in Chapter 1, there are several strands to social constructionism, one of which is *critical psychology*, devoted to challenging the unthinking use of social constructs within psychology. Coming from a critical psychological perspective, Cernovsky (1997) suggests that intelligence research is just one way in which psychologists have helped maintain the status quo in society, hence perpetuating social inequalities. Cernovsky cites the example of an intelligence test called Raven's progressive matrices that has been used to compare the intelligence of black Africans from poor ghettos with that of highly educated white Europeans (e.g. Rushton, 1988). Even though the test contains mathematics the white Europeans but not the black Africans had learnt at school, Rushton's results, showing that the Europeans do better on this test, have been used to claim genetic superiority for white people, thus justifying racism.

The concept of intelligence has also been used to prop up the British class system. In principle, the twentieth century saw a shift towards the acceptance of meritocracy, the idea that ability rather than birthright should determine the social position of any individual. However, research has consistently found that IQ is associated with socio-economic status; children of middle-class parents generally score more highly than those of working-class parents. This means that the middle classes have effectively had a monopoly on 'merit', and so the class system continues intact. Although there are various psychological explanations for the relationship between socio-economic status and IQ, at a *social* level of explanation, one reason why intelligence and IQ are considered so important is that they can be used to justify social stratification.

Historically, it would seem that critical psychologists are justified in their concern about the use of the word 'intelligence'. Although IQ tests were first developed with the aim of identifying children who would benefit from special education, their history throughout the twentieth century was largely one of justifying human rights abuses. The *eugenics* movement, begun by Francis Galton (1884), proposed that as 'intelligence' ran in white, middle-class families, it should be possible to raise the intelligence of a nation by preventing the intellectually 'inferior' from breeding. This theory underlay the Nazi extermination of Jews and Romanies, as well as those with physical and psychological disabilities, who were felt to be genetically inferior and at risk of polluting the Aryan gene pool. It also underlay the social policy of compulsory sterilisation of those defined as 'retarded' by their low score on standard IQ tests, still practised in some parts of Europe today.

It is largely because of its at best chequered history that the word 'intelligence' raises the hackles of many teachers and psychologists. However, the fact that the concept of intelligence is open to abuse is not to say that it is inherently abusive; this chapter explores some educational applications of modern views on intelligence.

Cultural variation in understandings of 'intelligence'

One reason why we might think of intelligence as a social construct rather than a real entity is the extent to which it is perceived differently in different cultures. The popular British view of intelligence as fixed is far from universal. Asian cultures tend to see effort and motivation as aspects of intelligence rather than additional factors affecting achievement (Stevenson *et al.*, 1990). This is important because it means that intelligence is seen as continuously variable rather than a fixed entity. Hsueh (1998) compared the beliefs of American and Taiwanese children about intelligence. It emerged strongly that the American children had a greater tendency to see intelligence as fixed and unchangeable, whereas the Taiwanese children tended to see intelligence as malleable. Presumably because of this, the Taiwanese children were more motivated than the Americans to take on challenging puzzles and mathematics. Presumably the American children did not see the point of stretching themselves when they saw their intelligence as unchangeable. Findings like this have important implications for enhancing achievement, because it is possible to manipulate children's beliefs about intelligence in order to motivate them.

45

The importance of beliefs about intelligence

Regardless of whether we choose to see intelligence as 'real' or as a social construct, it can be instructive to examine people's beliefs surrounding intelligence. Individual and cultural variations in such beliefs are not merely of academic interest, but can actually be applied to enhance learners' abilities. We owe much of our understanding of this to American psychologist Carol Dweck and her colleagues. Bandura and Dweck (1981) speculated that the preoccupation about intelligence they noted among their students appeared to be related to the students' belief that intelligence was a fixed quantity. The idea that we have a limited quantity of intelligence and that it may or may not be enough to achieve our goals provokes considerable anxiety among learners. Dweck *et al.* (1995) developed a tool for measuring learners' implicit beliefs about intelligence. Box 3.1 shows the children's version of the Implicit Theories of Intelligence Scale.

Box 3.1

Read each sentence below and circle the one number that shows how much you agree with it. There are no right or wrong answers.

1. You have a certain amount of intelligence and you can't do much to change it

1	2	3	4	5	6
Strongly Agree	Agree	Mostly Agree	Mostly Disagree	Disagree	Strongly Disagree

2. Intelligence is something about you that you can't change very much

1	2	3	4	5	6
Strongly Agree	Agree	Mostly Agree	Mostly Disagree	Disagree	Strongly Disagree

3. You can learn new things but you can't really change your basic intelligence

1	2	3	4	5	6
Strongly Agree	Agree	Mostly Agree	Mostly Disagree	Disagree	Strongly Disagree

4. No matter who you are, you can change your intelligence a lot

1	2	3	4	5	6
Strongly Agree	Agree	Mostly Agree	Mostly Disagree	Disagree	Strongly Disagree

5. You can always greatly change how intelligent you are

1	2	3	4	5	6
Strongly Agree	Agree	Mostly Agree	Mostly Disagree	Disagree	Strongly Disagree

6. No matter how much intelligence you have, you can always change it quite a bit

1	2	3	4	5	6
Strongly Agree	Agree	Mostly Agree	Mostly Disagree	Disagree	Strongly Disagree

To obtain a score, add up the numbers from Questions 1 to 3, and the reverse scores from Questions 4 to 6. You will have a score between 6 and 36. The higher your score, the more of an incremental theory you have.

On the basis of this and similar scales, Dweck and her colleagues have shown that children tend to adopt one of two approaches to their intelligence. *Entity theorists* see intelligence as fixed. *Incremental theorists* by contrast see it as changeable. Belief in the incremental theory has been shown in a number of studies to be predictive of high achievement (e.g. Faria, 1998). Studies have also shown that younger children and those from lower socio-economic groups are more likely to adopt an entity theory (Faria and Fontaine, 1997). This points towards a practical application in improving the motivation of young working-class learners. A number of successful studies have looked at the potential of manipulating learners' views of intelligence in order to improve their motivation, achievement and in turn their abilities. This is explored further in Chapter 6.

Reflection point

Assess yourself using the Implicit Theories of Intelligence Scale (Box 3.1). Are you an entity theorist or an incremental theorist? How might this affect the way you deal with learners who you judge to have particular levels of ability?

IQ testing

At the social and cultural levels of explanation there are good reasons to question whether intelligence is a valid construct. However, at the level of the individual, with which psychology has traditionally been most concerned, it has proved possible to assess cognitive abilities and to construct a profile of these abilities that we might call 'intelligence'. Indeed a fundamental principle of intelligence is that it is measurable. Psychologists measure intelligence using a variety of tests called *intelligence quotient* (IQ) tests. These measure a variety of mental abilities and give a total score or IQ. IQ can be calculated in two ways. Stern (1912) first developed the idea of IQ, originally defined as the relationship between mental age and actual age:

$$IQ = \frac{\text{mental age}}{\text{actual age}} \times 100$$

For example, if a 10-year-old child gained the score that represented the average score for nine-year-olds, their IQ would be

$$9/10 \times 100 = 90$$

The Stanford–Binet test

Building on the work of Binet and Stern, Terman (1916) produced the first true IQ test, the Stanford–Binet test. Early versions of the Stanford–Binet test used Stern's formula to calculate IQ, although the latest versions use the

Wechsler method (see below). The Stanford–Binet test measures a variety of abilities, including defining words, counting, reasoning, word naming and understanding the sequences in groups of numbers. Each of these includes items varying in difficulty. For example, words to be defined range from 'orange' to 'homunculus'. Detailed information on scoring with exemplars of acceptable and unacceptable answers for the reasoning problems is provided.

The Wechsler test

Wechsler (1939) produced an alternative IQ test, which had two major advantages over the Stanford–Binet test. First, it tested a wider variety of cognitive abilities, divided into verbal and performance abilities. These are shown in Box 3.2.

   The other main advantage of the Wechsler system was its method for calculating IQ, which could then be used for adults. This approach depends on the fact that intelligence, like all human abilities, has a normal distribution throughout the population (Figure 3.1).

   Using this system, we take the mean test score from a large and varied population and call it an IQ of 100. IQ scores of individuals can then be calculated according to where they fall on the normal distribution curve. For example, we know from looking at the normal distribution curve that 97.5% of the population score over 70 and that 2.5% score below. Therefore a score that appeared 2.5% of the way up from the lowest score in the population would be given an IQ score of 70. This is the method now generally used to calculate IQ, including the modern version of the Stanford–Binet test. The concept of mental age (MA) is still used in modern psychology, but is no longer so closely associated with IQ. Each generation does better on tests of IQ than the last, therefore psychologists have to regularly test large groups of people and work out the average score, which is then set at 100.

Box 3.2

The verbal and performance scales from the Wechsler test

Verbal scale
1. General questions
2. Text comprehension
3. Arithmetic
4. Similarities
5. Vocabulary
6. Digit span.

Performance scale
1. Picture completion
2. Picture arrangement
3. Block design
4. Object assembly
5. Maze escape.

Number of scores

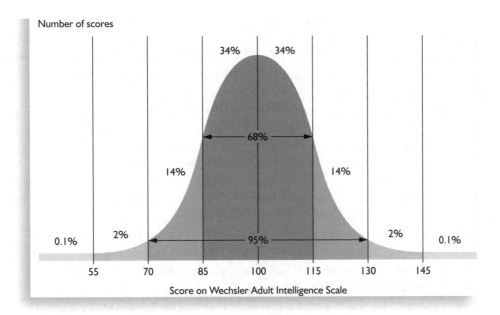

34%   34%

68%

14%   14%

0.1%   2%   95%   2%   0.1%

55   70   85   100   115   130   145

Score on Wechsler Adult Intelligence Scale

Figure 3.1 **Distribution of IQ across the population**

The British Ability Scales

Both the Stanford–Binet and Wechsler tests of IQ were developed in the US. In the 1970s the British Psychological Society sought to develop a British IQ test. The result was the British Ability Scales (BAS). BAS assesses 24 aspects of intelligence, grouped into five major abilities: reasoning, spatial imagery, perceptual matching, short-term memory and retrieval, and application of knowledge. Although there are some advantages to BAS, it has remained less popular than the Stanford–Binet and Wechsler tests (Richardson, 1991).

What use is IQ?

Forty years ago it was believed that IQ tests were the final word in educational psychology, that we could truly sum up a person's potential in an hour-long test. This now seems hopelessly naive in light of our understanding about the malleability of cognitive abilities, learning styles and the importance of social, motivational and emotional factors affecting achievement. Although modern IQ tests allow us to make extremely accurate measurements of a person's cognitive abilities in an artificial test situation, it is now widely acknowledged that this does not necessarily allow us to predict how well that person will function in real-life situations, such as education.

Recent studies suggest that IQ is only very modestly associated with scholastic performance. In one study, Dal Vesco *et al.* (1998) found no correlation between IQ and school performance in Brazilian 8–13-year-olds.

Similarly, Cote and Levine (2000) found that IQ did not predict academic success in Canadian university students and that motivation was the most important factor influencing how well the students did in their degrees. It seems that in most real-life situations, motivation and expertise are more important than IQ in affecting performance, so we would be unwise to take our IQ scores too much to heart. Sternberg *et al.* (2001) have reviewed the predictive value of IQ and concluded that it can be useful in predicting achievement, but only in conjunction with a range of other factors.

Rapport *et al.* (2001) have suggested one way in which IQ interacts with other factors in the classroom. IQ is associated with classroom performance, but so is earlier achievement independent of IQ. Earlier achievement is affected not only by IQ but other variables such as behavioural problems, thus IQ becomes less predictive of academic success once other important influences become introduced. It also seems that the association between IQ and later achievement is exaggerated by the influence of IQ on early achievement. This is significant because it suggests that if we manipulate early achievement then we should be able to boost achievement beyond that predicted by IQ.

General intelligence and multiple intelligences

There is considerable confusion surrounding the fact some commentators speak of general cognitive ability or g, while others talk about 'multiple intelligences'. The former approach suggests that intelligence is a single factor, whereas the latter emphasises our range of mental abilities. Note that the term 'cognitive ability' is now widely used in preference to 'intelligence'. This is because the term 'intelligence' comes with so much historical and political baggage; 'cognitive ability' is widely felt to be a more neutral term.

In fact, different as they may sound, the general and multiple abilities approaches are not mutually exclusive. Intelligence researchers correctly point out that when they measure a range of mental abilities using standard IQ tests like the Stanford–Binet, Wechsler or British Ability Scales, a positive correlation can be seen between the scores on different abilities, i.e. the same people tend to score highly in their verbal and performance scores (Cooper, 1999). This indicates that there *is* such a thing as general intelligence. However, such correlations should not blind us to the fact that individuals also have particular strengths and weaknesses in their profile of mental abilities. General intelligence is only moderately associated with academic success, and thinking of learners in terms of a single intelligence can obscure teachers' understanding of their strengths and weaknesses. Many educationalists therefore believe that it is more fruitful to focus on individual profiles of mental abilities rather than to label learners with a single figure. This line of thinking owes much to the work of Howard Gardner.

Gardner's multiple intelligences

Howard Gardner's (1983, 1993) aim has been to enrich education by showing us how to take account of and value the full range of learners' mental abilities. Whenever we talk about or measure intelligence, we are taking account of quite a wide range of mental abilities. For Gardner (Figure 3.2) this raises the question of whether there is any point in speaking of a single entity called 'intelligence'. Gardner's approach to cognitive development is a *modular* approach (Gardner, 2003), as described in Chapter 2.

To understand Gardner's position it is crucial to bear in mind that his critique of traditional views of cognitive ability questioned not so much the *existence* of general intelligence but rather its *usefulness*, particularly in education. Instead of taking a psychometric approach to intelligence, which measures abilities then classifies them, Gardner used a variety of sources of information when devising the multiple intelligences (MIs). He drew on cases of brain damage in which one mental ability became impaired but others were undamaged, developmental conditions like autism in which some mental abilities are much more impaired than others, and studies of prodigies who demonstrated exceptional abilities in one area but were more average in others. All these sources of evidence illustrate the tremendous disparities that can exist between levels of particular cognitive abilities within the same indi-vidual. In the light of these disparities, Gardner has suggested a range of separate intelligences (Table 3.1). Different versions of Gardner's theory show different numbers of MIs. In the original theory there were seven. It is likely that more will be added as Gardner's evidence accumulates.

Each of the intelligences can be linked to preferences for particular activities that involve different ways of processing information. As Gardner put it, the challenge in fulfilling human potential lies in 'how to best take advantage of the uniqueness conferred on us as a species exhibiting several intelligences' (Gardner, 1999, p. 45). Thus a learner strong in linguistic intelligence will probably orient towards learning situations where information can be assimilated in verbal form. A more kinaesthetic learner may find practical tasks more to their liking and a visual learner may make the best use of diagrams, tables and pictures.

Figure 3.2 **Howard Gardner**

Table 3.1 **Gardner's multiple intelligences**

Intelligence	Description
Linguistic/verbal	The ability to use language in written and oral forms
Logical/mathematical	The ability to reason logically and manipulate numbers
Visual/spatial	The ability to recognise and produce visual images
Kinaesthetic	The ability to coordinate the body and use it to express and achieve goals
Musical	The ability to recognise and produce music
Naturalist	The ability to recognise and interact with the natural world
Interpersonal	The ability to understand the motives, emotional states and intentions of others
Intrapersonal	The ability to understand one's own motives, characteristics, strengths and weaknesses

Assessing multiple intelligences

Part of Gardner's critique of traditional approaches to intelligence concerns the ways IQ is measured. Indeed measurement is not a high priority in his approach. Gardner suggests that a valid measure of each intelligence would take place in its own domain. Thus assessment of kinaesthetic intelligence would be entirely by bodily tasks. The implication of this is that traditional question-and-answer tests are flawed because they are inevitably mediated by the linguistic and logical abilities needed to interpret and respond to the tasks. This is one reason why, within Gardner's philosophy, intelligences do not lend themselves to their popular use in the UK as a learning styles classification system. That said, a number of writers influenced by Gardner's ideas have produced self-rating inventories to measures MIs. One such inventory comes from Christison (1999). Learners respond to six or seven items to assess each of the eight intelligences. The items for linguistic/verbal and logical/mathematical intelligences are shown in Box 3.3.

It is important to note that this type of self-rating inventory measures *preferences* rather than abilities, measured by IQ tests. Whereas IQ tests are *normative* in nature, i.e. they assess the individual relative to the norms of the population, MI tests are *ipsative*. This means that each individual is assessed in isolation and not compared to others. This is important because it means that someone who scores 7 out of 7 in logical/mathematical intelligence does not necessarily have greater logical abilities than someone else who scores 4, merely that they judge their logical/mathematical intelligence to be particularly strong compared to their other abilities. This was confirmed in a study by Chan (2001), where 192 Chinese students assessed themselves on seven multiple intelligences and were then assessed by standard measures. There was little relationship between self-rated MI and ability measures.

Box 3.3

Items from Christison's test of multiple intelligences

Directions
Rate each statement 2, 1 or 0. 2 means you strongly agree. 1 means you are
in the middle. 0 means you disagree. Total the points for each intelligence.
Compare your scores on the different intelligences.

Verbal/linguistic intelligence
1. ____ I like to read books, magazines or newspapers
2. ____ I often write notes and letters to my friends and family
3. ____ I like to talk to people at parties
4. ____ I like to tell jokes
5. ____ I like to talk to my friends on the phone
6. ____ I like to talk about things I read

Logical/mathematical intelligence
1. ____ I can do arithmetic easily in my head
2. ____ I am good at doing a budget
3. ____ I am good at chess, checkers or number games
4. ____ I am good at solving problems
5. ____ I like to analyse things
6. ____ I like to organise things
7. ____ I like crossword puzzles

Applying multiple intelligences to education

Gardner's theory has proved more popular with teachers, indeed more so
than with psychologists. Many educationalists, particularly in the US, have
applied his ideas in a range of ways. Some attempts to apply MI theory have
been extremely simplistic, and are perhaps best thought of as 'pop
psychology' rather than the systematic application of Gardner's theory. Some
examples of these 'pseudo-applications' are shown in Box 3.4.

The heuristic value of MI theory
So does Gardner's system have legitimate practical applications as a
classification of learning styles? Certainly it has good *face validity*, i.e. it
makes intuitive sense to teachers, corresponding neatly with their everyday
experience of learners. As Kornhaber (2001) puts it: 'The theory validates
educators' everyday experience: students think and learn in many different
ways. It also provides educators with a conceptual framework for organising

Box 3.4

Some 'pseudo-applications' of MIs

- Using contrived classroom techniques in an attempt to apply every MI to every subject.
- Simply stimulating the senses during lessons, such as playing music or encouraging movements in the belief that this activates different intelligences.
- Misunderstanding the intelligences and their implications. For example, suggesting that learners high in interpersonal intelligence prefer learning with others – virtually all learners prefer it – and that those high in intrapersonal intelligence learn best alone, which has no basis in MI theory.
- Using MIs simply as memory aids. Constructing diagrams or making up rhymes may be useful mnemonic techniques, but this is not the same as using visual or musical intelligence.
- Labelling children with a single learning style based on the MI in which they score most highly.

and reflecting on curriculum, assessment and pedagogical practices' (2001, p. 276).

MI theory is a useful approach for teachers but what of learners? If learners do indeed orient towards learning in particular modalities then understanding this may enhance their personal metacognition, i.e. their awareness of their own learning processes (p. 101). Cornwell (2001) looked at the effect of increased insight into 10 adult learners' use of their MIs in her work developing basic skills as part of the American Even Start project. She introduced learners to MIs (using a jargon-free system of 'word-smart', 'picture-smart', etc.) and completed MI profiles with them to help them acquire insight into their current strengths and weaknesses. Although most learners were initially resistant to MIs and learning, it was possible to overcome resistance by varying tasks whenever a student's anxiety became too great and explaining this in MI terms. By the end of the project, the students had an awareness of their cognitive strengths and were able to use them to approach problems with a range of strategies.

The values-led curriculum

MI theory has practical applications in terms of curriculum development. Although often cautious about the range of ways MI theory can be applied in education, Gardner (2002, 2003) stresses the possibility of rethinking teaching and assessment to take more account of individual needs. MI theory implies that a wide range of activities should be included and valued in the curriculum. Thus as teachers we should put a value on the musical intelligence demonstrated by talented musicians and the kinaesthetic intelligence demonstrated by athletes and dancers to the same extent as that accorded to verbal and mathematical abilities. In this sense, MI theory is as much a value system as a psychological theory. Moreover, like Sternberg's triarchic theory (p. 57), MI theory suggests that the same topic should be taught in a number of ways, thus the curriculum should favour depth of coverage of each topic over breadth of topic areas. In the UK this would mean a radical departure from the current content-heavy National Curriculum. However, the depth-over-breadth principle and the accordance of value to a range of courses *is* reflected in the ethos of more teacher-led domains such as adult education.

Multisensory learning

As regards classroom practice, MI theory informs *multisensory learning*, i.e. learning using a range of sensory modalities. At its most crass, this can mean the determined attempt to use all eight intelligences in every learning situation. However, there is little doubt that using different modalities can enhance teaching. Gardner (1997) gives an example: 'a teacher might say, "Look, Benjamin, this obviously isn't working. Should we try using a picture?" If Benjamin gets excited about that approach, that's a pretty good clue to the teacher about what could work' (Gardner, 1997). Numerous commentators have noted that teachers tend to rely principally on verbal techniques, and that learners frequently benefit from more visual, kinaesthetic and interpersonal techniques. Some examples of key words that can help design appropriate multisensory techniques are shown in Table 3.2.

Table 3.2 **Cues for multisensory activities**

Intelligence	Techniques
Verbal	Word search, story, essay, debate, letter, report, leaflet, advert, list
Visual	Illustration, diagram, drawing, flow chart, map, picture search, graph, chart, table
Kinaesthetic	Design, experiment, organise, pilot, carry out, research, move
Interpersonal	Role-play, peer tutoring, group work, question and answer, debate

Rocka (2001) has recorded her use of MI theory to enhance her multi-sensory teaching of reading, using Connie Porter's *Meet Addy*, which describes a teenage slave's escape to freedom. After reading a section students were given the following activities:

1. Draw a picture or model in play dough any part of the paragraph.
2. Pick a song or chant that would comfort the learner were they in such a frightening situation.
3. Draw a map of Addy's journey.

4. Write or discuss with a partner an interesting part of the paragraph.
5. Role-play the events described in the paragraph.
6. List the places in which Addy hid.
7. Design their own project concerned with the section.

The relationship between multiple intelligences and achievement

As an ipsative test, measuring self-rated preferences rather than abilities, we would not expect MI scores to be strongly predictive of educational performance. Nonetheless, there is a modest body of such findings. Snyder (2000) found a positive correlation between grade average and visual intelligence scores in 128 American high-school students, suggesting that a visual learning style advantages students in conventional educational settings. Other MIs are more associated with particular subjects. Thus musical intelligence is associated with musical ability and logical/mathematical intelligence with maths scores. It may also be the case that visual learners are particularly advantaged by the use of information learning technology. S. M. Smith and Woody (2000) compared the progress of a psychology class using traditional teaching methods with that of a multimedia-based class across a term. The multimedia class slightly exceeded the traditional class at the end of a term; the difference was explained by the significantly better performance of visual learners in the multimedia condition. Taken together, the results of studies like these suggest that both standard and multimedia learning environments are particularly suited to visual learners. Studies like these also support the predictive validity of self-rating inventories at least in the assessment of visual intelligence.

Discussion of Gardner's contributions

Gardner's theory is one of the most misunderstood in psychology. Rather than rejecting the widely agreed notion of general intelligence, as is often said of him, what Gardner has actually done is to focus on the value of emphasising discrete cognitive abilities. Had he not used the term 'intelligence' to describe each of several abilities, and instead framed his ideas purely using the language of modular cognitive development, Gardner's work would probably never have achieved its current influence. Neither, however, would it have been so misrepresented by other psychologists and so misunderstood by practitioners. Applications and critiques of MI theory have therefore been predicated on fundamental misunderstandings. Whether used as a heuristic system for learners and teachers, applied in multisensory learning or as a predictor of academic success in particular situations, MI theory can be of considerable value to educationalists. Be aware however of the risks of crass 'pseudo-application' in the classroom and of uninformed commentary in the literature.

Sternberg's triarchic theory of intelligence

Like Gardner, Robert Sternberg (Figure 3.3) has proposed a radical alternative to the notion of general intelligence. Sternberg (1985) proposed that, rather than think about general intelligence, we should think instead of three elements or *subtheories* to intelligence: componential intelligence, experiential intelligence and contextual intelligence.

Componential intelligence

Componential intelligence concerns the basic cognitive mechanisms underlying intelligent functioning. Sternberg suggested three types of component: knowledge acquisition components, performance components and metacomponents. Knowledge acquisition components involve curiosity and affect our learning strategies. Performance components determine our actual abilities, such as counting, comprehension and reasoning. Metacomponents are the partly conscious higher mental processes we use during information-processing tasks, including planning, problem-solving and decision-making.

Figure 3.3 **Robert Sternberg**

Experiential intelligence

Experiential intelligence concerns the impact of experience on the ability to perform mental tasks. To Sternberg, experience has two major effects on the ways we process information. First, we learn to deal with the demands of familiar situations. This is why IQ score predicts how quickly we learn new skills in the workplace, but *not* how expert we become over time (Kamin, 1995). Second, we *automatise* certain information-processing functions. Thus, when we have had sufficient practice at a task, we become able to carry it out quickly and efficiently because it has become automatic.

Contextual intelligence

Contextual intelligence considers intelligence within its cultural context, and recognises that what we actually use intelligence *for* is as important as its cognitive components. Even if human mental abilities are universal, the cognitive tasks we carry out will vary considerably according to our culture. Particular cognitive abilities such as critical thinking are more highly valued and hence often more highly developed in some countries than others. The corollary of this is that the same components of intelligence may be equally developed in different cultures but may show themselves in the performance of quite different tasks.

Applying triarchic theory to education

Like Gardner, Sternberg has aimed to maximise learning by making use of as many aspects of intelligence as possible. Sternberg (1997) has thus proposed a triarchic model of teaching, designed to make use of componential, experiential and contextual aspects of our intelligence. The triarchic model emphasises that teaching should involve not only learning of facts but also critical thinking, creative thinking and practical thinking. None of these elements is unique to Sternberg's approach, but he has provided a neat way of understanding how they fit together. Here are some examples of these activities (Sternberg, 1999).

Critical-thinking activities
- Compare and contrast two explanations.
- Evaluate a tool.
- Read and criticise a piece of text.
- Analyse how a tool can be used in a particular situation.
- Compile the arguments for or against a position.
- Assess the usefulness of a particular source of evidence in the courtroom.

Creative activities
- Create an imaginary debate between two people with different views.
- Invent a test to measure something.
- Imagine you have to find something out.
- Design an experiment to test an idea.
- Put together your own theory to explain something.

Practical activities
- Show how you would apply what you have learned to achieve a particular result.
- Explain how we could use a principle to achieve a particular result.
- Implement a strategy to achieve a particular result.
- Give an example of how a principle holds true in the real world.
- Demonstrate the usefulness of an idea.

One thing all these tasks have in common is that they require the learner to actively engage with the material rather than passively take it in and attempt to learn it. A strength of using all elements of the critical, creative and practical triarchy is that it creates a variety of activities that allow individuals, both teachers and learners, to play to their own strengths and either develop or compensate for their weaknesses.

Sternberg's theory and IQ testing

It is well established that IQ tests are now extremely reliable, i.e. they consistently measure cognitive ability but that they are of limited use in predicting real-life performance. Sternberg's theory offers a way of understanding this and of improving measures of IQ. The tasks that make up IQ tests are in principle meant to measure componential intelligence, but results are inevitably contaminated by experience and culture. Moreover, if we wanted to predict performance in real-life situations, it would be essential to systematically assess contextual and experiential intelligence. In other words, current IQ tests are flawed because they fail to take into account two of the three aspects of intelligence.

Evidence for the effectiveness of triarchic teaching

Triarchic teaching was developed for the teaching of introductory psychology, and its usefulness probably varies from one subject to another, according to the scope each provides for critical, creative and practical thinking. There is a small but respectable body of research to suggest that, in psychology at least, the triarchic approach is effective. Sternberg and Clinkenbeard (1995) assessed 199 American college students on their preferences for critical, creative and practical thinking and designed a course in introductory psychology that either corresponded or failed to correspond to these preferences. When assessed, students whose learning activities had been congruent with their preferences did significantly better, supporting the idea – central to triarchic theory – that individuals have strengths and weaknesses across the three domains. Sternberg et al. (1998) went on to compare a triarchic model of teaching with a traditional memory-based model of teaching and a critical-thinking model, which focused on critical evaluation of material without creative or practical tasks. A total of 141 American high-school children were taught introductory psychology at a university summer school in memory-based, critical thinking and triarchic groups. Assessments showed that the triarchic group did best, followed by the critical-thinking group and finally the memory-based group.

More recently, research has supported the usefulness of the triarchic model in teaching a range of subjects. Grigorenko et al. (2002) report two studies, conducted in primary, middle and secondary school settings, and involving subjects as diverse as languages, maths and history. A total of over 1300 children took part. Results were consistent across a range of age groups and subjects – triarchic teaching improved achievement significantly.

Discussion of triarchic theory

Like Gardner's MI theory, the triarchic theory of intelligence is of great heuristic value to teachers. Taking account of context and culture rings true for teachers and provides a way of bypassing the notion of general intelligence that, while valid in the psychometric sense, represents an educational dead end. In particular, triarchic theory points the way towards a variety of tasks to involve the individual learner in actively exploring and using information. This is perhaps of particular benefit to teachers who would like to expand their repertoire of teaching activities but, because of their own learning style (Chapter 4), require a theoretical underpinning to do so. The body of research supporting triarchic teaching is relatively small and dominated by one research team, so a little caution is needed at this point. However, the approach appears extremely promising.

Reflection point

Think of a topic you know well or have taught or observed recently. Design two lessons, one based on MI theory and one based on triarchic theory. The emphasis in the MI lesson will be on multisensory teaching and the emphasis in the triarchic lesson will be on providing opportunities for critical, creative and practical thinking. Critically compare your two lessons.

Developing intelligence and educational ability

The nature–nurture debate in the twenty-first century

Before looking specifically at attempts to develop individual intelligence, it is important to understand a little about where our intelligence comes from in the first place. The nature–nurture debate surrounding intelligence has been a long and bitter one, but in the new millennium it should be possible to move beyond this and acknowledge a role for both genes and environment. To teachers and psychologists, the environmental aspects of intelligence are clearly more salient, because it is our business to manipulate the environment, whereas short of selective breeding or genetic modification at the molecular level, there is little we can do about the genetic basis of intelligence in the classroom. This is not to say, however, that teachers should be threatened by the idea of a genetic component to intelligence. There are three fundamental misunderstandings that underlie such sense of threat:

- If genes are involved in intelligence, then the environment becomes less important and the importance of education is consequently diminished.
- If intelligence has a genetic basis, then it must be unchangeable and an individual's potential is predetermined at birth.
- If a genetic element to general intelligence is discovered, then this applies equally to all mental abilities.

Actually all these very common beliefs are quite mistaken. There are multiple influences on the development of mental abilities, involving interactions between a range of genes and environmental variables. Twin studies, a common technique for investigating the role of genes and environment on psychological variables, have consistently uncovered both genetic and environmental influences. For example, a study by Grigorenko and Carter (1996) compared IQ in 60 pairs of identical twins and 63 pairs of fraternal twins of Russian adolescents. It was found that the identical twins were significantly more similar in IQ, but also that IQ was associated with parenting style, level of the mother's education and the socio-economic status of the family.

Moreover, there is not necessarily a close link between the influence of genes on intelligence and abilities and the extent to which they are changeable. Genes appear to influence people's starting point in developing their cognitive abilities. This does not mean that their environment does not then affect them. M. J. A. Howe (1998) has suggested that there are several sources of evidence to support the idea that we can increase a child's IQ. These are shown in Box 3.5.

Twin studies have also shown that genes may be more important in the development of some abilities than others. In a large-scale study, Reznick *et al.* (1997) compared general intelligence, verbal ability and non-verbal abilities in 408 pairs of identical and fraternal twins. General intelligence was somewhat more similar in the identical twins, suggesting both genetic and environmental influences. There was very little difference between identical and fraternal twins in verbal ability but a dramatic difference in non-verbal ability. This suggests that verbal ability is primarily environmental in origin whereas other abilities are strongly influenced by genes. A highly controversial study suggests that language stimulation may be the factor underlying the

Box 3.5

Evidence for the changeability of intelligence

- Adoption studies have shown that when adopted into a highly stimulating environment, children's IQ increases and can become considerably higher than the IQs of their biological parents.
- Attempts to boost the IQ of disadvantaged children have resulted in substantial increases.
- Education research has shown a relationship between amount of time spent at school and IQ.
- Medical research has shown that improving nutrition can lead to increases in IQ.
- Where educational and social opportunities increase from one generation to the next so does IQ.

relationship between IQ and socio-economic status. Hart and Risley (1995) observed three-year-old children in families categorised as either professional, working class or on benefits, counting the number of words that were directed towards each child in a week. The difference was dramatic: children in professional families had up to 15 000 more words directed towards them in a week than the children from families on benefits. Extrapolating from this week to the children's first three years, the researchers estimated that the children from professional homes had 30 million words spoken to them as opposed to 20 million in the working-class homes and 10 million in the families on benefits.

Reflection point

We are now in very sensitive territory. Monitor how reading about issues like the heritability of intelligence and its relationship to socio-economic status make you feel. You may be experiencing *ideologic strain*, as the ideas presented here may challenge your political beliefs. Be aware of how your politics affect your academic opinions concerning issues like this.

Preschool intervention programmes

The original Operation Headstart project began in 1965 in America, with the aim of targeting regions where poverty appeared to be affecting children's early environment and to compensate for their impoverished environment. For a year before entering kindergarten, children received extensive intellectual and social stimulation accompanied by dietary supplements. After one summer the children in the Headstart group had an average of 10 IQ points advantage over their peers. Lazar *et al.* (1982) followed children up to primary education and found that the difference in IQ disappeared. Seitz (1990) set out to investigate why this might be. She followed up children from an earlier study (Zigler and Seitz, 1982), and found that the problem lay in the children's later education. The programme studied by Zigler and Seitz emphasised mathematical skills, and the children were simply not given enough later mathematical education to maintain their early gains. Interestingly, however, Seitz (1990) found that the benefits to IQ had partially reappeared by adolescence, suggesting that early intervention did have a substantial long-term effect.

Despite the apparent success of the Headstart project, there were problems. The programmes were implemented in several places and not all reported success. There was also considerable cost involved for relatively small gains. Since the original Headstart project, attempts have been made to refine the process. In the Milwaukee project, infants with mothers having an IQ of less than 75 were given extra stimulation in day care from three months.

The mothers were also given help in work and parenting skills. Garber (1988) followed up the children to 14 years and found that they had an average IQ 10 points higher than their peers. A review of 38 studies (Barnett, 1998) focusing on costs and benefits concluded that, in the long term, early intervention programmes are extremely cost effective. Ramey *et al.* (1999) reviewed 10 studies that randomly allocated children to the two conditions and concluded that there was firm evidence Headstart did boost IQ and that the greater the deprivation suffered by the children, the greater the gains achieved by Headstart. Gorey (2001) carried out a meta-analysis of 35 studies and found large effects, maintained over a long period. Some 70–80% of children in preschool programmes did better at school than those in control groups. Moreover, those who had attended preschool had lower rates of unemployment, poverty and criminality as adults. At the time of writing, Surestart, a major project based on American successes, is being rolled out across the UK. This aims to provide free preschool childcare in order to guarantee a stimulating environment for large numbers of children, in particular those judged to be at risk of a suboptimal home environment, perhaps due to poverty.

Hothousing

Whereas the aim of Headstart projects is to enrich the environments of disadvantaged children in order to raise them to 'normal' levels of intellectual functioning, hothousing seeks to take 'normal' or bright children and boost them to a level of intellectual functioning *above* the norm. Sigel (1987) first used the term 'hothousing' as an analogy with the way in which vegetables are forced to ripen earlier than normal by placing them in a greenhouse.

There have been many case studies where children have been taught skills such as reading at a very young age and have later exhibited very high IQ. However, this type of case study has the problem that the children may have already been exceptionally intelligent and this may have enabled them to learn to read early. Another approach to deciding whether exceptional skills can be developed by hothousing is to look at the early lives of particularly talented people. M. J. A. Howe (1988) has provided support for the principle that intensive early enrichment can enhance specific abilities. He reviewed biographical accounts of a wide variety of exceptionally talented and successful individuals, including the composer Mozart, the writer Dickens and the chemist Kekule. Howe found that in every case he studied, the early childhood of the individual was characterised by intensive training in their particular skill at an earlier age than is typical. Church (2000) has challenged Howe, suggesting that just because intensive training and practice are *necessary* for the development of exceptional talents, this in itself does not mean that training and practice are *sufficient*. It may be that these individuals had innate talents which were developed by their hothousing, and it seems unlikely that we can hothouse just anyone and produce another Mozart or Dickens.

Some psychologists and parents are concerned that intensive early training may interfere with children's social and emotional development. Certainly the stereotyped view of hothousing in which a child is forced to stay in and practice a skill for untold hours when their friends are out playing may cause a child to suffer problems. However, there are now methods of enhancing intellectual development that do not involve enormous numbers of practice hours. Fowler (1990) devised a programme of accelerated language development in which parents were trained and taught their children at home. Parents were trained to spend more time talking to their infants and at more regular intervals than is usual, to point to objects and speak names earlier than would normally be done, and to frequently play games like peekaboo, which involve intensive and lively interaction with the child. Fifteen babies were followed up from five months and their development assessed. The results were dramatic. By 24 months all the children could use five-word sentences, although typically this becomes possible for children at around 32 months. The average language quotient for the group was 139 (remember that the average for the population is always 100). At five years follow-up, the advantage for the children who had had the Fowler programme was maintained.

Ability grouping

Ability grouping is an important and long-running controversy surrounding the optimal conditions for the development of abilities in individual learners. The extent to which learners have been selected and grouped in British education has fluctuated throughout the last century, influenced by ideological shifts and changing beliefs about intelligence and educational effectiveness (Ireson and Hallam, 2001). There are two broad hypotheses underlying ability grouping. The first holds that learners benefit from clustering with others of similar ability. This is predicated on the common sense assumption that a school or class of homogeneous ability can receive material at the optimum level of complexity and learning tasks targeted at their common level of understanding (Lou *et al.*, 1996). However, there are theoretical and ideological objections to this proposition, and there is an alternative view that mixed-ability classes are more effective. On the theoretical level, social constructivist theory (Chapter 2) emphasises the role in learning of the communication of knowledge from individuals with more sophisticated understanding to those with less expertise. Clearly this process benefits from the cooperation of individuals of differing ability. Ideologically, both selection and ability grouping can be seen as objectionable because they can be seen as 'writing off' the potential of learners currently not achieving highly. There are several ways in which learners can be grouped by ability

Table 3.3 **Options for grouping learners by ability**

Name	Description
Selection	Learners are taken on by different institutions according to their general ability, so particular schools or colleges specialise in catering for learners of particular abilities
Streaming	Learners are put into classes that reflect their general ability and remain in these classes for all subjects
Banding	Learners are put into bands that reflect their general ability, but for different subjects they may be in different classes within the band
Setting	Learners are put into classes for each subject based on their ability in that subject rather than their general ability
Random mixed-ability	Ability is not considered when assigning learners to classes, so each class comprises a different mix of ability
Systematic mixed-ability	Learners are systematically allocated to classes so that each class contains a mixed profile of ability

and they have subtly different implications. Some of these options are shown
in Table 3.3.

Selection is the most controversial option, and is felt by many educationalists to reflect a perpetuation of the British class system, whereby children
from working-class backgrounds are channelled into institutions where there
are neither the expectations nor the opportunities for them to achieve highly
enough to realise upward social mobility. Streaming and banding are based
on the assumption that learners have a general academic ability that determines their potential achievements. This assumption in turn reflects the
traditional British cultural belief in general and immutable intelligence.
Setting reflects the belief in a variety of mental abilities that affect ability in
particular subjects. There are clear parallels between this ethos and
Gardner's view of multiple intelligences. Random mixing of abilities can
reflect a rejection of the importance of ability in educational effectiveness or
may simply be a pragmatic response to timetabling logistics. Systematic
construction of mixed-ability groups may be founded on social constructivist
principles of cooperative learning or ideological objections to classifying
learners as low in ability.

Research into ability grouping

Despite the passions aroused by selection and ability grouping in schools,
there has been a relatively small body of research conducted into their
effectiveness, and that research has found surprisingly little effect for alternative strategies. Studies into setting in secondary schools that have compared
achievement in national qualifications such as GCSEs and A levels have found
no consistent advantage for local authorities where selection has been
practised or where it has not. Jesson (2000) conducted a value-added analysis
of secondary schools comparing a range of local education authorities (LEAs).

A value-added study looks at results relative to qualifications on entry as opposed to raw results. None of the country's top 10 and four of the bottom 10 LEAs according to value-added figures had a policy of selection for secondary schools. This suggests that selection does not have a generally beneficial effect on secondary-school achievement and may indeed have an overall deleterious effect on achievement, although not necessarily on the minority selected for high-level secondary establishments such as grammar schools. Ireson and Hallam (2001) conclude that there is clear evidence for a negative effect of streaming on the achievement of learners put into bottom streams, but that setting appears to have little effect.

Reflection point

Ability grouping can be approached from either a strict psycho-logical perspective or from more of an ideological stance. Which do you think has been more influential in policy decisions, and on which do you place more personal emphasis?

Giftedness

Some children demonstrate exceptional abilities. We can call such individuals 'gifted'. There are a range of definitions for giftedness. Some children are considered as gifted because they display highly specific mental abilities, such as in maths or music. Others are identified by their particularly high IQ (Figure 3.4). It is worth stepping back for a moment from the range of psycho-logical definitions of giftedness and considering the implications of the term itself. The concept of ability as a 'gift' has clear Christian roots and suggests innate rather than environmental origins. Giftedness is the most commonly used term, and there is no obvious equivalent that carries fewer connotations. However, be aware that using the term indiscriminately may bias perceptions of the origins of ability and so have implications for other learners.

The BFLPE

Gifted children represent a challenge to teachers and psychologists. One important question concerns whether to integrate them into the mainstream or to provide tailor-made provision. According to common sense, we might think of this as a trade-off between the best social environment (integrated) and the best educational environment (segregated). This is an important issue for parents of gifted children, who have to decide whether to place their child in a mainstream school where they will stand out or to enrol them in a more academic institution where their peers will be as bright as they are and where teaching can be geared to the high ability of the children. Actually the social/educational distinction appears to be a false one, largely because of a phenomenon known as the big fish little pond effect (BFLPE). Zeidner and Schleyer (1999) tested the big fish little pond effect in 1020 gifted

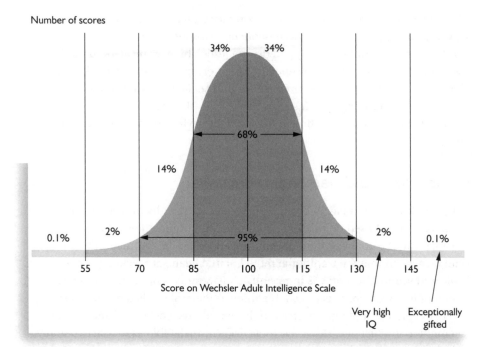

Figure 3.4 **Identifying gifted children using the normal distribution curve**

9–12-year-olds. Half were enrolled in mixed-ability classes and half were in special classes for high-ability children. Anxiety before tests, overall achievement and self-concept were compared in the two groups. Self-concept and performance were better and test anxiety lower in the mixed-ability classes, supporting the idea that children do better as big fish in small ponds.

Psychological well-being of gifted children

A further issue concerns the psychological well-being of gifted children. There are two stereotypical views of the gifted child in psychological literature: the highly resilient child whose social skills and emotional development mirror their intellectual development, and the very vulnerable and socially retarded child. Neihart (1999) reviewed the evidence and concluded that either stereotype can be true, depending on the nature of the gift, the appropriateness of the child's education and their temperament. There is no reason why children with a resilient temperament and who have positive educational experiences should be socially disadvantaged by their unusual abilities. However, an already vulnerable child who is then made to feel like a freak at school because of their abilities is likely to be scarred by the experience.

Much may depend on how gifted children perceive themselves and their gifts. J. D. Lewis and Knight (2000) investigated the self-concept of 368 gifted

American children in primary and secondary education. Interestingly, it was found that the children's self-concept was positive in primary school and high school, but that it dipped during junior high, equivalent to the UK secondary school. Boys were reported as suffering more than girls, being lower on scores of perceived intelligence and social status at school, and higher on scores of anxiety. It seems likely, then, that gifted girls have a somewhat easier time in fitting in during their early adolescence than gifted boys.

Conclusions and personal reflections

The whole area of intelligence and ability is fraught with controversy, but much of this is based on misunderstandings and outdated debates. Historically, the concept of intelligence has been politically misused, and it can be argued that the traditional model of intelligence as a single, measurable and immutable entity is inherently abusive; this is not true of modern views of intelligence. There *is* such a thing as general intelligence (at least according to psychometric tests) and there is almost certainly some genetic element to intelligence. However, those facts, unpalatable as they are to many psychologists and educationalists, need not be a source of too much concern. Multiple intelligence and triarchic theories are almost certainly more useful than g as tools for educationalists to think about intelligence, and the likely existence of a genetic element to intelligence takes nothing away from the importance of the environment and the opportunities afforded by education to develop an individual's mental abilities.

Modern intelligence research has produced a range of practical applications in the classroom. Understanding implicit theories of intelligence allows us to avoid demotivating learners by encouraging a conception of their abilities as fixed. MI theory and triarchic theory have given us strategies to make lessons more lively, inclusive and effective. Our understanding of environmental influences on intelligence has allowed the development of effective early intervention programmes, and research into giftedness has shown that the development of gifted children is not best served by common sense solutions. Teachers' understandings of academic ability are founded on beliefs about intelligence. Ability grouping is one way in which beliefs about intelligence have been applied to education. Although such grouping has attracted huge controversy, there is little evidence for strong effects on the development of learners' ability.

Self-assessment questions

1. To what extent do modern psychological theory and research support the traditional view of intelligence as a real, single, measurable, inborn and unchangeable entity?

2. Discuss the view from critical psychology that the concept of intelligence is inherently abusive in the light of traditional and contemporary theory.

3. Compare the usefulness of IQ, self-rated multiple intelligences and implicit theories of intelligence.

4. Critically compare multiple intelligence theory and triarchic theory.

5. What are the educational implications of the modern nature–nurture debate surrounding intelligence?

Further reading

•••••• Cooper, C. (1999) *Intelligence and Abilities*. Routledge, London.

•••••• Dweck, C. (2000) *Self-theories: Their Role in Motivation, Personality and Development*. Psychology Press, Philadelphia PA.

•••••• Gardner, H. (1993) *Frames of Mind*. Harper Collins, New York.

•••••• Gorey, K. M. (2001) Early childhood education: a meta-analytic affirmation of the short- and long-term benefits of educational opportunity. *School Psychology Quarterly*, **16**, 9–30.

•••••• Howe, M. J. A. (1999) *The Psychology of High Abilities*. Macmillan, Basingstoke, Hants.

•••••• Ireson, J. and Hallam, S. (2001) *Ability Grouping in Education*. Paul Chapman, London.

•••••• Neihart, M (1999) The impact of giftedness of psychological well-being: what does the empirical literature say? *Roeper Review*, **22**, 10–17.

•••••• Sternberg, R. J., Grigorenko, E. L. and Bundy, D. A. (2001) The predictive value of IQ. *Merrill-Palmer Quarterly*, **47**, 1–41.

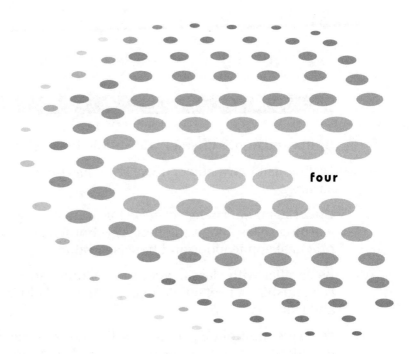

four

Styles of Thinking, Learning and Studying

Styles of Thinking, Learning and Studying

learning objectives

By the end of this chapter you should be able to:

• • • • • Distinguish between cognitive style, learning style and learning strategy.

• • • • • Understand alternative criteria for evaluating systems of learning styles, including their psychometric properties, practical applications and heuristic value.

• • • • • Be familiar with classifications of cognitive style and assess the relationship between field dependence or field independence and learning.

• • • • • Describe multidimensional classifications of learning styles, including those by Riding and Rayner, Honey and Mumford, and Felder and Silverman and evaluate their relative strengths.

• • • • • Explain the concept of learning strategies with particular reference to Entwistle's classification and ASSIST.

• • • • • Discuss research into the relationships between learning styles and academic preferences, pedagogical preference and academic success.

It is now widely acknowledged that, regardless of their age, general cognitive ability and motivation, individuals vary in the ways they respond to different classroom situations, different ways of presenting information and in the approaches they take to studying. In the past 15 years there has been an explosion of research into these individual differences, all of which fall under the very broad umbrella of *learning styles*. Understanding what makes the individual learner 'tick' has become something of a Holy Grail for many researchers, but it has proved extremely difficult to pin down the nature of individual learning styles. Consequently, there are a plethora of learning style classifications on the market. For reasons of space, only a handful can be considered in any depth, but the overlap between different systems means that this chapter still gives a fair idea of the nature of the field. Before looking at the specifics of learning style classifications, let us consider three very common scenarios in which individual learners are failing to reach their potential because their particular styles of learning are not adequately catered for.

Box 4.1

Case examples

- *Emily* is in year 6. She excels in art and other subjects like geography in which there is plenty of information in visual form. However, she is not a strong reader and finds English a particularly difficult subject.
- *Aaron* has just taken his mock GCSEs and is shocked and upset by his low grades. Until now he has relied on his innate abilities rather than good study habits and has passed exams with cursory revision.
- *Tom* has just started AS levels. He has opted predominantly for arts subjects but is also taking psychology. He is surprised at how scientific psychology is, and finds this way of thinking very difficult to get used to.

We can explain each of these very common problems in terms of individual differences in styles of learning and studying. Emily (Box 4.1) has a distinctive profile of abilities, in which her weakness seems to be handling verbal information. By contrast, she is adept at handling visual information. She can be helped in English by the use of visual teaching strategies that use her strengths. Aaron's learning strategies are not highly developed. Up to Key Stage 3 this was not a problem as he has good memory and analytic skills, but to progress to more advanced study he needs to learn more efficient ways to understand and learn information, i.e. to develop his *learning strategies*. Tom is faced with a mismatch between his innate style of thinking or *cognitive style* and the demands of a science subject. He might opt for arts subjects that match his thinking style, which might be termed field dependent, wholist or intuitive, according to alternative theories of style. Alternatively, he might attempt to modify his cognitive style.

Defining terms: cognitive style, learning strategy and learning style

Before defining cognitive style, learning strategy and learning style, it is important to be aware that they have not been used consistently in the education literature. Thus the same classifications of individual differences may be called 'cognitive styles' within some research traditions and 'learning styles' in others. However, in principle if not in practice, each term has a distinct meaning.

Cognitive style refers to 'the way the individual person thinks' (Riding and Rayner, 1998, p. 7). Cognitive style is widely believed to be 'hard-wired' into the individual, thus it is either innate or determined early in development and thus difficult to modify by the time formal education is under way. Our cognitive style leads us to process information in particular ways. Thus some of us find it easier to break down a problem and think logically through each part, whereas others tend to consider it as a whole. Some people tend to seek out and apply conventional procedures to tasks, whereas others prefer to find their own, more novel approaches. Some learners think largely in images, whereas others make more use of verbal information. Some people have a strong need to 'do something' with information rather than understand it from verbal or visual representations. Our cognitive style can impact on many aspects of our learning, ranging from our ability to use diagrams, text and practical tasks to the sorts of subject we orient towards. This chapter examines one 'pure' cognitive style system, concerning field dependence and field independence. Cognitive style is also a major factor underlying the learning style classifications of Riding and Felder and Silverman, also reviewed in this chapter.

Learning strategies are the ways individuals adapt to the learning tasks at hand and the environment they are in. Given any learning task, we are faced with a choice of how we go about tackling it. This is influenced in part by our cognitive style, but also by habit, experience, motivation and practical constraints such as the study time we believe to be available. We may therefore opt for an individual mode of study or prefer to work cooperatively. One learner might habitually work at a relatively 'surface' level, making the most of minimal information, whereas another will tend to seek a more in-depth understanding of the task at hand. Unlike cognitive styles, learning strategies are habits rather than innate characteristics and are thus probably amenable to change, even though it may not be easy to change them. Such change requires a degree of insight, and there is growing interest in ways of informing learners about their current learning strategies and the ideal strategies for their situation.

The term 'learning style' is the most difficult to define because it is the least consistently used. This chapter takes a fairly broad view, and 'learning style' is used as an umbrella term for all the systems of classifying individual differences in learning, including those closely based on cognitive style and those more oriented towards learning strategies. In some circles the 'learning styles' construct has fallen into disrepute due to the inconsistency with which it has been used, and because it defies precise definition and lacks a single, agreed theoretical basis (e.g. Reynolds, 1997). Nonetheless, it is worth bearing in mind that both cognitive style and learning strategy are widely agreed to be robust concepts (Sadler-Smith, 2001).

What makes a good system for classifying learning styles?

Given the myriad of alternative systems available for classifying and assessing learning styles, finding an appropriate system for a particular situation can be extremely daunting for the teacher and the researcher. There is no single criterion that consistently allows us to identify the most appropriate system for a given situation, but the learning styles literature will probably make more sense with a grasp of the alternative ways in which learning style systems might be judged. Each classification system depends on a theoretical idea and an instrument of measurement, and both are open to evaluation. A system also has to have a practical application, perhaps as a tool of metacognition, providing insight for the teacher and learner or as a guide to inform pedagogical practice.

Psychometric criteria

One common approach to evaluating learning styles involves testing the psychometric properties of its instrument of measurement. All psychometric tests are judged on their reliability and validity. Put simply, tests can be said to be *reliable* if they consistently measure the same thing and *valid* if they measure what they purport to. For example, we might look at the *internal reliability* of scales. The term 'internal reliability' refers to the extent to which each item in the scale measures the same quality. If the internal reliability of a learning style scale were good, we would expect every item to discriminate between people who score high and low in that variable. If this is not the case, the scale will not effectively discriminate between individuals with different learning styles. We might also look at *test–retest* reliability. This is the extent that the test will find the same learning style in the same person when presented to them on two occasions.

Psychometric tests, including learning style questionnaires, also need to meet the criterion of validity. A test has good *face validity* if it appears to the person taking it to be an appropriate measure of what they believe it aims to assess. This is important as if a test lacks face validity, then those taking it will not treat it seriously (Rust and Golombok, 1999). A test has good *predictive validity* if those scoring high and low on a scale can then be demonstrated to display some other difference not directly related to the content of the test. For example, researchers have investigated the extent to which subject preference and academic success can be predicted by learning style.

Another way of assessing systems for classifying learning styles concerns the theory or theories on which they are based. Psychometricians refer to this as *construct validity*. If a system used to classify learning styles is based on a theory that has little support, then it is unclear precisely what is being measured. If we are not clear what a test is measuring and have no faith in the logic underpinning the test, then it can be very difficult to know how to respond to the results. But a word of caution is needed. There is some controversy surrounding most psychological theories, and fashions in psychology and education change just like those elsewhere. Consequently, there is no ultimate arbiter of what theories are 'supported'. Beware of dismissing any psychological theory just on the basis of polemical attacks in the literature.

The applicability criterion

To the researcher, tests of learning style are primarily tools of measurement and must therefore have reasonable psychometric properties. However, classroom teachers tend to be great pragmatists and are most impressed by systems that have a clear educational application. This might be in the form of broadening the range of teaching styles used to 'reach' the full range of students. It might also involve testing teaching groups and targeting particular techniques, or indeed teachers, at them. Some learning style assessments can be useful in suggesting what courses or particular aspects of courses are likely to prove difficult for learners. Learning strategy assessments have the additional application of identifying learners at risk for poor study habits and intervening.

The heuristic criterion

Perhaps the most important application of learning styles systems is *heuristic*, i.e. they serve as mental tools, allowing the learner and the teacher to think about individual differences in learning. There is no reason why poor psychometric properties of a learning styles test should prevent it being used as a heuristic device (Loo, 1999). For the learner, understanding their own learning style can form an important aid to their personal metacognition, i.e. their awareness of their own mental processes and learning (p. 101). By studying learning styles, teachers can gain a better awareness of the impact of different pedagogical techniques and a greater appreciation of the difficulties faced by each learner in every learning situation.

Reflection point

The importance of these ways of evaluating learning styles classifications will be influenced by your own style. Which appeals to you the most? Do you adopt a hard-nosed scientific approach and emphasise psychometric properties or are you more philosophical, thinking in terms of the heuristic value of learning styles. Are you in fact purely pragmatic and going with applicability in the classroom?

Cognitive styles

Recall that the term 'cognitive style' refers to the more hard-wired and immutable aspects of the way the individual processes information and thinks. A range of systems have been devised to classify cognitive style; Table 4.1 shows some of the more influential ones. The systems devised by Hudson, Pask, Gregorc and Paivio have been particularly important in influencing the development of some of the most popular systems for measuring and classifying learning styles. They are covered later in this chapter, but it is worth paying particular attention to Witkin's distinction between field-dependent and field-independent individuals as this has remained a popular 'pure' cognitive style system with important educational applications.

Field dependence

Psychologists first noted the phenomenon of field dependence in the 1940s, during perception experiments in which it emerged that some individuals made more use than others of background information to determine whether an object was vertical. The field-dependent person makes more use of external information to draw conclusions of this sort, whereas the field-independent individual makes more use of internal information, and is thus less influenced by background information. The field dependence construct was later broadened to include a dimension of thinking as well as perception (Witkin, 1964). Thus the field-dependent person sees tasks and problems within specific contexts whereas the field-independent person sees them in isolation.

Table 4.1 **Examples of cognitive styles classifications**

Reference	Styles	Description
Witkin (1964)	Field dependent	Perception of an object or situation is altered by its context
	Field independent	Perception is more independent of context
Hudson (1966)	Converger	Logical deductive approach to problem-solving
	Diverger	Intuitive and imaginative image to problems
Pask (1976)	Serialist	Working through a task one piece at a time
	Wholist	Viewing a task or situation as a whole
Gregorc (1982) and Allinson and Hayes (1996)	Active Reflective/contemplative	Learns though experience Learns through reflection
Paivio (1971)	Verbaliser	Information is most easily processed in verbal form
	Visualiser	Information is most easily processed in visual form

After Riding and Rayner (1998)

Early research established that men tend towards field independence whereas women are more likely to be field dependent (Witkin *et al.*, 1962). This was initially conceived as a cognitive advantage for men, however, Spender (1980), cited in Hayes (1998), has pointed out that this is actually rather sexist, and that field-dependent people could equally be labelled 'context aware' and field-independents 'context blind'. From this perspective, the cognitive advantage lies with the typically female mode of information processing. Interestingly, recent studies (e.g. B. Pithers, 2000) have found that these sex differences in cognitive style no longer exist or at least are much diminished. This is significant as it suggests the origins of cognitive style are cultural and thus modifiable.

The Embedded Figures Test

The most commonly used assessment tool of field dependence is the Embedded Figures Test (EFT). The task here is to pick out concealed shapes from a perceptually similar background. Figure 4.1 shows an example. Field-independent people find it easier to spot or *disembed* the concealed figure. There are a range of published versions of the EFT. The original test, designed to be administered to adults on an individual basis, consists of 12 cards each showing an embedded figure. The children's embedded figures test consists of 25 figures, and is also designed for individual use. In addition there is a 25-item group EFT for administration to people in groups; it is standard practice to administer particular psychometric tests to either individuals or groups.

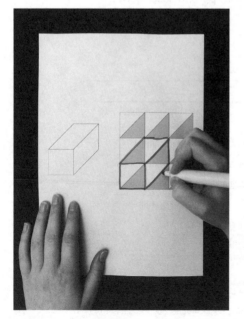

Figure 4.1 **An embedded figure**

Applying field independence to education

Field dependence has been applied to understanding the characteristics of teachers and learners, and to the interactions between them. Although findings are not entirely consistent, there is some evidence (e.g. Saracho, 1991) that field-dependent teachers are more socially skilled and more interested in people. These are clearly strengths in a profession depending on social interaction, but Saracho also found that field independents are more independent and better problem-solvers. Field-dependent teachers expressed more satisfaction in dealing with students, whereas field-dependent students expressed a strong preference for field-dependent teachers. This leads us to the possible practical application of matching field-dependent learners and teachers. However, B. Pithers (2000) has cautioned against this on the basis that if there is a degree of modifiability in field dependence, matching with a field-dependent teacher may reinforce field dependence in learners. By contrast, placing dependent learners with independent teachers may encourage the development of a more balanced cognitive style.

Riding and Cheema (1991) investigated differences in behaviour between the two types of teachers. They noted that field-dependent teachers and field-independent teachers had different attitudes toward the use of questioning. Dependents saw questioning as a way of checking on students' understanding, whereas independents tended to see it more as a technique for instruction. This is consistent with the field dependent's orientation towards social interaction and the field independent's orientation towards problem-solving. Both are legitimate uses of questions, but teachers can benefit from insight into how their understanding of everyday teaching techniques such as questioning varies according to their own cognitive style.

Given the different strengths of field-dependent learners and field-independent learners and the possibility of modifying cognitive style, would modifying this dimension of cognitive style confer a significant advantage on learners? Field independents tend to score higher on standard IQ tests, although bear in mind the controversies surrounding IQ testing (p. 42). We would perhaps expect this given that IQ tests are intended to be context-free measures of cognitive ability and that field independents are advantaged in the sort of problem-solving that characterises IQ measures. There is also some evidence that field independents do better in exams. Childress and Overbaugh (2001) gave 204 students on a computer literacy course the group EFT and tracked their progress. No difference emerged between dependents and independents during the course itself, but independents did significantly better in the final exam. This disparity in performance between coursework, where learners can make full use of contextual information and teacher support, and exams, in which these sources of information are unavailable, highlights the difficulties faced by field-dependent learners.

Discussion of field dependence

There is strong support for the construct validity of the field dependence–field independence dimension of cognitive style. However, a number of uncertainties remain. Riding and Rayner (1998) criticise the EFT as a measure of field dependence. Given that field dependence was originally conceived as a perceptual style and then reframed as a style of thinking and problem-solving, it seems that assessing the characteristic by a perceptual test is an outdated approach. Field dependence has a number of possible applications in education. Students express a preference for teachers with the same cognitive style, and this matching approach may make for more harmonious classrooms. On the other hand, research is now suggesting that cognitive style may be modifiable, and strongly field-dependent learners can benefit from exposure to field-independent teachers. As a heuristic device, field dependence can be useful in helping teachers understand their own use of pedagogical techniques and their relations with learners.

Multidimensional systems of learning styles

There are now a huge number of classification systems that assess learning style on one or more dimensions. Some systems are based closely on dimensions of cognitive style whereas others also draw on theories of personality, multiple intelligences and preferences for different learning environments. Some of the more influential classifications are shown in Table 4.2. It is not possible to review all these systems in detail, but it may be helpful to look in more depth at three systems: Felder and Silverman's pan-theoretical model, Riding's two robust dimensions, and the popular Honey and Mumford system. These represent very different philosophies of what makes a good learning styles classification, yet paradoxically they focus on fairly similar aspects of style.

Felder and Silverman's model

Richard Felder and Linda Silverman (1988) aimed for a comprehensive system of learning styles to help lecturers in undergraduate engineering

Table 4.2 **Examples of major learning styles classifications**

Author	Test	Dimensions or types
Kolb	Learning Style Index (LSI)	2 dimensions experiential–reflective, active–conceptual
Honey and Mumford	Learning Style Questionnaire (LSQ)	4 types activists, theorists, reflectors, pragmatists
Felder and Silverman	Index of Learning Styles (ILS)	4 dimensions active–reflective, sensing–intuitive, visual–verbal, sequential–global
Dunn and Dunn	Learning Style Inventory (LSI)	5 dimensions environmental, emotional, sociological, physical and psychological preferences
Schmeck	Inventory of Learning Processes (ILP)	4 dimensions synthesis–analysis, elaborative processing, fact retention and study methods
Riechmann and Grasha	Styles of Learning Interaction Questionnaire (SLIQ)	3 dimensions participant–avoidant, collaborative– competitive, dependent–independent
Riding	Cognitive Styles Analysis (CSA)	2 dimensions visual–verbal, wholist–analytic

better understand the needs of their students and adapt their teaching accordingly. In the initial version of their theory they proposed five dimensions of learning style: active–reflective, inductive–deductive, sensing–intuitive, auditory–visual and global–sequential. The auditory–visual dimension was amended in later versions to visual–verbal and the inductive–deductive dimension has not been included in the current psychometric test. The four dimensions currently measured are as follows.

Active–reflective

The active–reflective dimension is closely related to Carl Jung's idea of extra-version, assessed in the popular personality test known as the Myers–Briggs type indicator (MBTI); see Jarvis (2004a) for a review of Jung's theory and research using the MBTI. The dimension can also be found in the classifica-tions of Kolb and of Honey and Mumford. An active learner is most at home processing new information by doing something with it, such as discussion or experimentation. The reflective learner, by contrast, tends to manipulate information internally rather than externally and can therefore make better use of situations, like lectures, in which information is directly imparted.

Sensory–intuitive

The terms 'sensing' and 'intuiting' were first used by Jung, and are also assessed in the MBTI. The two terms describe the way information is perceived. Learners at the sensory end of the continuum prefer to rely on the evidence of their senses, whereas those at the intuitive end rely more on speculation, hunches and imagination. Felder and Silverman call this 'indirect perception by way of the unconscious' (1988, p. 676). This dimension can be thought of as an aspect of *epistemological style*, because it affects the learner's understanding of what comprises knowledge.

Visual–verbal

The verbal–visual dimension is a widely accepted distinction between prefer-ence to process information in visual and verbal form, recognised for example in Paivio's classification of cognitive style and in Gardner's multiple intelligences. Visual learners tend to understand and remember information better when in the form of diagrams, pictures, films and demonstrations. Verbal learners are more comfortable handling information presented in verbal form.

Sequential–global

The sequential–global dimension is based on Pask's distinction between serialist and wholist cognitive styles and is in some respects reminiscent of the field independent–field dependent distinction (van Zwanenberg et al., 2000). The sequential learner learns in steady, logical steps whereas the global learner may have difficulty with this, but is capable of great intuition and sudden leaps of understanding, and may be better at creative solutions and seeing 'the big picture'.

Assessing Felder and Silverman's dimensions

The Index of Learning Styles (ILS) is currently used to assess learning styles according to Felder and Silverman's system (Solomon and Felder, 1996). It comprises 44 items measuring the four dimensions of learning style on bipolar scales. The ILS can be taken in paper form or online. Each item requires a fixed choice between two options (A and B), each of which represents one point towards one of the opposing learning styles. Box 4.2 shows some examples of items from the ILS.

Box 4.2

Items from the ILS

1. I understand better if I	Active–reflective
(a) Try it out	
(b) Think it through	
2. I would rather be considered	Sensing–intuitive
(a) Realistic	
(b) Innovative	
3. When I think about what I did yesterday, I am most likely to get	Visual–verbal
(a) A picture	
(b) Words	
4. I tend to	Sequential–global
(a) Understand details of a subject but may be fuzzy about its overall structure	
(b) Understand the overall structure but may be fuzzy about the details	

Riding's model

Whereas Felder and Silverman's model of learning styles is truly multidimensional and its strength lies in giving maximum information to the learner and teacher, Richard Riding (Riding, 1991; Riding and Rayner, 1998) has focused on the two style dimensions he considers to have the strongest empirical support. His aim was to produce a simple, integrated measure of 'pure' cognitive style. Riding decided on the visual–verbal dimension and the wholist–analytic dimension as the most robust factors to emerge from previous theory and research. Essentially these are the two factors that are most independent of one another. The wholist–analytic dimension corresponds to the global–sequential and sensing–intuitive dimensions identified as separate by Felder and Silverman, and is closely related to field dependence. Interestingly, there is a weak correlation between scores on the sensing–intuitive and sequential–global scales of the ILS, suggesting that they are in fact related but not synonymous constructs; this is somewhere between the positions of the two teams of researchers.

Riding's styles are assessed by a computerised test called Cognitive Styles Analysis (CSA). There are three parts to the CSA. In the first, respondents are required to answer true or false to items requiring verbal or visual processing. Response times are recorded and the relative times needed to process visual and verbal information are used to indicate visual–verbal style. The remaining two parts to the test require respondents to disembed figures and spot differences between complex geometric patterns. The rationale for this is that wholist learners will find it easier to perceive the whole complex patterns whereas analytic learners will prove superior at picking out the parts within an embedded figure.

Honey and Mumford's system

Honey and Mumford (1992) developed the Learning Styles Questionnaire (LSQ) for use in management rather than education. However, it has been adopted enthusiastically by some educationalists. Rather than the bipolar scales favoured by Riding and by Felder and Silverman, the LSQ has four unidimensional scales each representing a learning *type*:

- *Activists* have a learning style characterised by the enjoyment of new experiences, are active and rely on intuitive decision-making and dislike structure (Box 4.3).
- *Theorists* have a learning style characterised by reliance on logic and a preference for systematic planning. They dislike making intuitive decisions.
- *Pragmatists* have a learning style characterised by a down-to-earth attitude and a like of group work and risk-taking. They tend to avoid deep reflection.
- *Reflectors* have a learning style characterised by a wish to observe and ascribe meaning. They tend to formulate and test hypotheses.

83

Box 4.3

Items from the activist scale of the LSQ

- *Item 2*: I quite like taking risks.
- *Item 5*: I often do things just because I feel like it rather than thinking about it first.
- *Item 8*: I actively seek out new things to do.
- *Item 15*: I like the challenge of trying something new and different.
- *Item 19*: I prefer to jump in and do things as they come along rather than plan things out in advance.

There are some similarities between the types described by Honey and Mumford and the bipolar dimensions identified by Felder and Silverman. Both systems refer to preference for active learning and both make a distinction for a preference towards logic or intuition.

Comparing the systems

The teams of researchers arrived at the four dimensions of the ILS, the four types defined by the LSQ, and the two scales of the CSA in quite different ways, reflecting their different aims. The ILS is *pan-theoretical*, drawing freely on a range of approaches to cognitive style, learning style and personality in order to be maximally informative to teachers and students. The CSA was devised in an attempt to isolate the two most 'pure' dimensions of cognitive style, and thus to cut through the confusing range of learning style classifications. Given these origins and aims, we might expect that the CSA has the best psychometric properties and that the ILS has the greatest heuristic value.

Psychometric criteria

The psychometric properties of the ILS and the LSQ are fairly typical for learning styles inventories – rather poorer than the norm for standard tests of personality and IQ. Van Zwanenberg *et al.* (2000) carried out a major analysis of the ILS and LSQ. Some 284 university students of engineering and business studies completed the ILS and a further 182 completed Honey and Mumford's LSQ. Internal reliability of each of the subscales was measured. Results are shown in Tables 4.3 and 4.4.

The figures in Tables 4.3 and 4.4 are correlation coefficients. A score of 1 would represent a perfect relationship between each test item and the rest of the items; this would be ideal but extremely unusual in a psychometric test. A score of 0 would represent no relationship between items; this would indicate an extremely poor test. According to this criterion, the LSQ does somewhat better than the ILS. None of the four dimensions of the ILS or the LSQ was predictive for end-of-year marks or number of units failed. The *orthogonality* of the four dimensions of each test was also assessed, i.e. the extent to which

Table 4.3 **Internal reliability of the ILS**

Dimension	Reliability
Active–reflective	0.51
Sensing–intuitive	0.65
Visual–verbal	0.56
Sequential–global	0.41

Source: Van Zwanenberg *et al.* (2000)

Table 4.4 **Internal reliability of the LSQ**

Dimension	Reliability
Activist	0.74
Pragmatist	0.59
Theorist	0.64
Reflector	0.68

Source: Van Zwanenberg *et al.* (2000)

they measure separate attributes. The active–reflective and visual–verbal dimensions of the ILS did emerge as orthogonal, but a correlation of 0.41 was found between the sensing–intuitive and sequential–global scales, suggesting that they may not be entirely separate entities. These properties were slightly better than those of the LSQ, where a correlation of 0.52 was found between theorist and pragmatist scores. The ILS did distinguish clearly between the engineers and business studies students, supporting its validity.

The CSA has rather better psychometric properties than the ILS or the LSQ. The two scales have consistently been found to be orthogonal (Riding *et al.*, 1995). Moreover, a large body of research has linked the two dimensions with a host of education-related behaviours and characteristics, including stress, interpersonal interaction, optimism and occupational choice. Occupational choice has a clear application in careers counselling. In one study, Riding and Wheeler (1995) assessed 204 nurses using the CSA and found that job satisfaction was highest in general, orthopaedic and psychiatric nurses with different learning style scores. Analytic verbalisers were happiest in general nursing but unhappy in psychiatric nursing, among whom wholist imagers expressed most satisfaction.

Heuristic and practical application in educational settings

The different philosophies and strengths of the three models make for rather different applications. The ILS has tremendous heuristic value, providing learners with four tools for introspecting on their learning. By establishing norms for each scale, Felder and Silverman (1988) were able to demonstrate the mismatch between the needs of engineering students and the characteristics of their education. For example, most students were active rather than reflective, yet teaching was almost exclusively oriented towards reflective students. Most learners are visual rather than verbal, but most teaching is verbal in nature. The ILS can therefore be an effective tool to help teachers reflect on their teaching and on how well it matches with the learning styles of their learners. Felder and colleagues have explored the mismatch between learning styles of students and teaching modalities in various subjects, including science (Felder, 1993) and languages (Felder and Henriques, 1995). In using unipolar scales, the LSQ has an advantage over the ILS because it does not rely on the assumption that a learner cannot score highly in both ends of a continuum. On the other hand, the four dimensions are probably less useful as heuristic devices.

The better psychometric qualities of the CSA make it a better research tool than the ILS or LSQ. This has proved useful in understanding individual preferences in a number of situations. For example, Riding and Read (1996) used the CSA to understand which learners benefit most from cooperative learning. Seventy-eight 12-year-old children were assessed using the CSA and questioned about their preferences for solo, pair and group work. Although all categories expressed preferences for cooperative work, this was greatest in wholist imagers and least in analytic verbalisers. Achievement in different subjects can also be understood by reference to the two dimensions of the CSA. Analytic verbalisers do best in English whereas wholist imagers do best in maths and science (e.g. Riding and Pearson, 1994). Understanding the learning dimensions underlying achievement in different subjects and success in studying in different ways opens the way to improving achievement. For example, increasing the image content in English and the verbal content in maths and science should help compensate for the natural weaknesses of students who often underachieve in these areas. Interestingly, behavioural problems are also associated with style as measured by the CSA. Riding and Burton (1998) assessed learning style and behavioural difficulties in 341 year 10 and year 11 pupils from urban schools. Male wholists were the most disruptive category, suggesting that the frustration resulting from difficulty in following sequential lessons may contribute to behavioural problems. In support of this finding, Riding and Craig (1997) found that wholists and verbalisers were significantly over-represented in schools for children with behavioural problems.

Discussion of multidimensional systems

The contrast between these three classification systems is an excellent illustration of the trade-off between value as a heuristic system and as a research tool that has dogged the field of learning styles. The ILS is extremely useful, arguably the best test of its type, in helping students and teachers understand their own learning. In particular, adult returners to education, who tend to actively seek insight into their learning styles, benefit from having four dimensions to reflect on. The ILS is also useful for illustrating to teachers how serious a mismatch there can be between the style of their delivery and the preferred learning style of their students. This is not to say, however, that the CSA is merely of academic interest. The accumulated body of research linking its two dimensions to a variety of educational outcomes is impressive and highly relevant to developing better pedagogy.

Reflection point

Consider the three systems outlined above in relation to your own learning experiences. Which system do you find the most useful in understanding the sort of learner you are?

Learning strategies

The learning strategies approach represents a radical departure from the learning styles systems looked at so far in this chapter. Whereas classifications based on cognitive styles and multiple dimensions of learning focus on the relatively fixed characteristics of the learner and how best to adapt to them, learning strategies are seen as modifiable patterns of learning behaviour. In other words, we can classify learners according to how they go about learning and studying. The practical application of this is clear – we can identify learners likely to underachieve because of poor learning strategies and help them develop better strategies.

Deep and shallow learning

The distinction between deep and shallow learning has its roots in the cognitive psychology of the 1970s. In their *levels of processing* model of memory, Craik and Lockhart (1972) distinguished between information that is extensively processed for meaning (i.e. deeply processed) and is well remembered, and information that is processed less extensively for more surface attributes like sound or appearance (shallow processing). Entwistle *et al.* (1989) applied this idea to education, distinguishing between processing academic information for its surface attributes, and study using deep processing strategies. Shallow or *surface* learning involves relying on single sources of information and learning key points by rote. Learners adopting a surface strategy limit what they study and learn to the strict requirements of a syllabus. Deep learning by contrast is characterised by the motivation to understand at as deep a level as possible the material being studied. There is an association between depth of learning and motivation. Surface learning appears to be motivated by fear of failure whereas deep learning is based on a genuine interest in knowledge for its own sake. The key elements of deep learning are shown in Box 4.4 (McCune and Entwistle, 2000).

There is a moderate negative relationship between deep and surface learning in individuals. This means that we are fairly stable in our preference for either deep or surface strategies, but that we are all likely to vary our strategy according to the situation. Although we might speak of people as

---

Box 4.4

The elements of deep learning

- Intention to understand
- Active interest and personal engagement
- Relating ideas
- Gaining an overview
- Creating outlines and structures
- Questioning and using evidence critically
- Seeking the main point
- Drawing conclusions
- Seeing the purpose of a task or seeing it in wider context.

surface or deep learners, be aware that defining people this narrowly is a little too simple.

Strategic learning

A further dimension of learning strategy concerns how *strategic* learners are. The strategic learner is effective in organising their time and sources of information. They monitor the effectiveness of their strategies and are adaptable when their achievements do not live up to expectations. Nisbett and Shucksmith (1986) describe strategic learners as having a 'game plan' when approaching an academic task comparable to that of a football team approaching an important match. Weinstein and van Mater Stone (1996) see strategic learners as having four key areas of knowledge: awareness of individual characteristics as a learner, understanding of the demands of different academic tasks, knowledge of successful tactics for different learning tasks and situations, and awareness of contexts in which knowledge could be applied. The strategic learner will need to be able to apply these areas of knowledge to learning. This requires a degree of insight (metacognition), willingness to monitor progress and the self-control strategies (self-discipline) to set aside time and maintain focus on the task. A strategic learner typically displays a number of key behaviours when approaching a learning task (Box 4.5).

Box 4.5

Activities of strategic learners

- Creating a plan of action
- Selecting appropriate strategies
- Implementing the strategies in order to carry out the plan
- Monitoring progress and modifying the strategies or even the plan, as appropriate
- Evaluating the outcome to inform future learning experiences.

Assessing learning strategy

Noel Entwistle has developed a series of self-rating inventories to measure individual tendencies for deep, surface and strategic learning. The Approaches to Studying Inventory (ASI) was a 64-item test measuring 16 aspects of learning (Entwistle *et al.*, 1979). Entwistle and Tait (1994) developed a shortened revised version, RASI. Items from the RASI are shown in Box 4.6.

Box 4.6

Items from the RASI

	✓	✓?	??	X?	XX
I'm not just prepared to accept things I'm told; I have to think them out for myself	5	4	3	2	1
One way or another I manage to get hold of books or whatever I need for studying	5	4	3	2	1
Often I feel I'm drowning under the sheer weight of material we're having to cope with on this course	5	4	3	2	1
Sometimes I find myself thinking about ideas from the course when I'm doing other things	5	4	3	2	1

Currently the most used system for assessing learning strategy is the Approaches and Study Skills Inventory for Students (ASSIST), developed by Noel Entwistle. This assesses the learner's view of what learning is (part A), their study habits and strategies (part B) and their preferences for different

Box 4.7

Part A of ASSIST

When you think of the term 'learning' what does it mean to you?

	Very close	Quite close	Not so close	Rather different	Very different
a. Making sure you remember things well	5	4	3	2	1
b. Developing as a person	5	4	3	2	1
c. Building up knowledge by acquiring facts and information	5	4	3	2	1
d. Being able to use the familiarity you've acquired	5	4	3	2	1
e. Understanding new material for yourself	5	4	3	2	1
f. Seeing things in a different and more meaningful way	5	4	3	2	1

learning activities (Part C). Part A is shown in full in Box 4.7 and items from Parts B and C are shown in Boxes 4.8 and 4.9. There are 52 items in Part B and eight in Part C. Part C serves as an additional measure of preference for deep or surface learning. Items (a) and (c) assess surface learning whereas items (b) and (d) are associated with deep learning.

Box 4.8

Items from Part B of ASSIST

1. I manage to find conditions for studying which allow me to get on with my work easily.
2. When working on an assignment, I'm keeping in mind how best to impress the marker.
3. Often I find myself wondering whether the work I am doing here is really worthwhile.
4. I usually set out to understand for myself the meaning of what we have to learn.
5. I organise my study time carefully to make the most of it.

Box 4.9

Items from Part C of ASSIST

	✓	✓?	??	X?	XX
a. Lecturers who tell us exactly what to put in our notes	5	4	3	2	1
b. Lecturers who encourage us to think for ourselves and show us how they themselves think	5	4	3	2	1
c. Exams which allow me to show that I've thought about the course material for myself	5	4	3	2	1
d. Exams or tests which need only the material provided in our lecture notes	5	4	3	2	1

Evaluation of the learning strategies approach

Psychometric properties of learning strategy tests

The properties of the ASI were typical of learning styles assessments; its reliability is somewhat less than desirable for a research instrument. The RASI fared rather better, with Duff (1997) finding internal reliability figures of 0.80–0.82 for the three scales. ASSIST has even better psychometric properties, arguably the best of any of the measures that fall under the broad umbrella of learning styles assessments. In a study of 1284 undergraduate students sampled across a range of UK universities, McCune and Entwistle (2000) found reliability ratings for each of the three strategies on a par with those of standard personality tests, a rare achievement in learning styles research. These are shown in Table 4.5.

Table 4.5 **Reliability of ASSIST dimensions**

Dimension	Reliability
Deep approach	0.84
Surface approach	0.8
Strategic approach	0.87

Moreover, a number of studies have demonstrated that learners scoring highly in deep and strategic learning achieve good grades, whereas surface learning is associated with poor performance. ASSIST and other scales of its type can therefore be said to have good predictive validity.

Heuristic value

There seems to be little doubt that if learners can identify their surface learning strategies and replace them with deeper learning strategies, they will improve their learning. As a starting point, it is certainly helpful to identify poor study habits. However, an over-reliance on surface strategies is associated with motivational factors, and we cannot assume these can be consciously modified simply in response to seeing the results of a test like ASSIST. To develop deep learning strategies in learners we would have to impart to them a love of knowledge and thus the intrinsic motivation to study. There are opportunities to achieve this, such as at the start of post-compulsory education when students opt for subjects that particularly interest them. Although not currently researched, the transition from compulsory to post-compulsory education might be an excellent stage at which to build deep learning strategies. Research into deep learning has currently focused on undergraduates and has found that insight into learning strategy is associated with modest change. McCune and Entwistle (2000) followed up 19 undergraduates over the course of their first year at university to see whether they managed to modify their learning strategies. It emerged that although some students made some significant changes, in general it proved quite difficult to modify learning strategy.

Practical application: developing strategic learning

It may be that strategic learning is more open to modification. Strategic learning can be developed by the use of metacognitive strategies, i.e.

approaches to teaching which make clear to students how and why they are learning. This is explicit in vocational courses such as GNVQ and AVCE, where learners are regularly required to draw up action plans, name the strategies to be used, gather information and review the task. This 'plan, do and review' approach is closely related to the key activities of strategic learners shown in Box 4.5. Learners can also be taught time management strategies, such as using timetables with evenings and weekends blocked so that quality study time can be built into the week. Fisher (1995) has suggested that even quite young children can be taught how to plan by providing appropriate examples of plans. He suggests a three-stage strategy for teaching planning:

- *Direct instruction stage*: teacher explains planning and shows learners examples of plans.
- *Facilitation stage*: learners put plans into their own words.
- *Self-generation stage*: learners construct their own plans.

Riding and Rayner (1998) suggest an alternative approach to developing strategic learning, by adjusting learning activities to fit better with the cognitive style of the individual learner. Thus visual learners can actively seek out and use visual strategies in learning. Riding and Watts (1997) demonstrated that when information is freely available in alternative formats, they opt correctly for the format that best matches their learning or cognitive style. Secondary-school pupils were offered a handout on study skills in three formats: verbal unstructured, verbal structured and diagrammatic. None of the children took the unstructured verbal handouts, and the majority correctly chose the format corresponding to their visual or verbal style. It appears, however, that when such direct choices are not obvious to learners, they are less good at selecting the strategies most congruent with their style. A simple way to help learners develop better learning strategies is therefore to explain the importance of learning 'their way'. Teachers who direct all students towards a single 'best' way of learning are not taking account of the range of learning styles.

Conclusions and personal reflections

The term 'learning style' is at once a buzzword, reflecting the growing acknowledgement of qualitative differences in individual learning, and at the same time a source of frustration, being overused, vague and poorly defined. Anyone tackling the literature of learning style, cognitive style and learning strategy cannot help but be daunted by the variety of alternative conceptions of style and by the lack of consistency in the use of terms. This chapter has probably contributed to this inconsistency by identifying Riding's CSA as a learning style system when it was intended as an approach to cognitive style.

The consequence of this aura of importance combined with the lack of clarity surrounding the field is that many teachers are either unclear as to what they should be doing about learning styles, or they adopt a single model of style classification, perhaps applying it inappropriately, and at best missing out on the potential benefits of applying a range of models. It is certainly helpful for teachers to think of learners in terms of the qualitative as well as the quantitative differences in their learning, and an understanding of the nature of these differences is helpful in encouraging teachers to vary their delivery and match delivery to the styles predominant in a learning popula-tion. Learners too can benefit from a better understanding of how they learn and from help in developing strategic learning. There is little doubt that a better understanding of learning styles is of potential benefit to education.

One issue of concern is the disparity between the emphasis placed on learning styles in schools and colleges and the corresponding emphasis on learning *strategies* in higher education. This no doubt reflects the greater autonomy and maturity of university students, but perhaps also a cultural difference between sectors that sees responsibility in schools as lying with the teacher to change their pedagogy, and in higher education with students to modify their study habits. Without becoming embroiled in the political domain, it is worth considering whether this imbalance of emphasis risks a lack of development of awareness and corresponding good practice in learning strategy in schools and learning style in higher education.

93

Self-assessment questions

1. Distinguish between cognitive style, learning style and learning strategy. How well do such distinctions hold up under examination?

2. Discuss the extent to which field dependence or field independence affects the learning process.

3. Compare and contrast two multidimensional systems for classifying learning styles.

4. Consider how useful the concepts of deep, surface and strategic learning have been in assisting learners in developing better learning strategies.

Further reading

•••••● Bagley, C. and Mallick, K. (1998) Field independence, cultural context and academic achievement: a commentary. *British Journal of Educational Psychology*, **68**, 581–587.

•••••● Felder, R. M. and Silverman, L. K. (1988) Learning and teaching styles in engin-eering education. *Engineering Education*, **78**, 674–681.

•••••● Mahlios, M. C. (2001) Matching teaching methods to learning styles. In *Children and Stress* (ed. Stanford, B. H. and Yamamoto, K.). Association for Childhood Education, Olney MD.

•••••• McCune, V. and Entwistle, N. (2000) The deep approach to learning: analytic abstraction and idiosyncratic development. Paper presented at the Innovations in Higher Education Conference, Helsinki.

•••••• Riding, R. and Rayner, S. (1998) *Cognitive Styles and Learning Strategies*. David Fulton, London.

•••••• Sadler-Smith, E. (2001) A reply to Reynolds's critique of learning style. *Management Learning*, 32, 291–304.

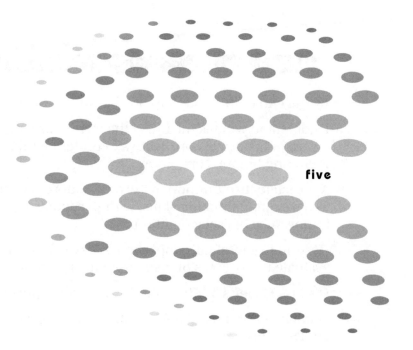

five

Thinking
Skills

Thinking Skills

learning objectives

By the end of this chapter you should be able to:

- Understand what is meant by the term 'thinking skills' and be aware of historical approaches to understanding thinking, including Bloom's taxonomy.

- Appreciate the common features of different current approaches to developing thinking skills, with particular regard to the importance of metacognition.

- Describe Feuerstein's approach to develop thinking skills and evaluate the success of instrumental enrichment programmes.

- Discuss Fisher's 'philosophy for children' approach.

- Outline and evaluate the activating children's thinking skills (ACTS) approach.

- Understand the rationale behind cognitive acceleration and evaluate the success of cognitive acceleration projects, including CASE.

- Outline current thinking on the development of critical thinking skills in higher education.

In recent years, a number of influential psychologists and educationalists have challenged the traditional view of education as transmission of knowledge. They argue that the primary aim of education should be to develop the thinking skills of learners. This is not a new idea; as far back as Ancient Greece, educators have seen education as the development of intellect. As a philosophy, this is entirely compatible with the ideas of Piaget (p. 19), Vygotsky (p. 27) and Sternberg (p. 57). However, in the light of the crowded curricula of the twentieth century, where educational institutions and individuals have been increasingly judged on exam performance rather than the long-term benefits of their teaching, emphasis on thinking skills assumed the status of a radical, even subversive, perspective. The past decade, however, has seen a shift in attitudes, and developing thinking skills is becoming an increasing priority. Much of the theory and research discussed in the previous three chapters is highly relevant to an under-standing of thinking skills, and it would be a mistake to think of work on the development of thinking skills in isolation. Much of the work reviewed in this chapter owes much to Piagetian and Vygotskian ideas. However, there is now sufficient work aimed specifically at enhancing the thinking skills of learners to warrant a separate chapter.

If developing thinking skills is to be an educational priority, then we would expect such skills to convey an advantage to society. Richard Paul has eloquently addressed this, pointing to 'deep-seated problems of environmental damage, human relations, overpopulation, rising expectations, diminishing resources, global competition, personal goals and ideological conflict' (Paul, 1993, p. 1) that face future generations and will require imaginative and critical thought to tackle. On the level of the individual, Wilson (2000) suggests that a broad range of higher thinking skills is beneficial on the grounds of cognitive efficiency; the volume of information we are required to process is ever-increasing, so we simply cannot store sufficient information to respond to every situation without being able to transfer skills from one situation to another.

What are thinking skills?

The term 'thinking skills' is not a clear one, and some commentators have questioned whether we are technically correct to think of cognitive processes as skills that can be learned in the same way as motor skills (Wilson, 2000). Helpfully, Wilson has redefined the central question facing teachers and researchers as 'can children [or any other learners] be taught to think more effectively?' (ibid., p. 2). When we speak of 'thinking' in this context, we are not referring so much to the stream of consciousness that describes our moment-by-moment experience of thinking, but rather a set of *higher-order* mental processes. There have been a number of attempts to classify such higher-order processes. Figure 5.1 shows an influential taxonomy from Bloom (1956).

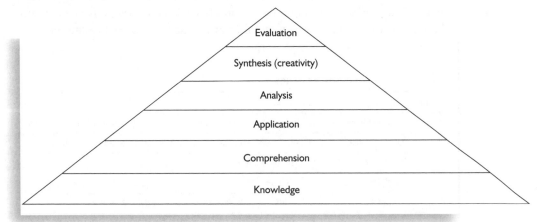

Figure 5.1 **Bloom's taxonomy**

To Bloom and his colleagues there were six levels of thinking, which we can treat as the cognitive goals of education. These were seen as an ascending hierarchy; the most basic was knowledge and the highest was evaluation. The Bloom approach has been enormously influential in curriculum design and assessment. Consider the assessment objectives adopted by the awarding bodies for post-2000 A and AS levels. These are framed in terms of assessment objectives, one representing the Bloom basic levels of knowledge and understanding and another representing their higher goals. Take, for example, the specifications for psychology A level (Edexcel, 2000; AQA, 2000; OCR, 2000). AO1 is defined as knowledge and understanding. AO2, representing higher thinking skills, is worded as follows: 'analysis, evaluation and application' (OCR); 'application of knowledge and understanding, analysis, synthesis and evaluation' (Edexcel); and 'analyse and evaluate' (AQA). In keeping with the belief that analysis, synthesis and evaluation represent more advanced levels of thinking, the proportion of marks available for AO2 is greater at A2 level than at AS level.

Bloom's taxonomy has also proved useful in designing classroom activities and assessment tasks that develop and test a good range of thinking skills. Fisher (1995) has offered a set of cues to trigger thinking across the spectrum of processes suggested by Bloom and colleagues. An adapted version is shown in Table 5.1.

Valuable as the Bloom system has been, it does have its limitations. As any examiner knows, questions requiring evaluation are not necessarily those that pose greatest difficulty to learners. Assessments requiring comparison and problem-solving can be extremely challenging. Moreover, recall Sternberg's model of teaching based on his influential view of intelligence (p. 57), and his distinction between creative, practical and critical thinking. According to Sternberg, our practical, creative and critical thinking represent separate forms of intelligence, and as individuals we vary considerably in the relative ease with which we use them. Both Sternberg's work and the experience of examiners suggest that Bloom and his colleagues might have been too rigid in ascribing a hierarchy to the thinking skills they correctly identified.

Table 5.1 **Thinking process cues**

Level	Thinking skill	Cues for classroom exercises
1	Knowledge	Describe, outline, recall, repeat, define, identify, which, where, who, what
2	Understanding	Summarise, rephrase, explain, compare, conclude, relate, interpret, why
3	Application	Demonstrate, apply, use to solve, use to explain
4	Analysis	Identify the causes, reasons, problems, solutions, consequences
5	Synthesis	Develop, improve, design, create, put together, tell a story
6	Evaluation	Judge, criticise, evaluate the success, practical value, coherence, validity

Source: Adapted from Fisher (1995)

The hierarchical nature of the Bloom *et al.* taxonomy also renders it culture-bound. The belief that evaluation or critical thinking is the highest level of cognition represents the ideals of the European-American academic tradition. By contrast, the Japanese concept of intelligence is closely linked to conformity, and the word *oriko* 'smart' is often juxtaposed in Japanese discourse with *kashikoi* 'obedient' (Tobin *et al.*, 1989).

Reflection point

1. Think about your current practice or that of a teacher you have recently observed. To what extent do you or they use the terms shown in Table 5.1 to cue different thinking skills? Are you personally most skilled at practical, creative or critical thinking?

2. If you teach within the National Curriculum, look at the section on promoting skills across the curriculum. How do the thinking skills outlined there fit with taxonomies like that of Bloom?

Critical thinking

In the UK we place great value on being able to think critically, the skill Bloom and colleagues termed *evaluation*. Fisher (1995) identifies two essential elements to critical thinking:

- learning how to question, when to question and what questions to ask;
- learning how and when to reason.

Underlying these two elements is a common thread of open-mindedness and passion for the truth. The truth has the ideological connotation of fairness, and the critical thinker as conceived by Fisher is characterised by the ability to 'examine experience, assess knowledge and ideas, and to weigh arguments before teaching a balanced judgement' (ibid., p. 66). To achieve this balance means challenging the assumptions of common sense and the beliefs of others. It also means accepting the possibility of being wrong. The ideal critical learner is one who can appreciate and immerse themselves in argument while maintaining a sense of balance.

Creative thinking

Creativity corresponds approximately to the Bloom *et al.* category of synthesis, the ability to put ideas together. When we speak of highly creative individuals we are really thinking about those who bring original ideas or combinations of influences to bear on a problem. Sternberg (1988) has suggested that creative individuals are characterised by willingness to experiment, to reject their limitations, to appreciate the arts, to challenge social norms, to be unpopular and show curiosity. Like critical thinking, creative thinking is highly valued in Western culture. Fostering creativity in education is not easy, but Henson and Eller (1999) offer some simple practical suggestions:

demonstrate creativity in the teacher role, provide activities requiring creativity, and respond to creativity positively, bearing in mind that the unconventional nature of creative thinking may not lend itself to formal marking.

The rationale underlying current work on developing thinking

There is a range of contemporary educational approaches that aim to help develop the thinking skills of learners. In an influential report Carol McGuinness (1999) concluded that, irrespective of different theoretical bases, different approaches share the ultimate goal of bringing about qualitative change in the type of thinking of which learners are capable. In terms of their rationale for doing this they tend to share a number of core concepts:

- Learners are active creators of their knowledge, so they need to seek meaning and impose structure on learning material as opposed to passively absorbing it. Development of thinking skills is therefore closely related to the constructivist tradition (Chapter 2).
- A classroom focus on thinking skills is beneficial because it leads to development of activities that support active information-processing strategies.
- Learners can be and need to be taught the skills of higher-level thinking.
- Development of thinking skills requires a taxonomy of skills to be developed. Common features of most modern taxonomies include sorting, classifying, comparing, predicting, relating cause and effect, concluding, generating new ideas, problem-solving, solution-testing and decision-making.
- Effective teaching of thinking skills involves developing non-routine tasks, which require higher-level thinking to complete successfully.
- Learners need to develop better awareness of their own thought processes and to reflect consciously on them. This type of awareness is called *metacognition*.
- There are important social aspects to learning, and learners pick up thinking strategies from each other and from teachers. Social interaction should therefore be oriented towards a thinking skills perspective.
- Thinking takes place in a cultural context, and the culture of the learning environment must reflect the value placed on thinking skills, so questioning and challenge should be encouraged.
- Teachers and institutions can benefit from improvements in thinking skills as well as individual learners.

Metacognition

Perhaps the single most influential concept in contemporary research and practice in developing thinking skills is *metacognition*. Metacognition is at one level a deceptively simple idea, yet it describes a complex and advanced mental process. At its simplest, metacognition can be defined as the process of thinking about our own thinking. However, when we try to tease out this definition a little we soon find ourselves in much deeper conceptual water. Larkin (2002) provides a helpful definition of metacognition as 'a form of cognition, a second or higher-level process. It involves both a knowledge of cognitive processing (how am I thinking about this?) and a conscious control and monitoring of that processing (would it be better if I thought about this differently?)' (ibid., p. 65).

Flavell (1985) suggests that metacognition makes use of three categories of metacognitive knowledge: personal knowledge, task knowledge and strategy knowledge. *Personal knowledge* is the knowledge and beliefs learners have about their individual cognitive characteristics. This is one way of interpreting the importance of many of the concepts described in the previous two chapters. Personal knowledge might include information about implicit theory of intelligence, general intelligence, multiple intelligences, triarchic intelligence, cognitive style, learning styles and learning strategies. It might also involve awareness of subject preferences, responses to exam stress and even circadian rhythms. *Task knowledge* is what we know and believe about the learning task we are engaged in. We are aware that the task of writing an essay differs in its requirements to the task of solving a mathematical problem. *Strategy knowledge* refers to awareness about the strategies we have available to us to progress on a learning task and the ability to select the most appropriate strategy. Suppose we have the task of learning a body of information for a test. We would probably not select the same strategies to accomplish this as the strategies we would use to answer a series of questions on the text. Instead we might rehearse material, practice recall, use stimulus enhancement techniques like highlighting or underlining key points, or we might restructure material.

Good knowledge of our personal characteristics, the task at hand and the available repertoire of available strategies can be invaluable in becoming expert learners. It is likely that learners who face particular problems in getting to grips with the classroom are indeed those who lack metacognitive ability. Metacognitive ability increases as a function of age, but may also be fostered by teaching (Larkin, 2002). Table 5.2 gives examples of teacher prompts likely to elicit metacognitive responses.

Table 5.2 **Teacher prompts to elicit metacognition**

Metacognitive knowledge	Type of prompt	Example
Self	Focus on abilities	You really enjoy this sort of thinking, don't you?
	Focus on learning style	Does seeing it in a table like that make it easier?
	Focus on learning strategy	What do you do when you get homework like this?
	Focus on motivational style	Do you find it easier in small chunks like this?
Task	Focus on assessment criteria	What am I looking for when I mark this?
	Comparison with other tasks	What did you find last time we did this?
	Focus on critical thinking	Can you see anything dodgy about that?
	Focus on creative thinking	What can we do about that?
Strategies	Focus on thinking	Put your thinking cap on for a moment.
	Focus on planning	What's the first thing we have to do?
	Focus on checking	Good, now look back at what you've done.

Reflection point

Consider the types of question shown in Table 5.2. To what extent do you or teachers you have worked with use questions like this to stimulate metacognitive awareness? How good is your own metacognitive knowledge, and how might this have affected your experiences as a learner?

Programmes for the development of thinking skills

There are a number of programmes that aim to effect qualitative change in the nature of learners' thinking skills. Four particularly influential approaches are reviewed here:

- Instrumental enrichment (Feuerstein *et al.*, 1980)
- Philosophy for children (Fisher, 1995)
- Cognitive acceleration (Adey and Shayer, 1994)
- Activating children's thinking skills (McGuinness *et al.*, 1997).

Instrumental enrichment

Reuven Feuerstein, an Israeli clinical psychologist, began work in the 1950s on techniques to boost the intellectual ability of low-achieving children. For some time his work was rejected by mainstream educational psychology, probably because his assertion that 'intelligence' could be taught flew in the face of the dominant representation of intelligence at the time as innate and fixed (Sharron and Coulter, 1994). With the development of more modern views of intelligence it gradually gained more acceptance, and at the time of writing it is perhaps the best-known and most widely used system worldwide.

Cultural deprivation

The rationale of Feuerstein's work is highly reminiscent of Vygotsky's in that cognitive abilities are seen as culturally transmitted tools of learning, acquired during social interaction. There are, however, key differences, perhaps the most important concerning the role of language, emphasised by Vygotsky but not by Feuerstein. In addition, whereas Vygotsky saw basic cognitive processes as being innate and higher functions being acquired through social inter-action, Feuerstein found that even fairly basic perceptual processes like visual scanning and selective attention were lacking in culturally deprived groups and could be taught.

Feuerstein noted that different groups of immigrants to Israel varied considerably in their ability to learn, and that poor learning ability was associated with groups who had become culturally deprived through experiences of violent uprooting and poverty. Feuerstein proposed that without the founda-tion of a firm cultural base there is insufficient opportunity to develop the shared thinking and values that allow the individual to process information meaningfully. To Feuerstein, culture is actively imposed on children when adults selectively present material to children, emphasise and explain it. Note that Feuerstein did not equate cultural richness with urbanisation or industri-alisation. He gave the example of the Falasha from Ethiopia, a rural farming community who maintained a tradition of oral learning and studying hand-written books, and who adapted with ease to life in Israel. Based on this adaptability, Feuerstein proposed the idea that an individual with a firm cultural foundation can adapt to another culture, but those who lack any cultural foundation cannot flourish anywhere.

Mediation

The term 'mediation' is used in instrumental enrichment in a slightly different way than in social constructivist theory. To Feuerstein, mediation describes the role of adults in helping children make use of experience. In meaningful interactions between adults and children, the adult intervenes in the interaction between child and environment. This type of event is called a mediated learning experience (MLE). MLEs begin early as primary carers impose order on simple events like feeding by consistently ordering the sequence of events. Adults also provide meaning to the world when they explain what toys are and how to play with them, what aspects of the environ-ment are dangerous, etc. Cognitive abilities are internalised alongside cultural beliefs and values during mediated learning. Sharron and Coulter put it like this: 'the child is being invested with a series of thinking skills – a structure with which he can make sense of the world. By scheduling and sorting stimuli, the mother is giving the child a sense of time and space through which experience can be organised' (1994, p. 39). The key feature of educational intervention to improve thinking skills remains the mediated learning experience.

Enrichment and structured mediation

Feuerstein *et al.* (1980) suggest that structured mediated learning experiences can help to develop a range of cognitive skills:

- *Mediated focusing*: activities that help the learner develop better perceptual and attentional abilities, such as recognising patterns and maintaining selective attention. This helps the learner make the best use of visual and auditory information.
- *Mediated planning*: activities that instil the idea of routine and sequence. Once these concepts are internalised, the learner can plan and delay gratification.
- *Mediated self-regulation*: activities that overcome the tendency for impulsiveness and encourage instead thoughtful consideration of actions.
- *Mediated precision*: activities that emphasise the benefit of precision and accuracy, such as in choosing terms to describe a concept.

Instruments of enrichment

In practice, instrumental enrichment consists of a series of exercises in the form of games, each of which is oriented towards developing a particular cognitive skill. The exercises are undertaken with a teacher who mediates the encounter between learner and instrument with questions that encourage metacognition: What is the problem? Which do you think is the best? And so on. Successful instrumental enrichment leads to *bridging*, Feuerstein's term for taking the cognitive skills acquired in artificial paper-and-pencil exercises and generalising them to other situations, such as studying particular subjects. Feuerstein developed a number of instruments of enrichment. Here are some of the more important ones:

- *Organisation of dots*: a way of understanding spatial relationships. Tasks are given requiring the learner to make shapes from joining dots (Figure 5.2). The aim is to help the learner understand the cognitive processes needed to perceive order in apparent chaos.
- *Orientation in space*: also oriented to understanding spatial relationships, particularly the meanings of up, down, front, etc. The aim is to help the learner understand the relationship between each element in a system, such as between days, weeks and months.
- *Comparisons*: oriented towards understanding the idea of similarities and differences, such as between shapes (Figure 5.3). This aims to give the learner skills in identifying the key characteristics of an object or concept.

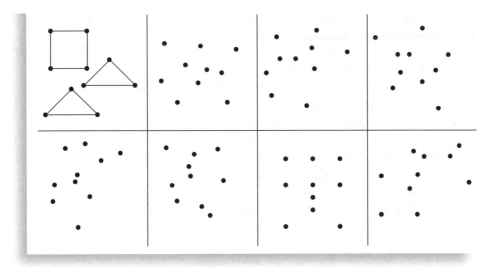

Figure 5.2 **An example of organisation of dots**

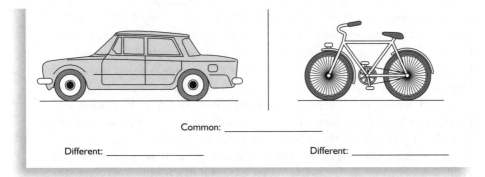

Common: _____

Different: _____   Different: _____

Figure 5.3 **An example of shapes to compare**

- *Analytic perception*: designed to develop the skill of seeing the constituent parts in a whole. This allows the learner to break down tasks to their component parts and so plan activities and approach problems in a systematic way.
- *Categorisation*: involves identifying the criteria by which objects can be placed in categories; for example, learning that tomatoes and bananas are more meaningfully categorised together because they are fruit as opposed to tomatoes and balls because they are both round. This teaches the skill of making logical deductions from information.
- *Family relations*: involves studying families in terms of the variety of relationships existing between different members. This aims to give

the learner an understanding of the different types of relationships between concepts, such as hierarchical and symmetrical.

● *Temporal relations*: involves mathematical problems which require the learner to think about time, such as the relationship between time elapsed, speed and distance. The aim is to improve the learner's subjective experience of time and the sequencing of events.

● *Numerical progressions*: involves identifying the patterns in sequences of numbers and predicting the next numbers in sequence. This aims to develop the skill of predicting outcomes and under-standing cause-and-effect relationships.

● *Instructions*: involves giving the learner a series of instructions to allow them to complete tasks. This allows the learner to clarify and test the meaning of ambiguity and make decisions.

The effectiveness of instrumental enrichment

There have been a number of studies which set out to evaluate the success of instrumental enrichment. McGuinness (1999) concluded that there is an extensive volume of literature demonstrating positive effects. In the original outcome study (Feuerstein and Rand, 1977) 218 Israeli children with IQ of around 70 (the cut-off point for retardation) were split into two groups. The experimental group underwent two years of instrumental enrichment, comprising five one-hour sessions per week; the control group had an enrichment programme based on extra subject tuition. All participants were assessed at the end of the programme with an IQ test and two years later using Israeli army assessments. The instrumental enrichment group scored significantly higher on IQ and over half scored above average in the army assessments, unlike the general enrichment group. These positive findings with low-ability adolescents have been repeated in a number of countries (Sharron and Coulter, 1994). More recently, Blagg *et al.* (1988) attempted to use Feuerstein's instruments of enrichment to boost the skills of able children in Somerset. No significant gains in IQ were reported, and in spite of some positive experiences, there were serious practical problems of integrating such abstract tasks into the curriculum. However, Blagg and colleagues went on to develop a series of exercises designed for more able students, based on pictorial tasks rather than abstract thinking, and reported a greater degree of success.

Philosophy for children

An alternative approach to developing higher thinking skills derives from the pioneering work of philosophy lecturer Matthew Lipman (1982), who bemoaned the rigid thinking of undergraduate philosophy students: 'I was beginning to have serious doubts about the value of teaching philosophy. It didn't seem to have any impact on what people did. I began to see that the problem I was seeing at the University couldn't be solved there, that thinking was something that had to be taught much earlier' (ibid., p. 35).

In the UK the leading exponent of philosophy for children has been Robert Fisher (1995, 2003). The rationale of philosophy for children is rather different from that of Feuerstein and instrumental enrichment practitioners. Rather than developing a full set of basic cognitive skills on which to construct more advanced ones, the aim of philosophy for children is more to develop flexibility in higher reasoning. It is well established by research that learners derive greater satisfaction from lessons in which they are challenged to think; Fisher quotes a 10-year-old as saying, 'I like those lessons where the teacher doesn't tell you what you already know, but you have to think it out for yourself' (Fisher, 2003, p. 7). Essentially, philosophy is used as a vehicle to develop tasks in which learners are challenged to think more deeply. 'Philosophy' is used less in the sense of teaching philosophy as a discipline than in the sense of teaching children to *philosophise*. The aim of this is to develop creative and critical modes of thinking. Table 5.3 gives some examples of the type of thinking developed by philosophy for children.

Table 5.3 **Everyday thinking and critical thinking**

Everyday thinking	Critical thinking
Guessing	Estimating
Preferring	Evaluating
Assuming	Justifying
Associating	Classifying
Accepting	Hypothesising
Judging	Analysing
Inferring	Reasoning

Source: Fisher (2003)

Discussion and the community of enquiry

The classic philosophy lesson, as outlined by Lipman and Fisher, involves discussion, stimulated by literature, and a key question or questions. The key element of discussion is the use of Socratic questioning. Socrates was an Ancient Greek philosopher. He is best remembered for formulating a method of teaching in which the teacher does not tell, but assumes a position of 'scholarly ignorance', asking a series of questions. An example of a classic philosophical question concerns the relationship between the mind and the brain. Fisher (2003) reports a dialogue with a group of 11-year-olds stimulated by *Harry Stottlemeier's Discovery* (Lipman, 1974), the story of a boy who, following a misunderstanding of an astronomy lesson, discovers a rule of logic. Selected extracts are shown in Box 5.1.

Box 5.1

Extracts from a discussion after reading *Harry Stottlemeier's Discovery.*

RF: Is your brain the same as your mind? Let's see if we can get closer
   to an understanding of that.

Tom: Well is it? I mean your brain controls your heart and your arms
   and everything that goes on in your body, but does your mind think
   'okay I'll move left' and do you think 'okay, brain, send messages down
   to the muscles to move'?

Mark: I think I'd agree with Tom that your mind is part of the brain.
   But . . . if you'd like to put one inside the other you'd put the mind
   inside the brain.

RF: So is the mind the same as the brain, but the brain just bigger than
   the mind, or is the mind different from the brain?

Melanie: Different . . . . Because it doesn't control anything. It just thinks.

Camilla: The mind I think is our thoughts rather than controlling our
   body . . . . I think the mind just contains our thoughts.

Jamie: And memories.

Source: Fisher (2003)

This is an example of effective use of Socratic questioning in which a
number of children joined in the discussion. Lipman and Fisher have both
stressed the importance of establishing a *community of enquiry*, i.e. a group
in which ideas can be explored frankly and without fear of embarrassment.
Fisher (1995) has emphasised the importance of the physical environment.
Philosophical discussion requires quiet, and just as the Ancient Greeks
maintained 'philosopher's gardens', Fisher recommends taking a class
outside to a quiet area for philosophical discussion.

Stories for thinking

Lipman and others have generated literature specifically for the purpose of
stimulating philosophical discussion. However, stories in general can be used
to stimulate thinking. Fisher (2003) suggested seven types of question that can
be asked about a story and which can stimulate thinking:

1. *Context*: asking questions can uncover information about the historical,
   geographical, political and cultural context in which a story is set.
2. *Temporal order*: asking what happened next and similar questions
   leads children to consider the meaning of events in a story, which
   reflect constructed 'human time' rather than simple chronological
   ordering.

3. *Particular events*: taking fictional incidents and asking what else characters could have done and then what might have happened, will stimulate thinking about the problematic nature of life.

4. *Intentions*: stories involve characters who act in particular ways in response to inner states of emotion, motivation, etc. Questions about characters' intentions can foster the development of an advanced theory of mind, i.e. an in-depth understanding of the mental processes of others. Flavell (1999) has suggested a close link between theory of mind and metacognition, central to the development of thinking skills.

5. *Choices*: stories involve choices, often with a moral dimension. Such choices can form the basis of moral analysis, using questions such as, Should she have done that?

6. *Meanings*: within any story there is a metadiscourse, in which the author puts across a message. For example, many stories concern wrongdoers who come to a bad end. The metadiscourse here is that crime does not pay. Learners can be questioned about the metadiscourse of a story.

7. *Telling*: there is a distinction between the plot of a story and its telling. Telling refers to the way in which the plot, which may be common to many stories, is put across. A literary genre is characterised by plots and telling. Questions can be asked concerning how a plot is put across.

Thinking about current affairs

One of the problems faced by practitioners faced with the reality of involving learners – many of whom may be disenchanted with education – in philosophical tasks is cynicism over the sources of stimulation, such as stories. One source of thinking material that may capture the imagination of learners is current affairs. Fisher (2001) offers some examples of recurring themes in news stories that may be helpful in stimulating discussion (Table 5.4).

Table 5.4 **Examples of using news stories to stimulate discussion**

Story	Theme	Key questions
Racist murder	Racism	Why did it happen?
		Why is this wrong?
		What can we do about it?
Drug smuggling	Drugs	What are drugs?
		Is taking drugs bad?
		Why?
Truancy	School	Is school a good thing?
		Should school be compulsory?

The effectiveness of philosophy for children

Some contemporary reviews of research into philosophy for children (e.g. McGuinness, 1999) have concluded that there is evidence in the form of small-scale experimental studies to support the effectiveness of philosophy for children. Wilson (2000) is more cautious, and points out that the wide-ranging goals of the programme and lack of agreed success criteria make it difficult to evaluate. In addition, where gains are reported it is not always clear exactly how the philosophy for children programme exerted its influence. It may be that reported gains are the product of improved self-esteem or academic self-efficacy rather than a direct influence on thinking capabilities. Although in one sense this takes nothing away from the value of the programme itself, it would be helpful to have clearer evidence on what elements of philosophy for children are useful.

Activating children's thinking skills

Activating children's thinking skills (ACTS) was a project in Northern Ireland, initially involving Key Stage 2 teachers (McGuinness, 2000). Since the original project, the ACTS methodology has been used in secondary education. The aim was a general transformation of thinking skills, in particular the development of the following, based on the R. Schwartz and Parkes (1994) taxonomy:

- *Finding order and imposing meaning on information*: sorting, ordering, sequencing and comparing.
- *Critical thinking*: predicting, concluding, seeking bias, distinguishing fact from opinion and establishing cause-and-effect relationships.
- *Creative thinking*: generating new ideas, brainstorming, using analogies, formulating an opinion.
- *Problem-solving*: defining problems and suggesting and testing solutions.
- *Planning*: breaking down goals to subgoals and monitoring progress.
- *Decision-making*: generating options and choosing a course of action.

Infusion

One important decision in introducing a thinking skills programme concerns its relationship to the curriculum. Instrumental enrichment and philosophy for children are bolt-ons to the existing curriculum, taking up a significant proportion of teaching time. By contrast, the ACTS programme adopts an *infusion* approach. Infusion involves identifying opportunities across the whole curriculum where particular thinking skills are especially salient and can be introduced. For example, opinion formation (creative thinking) can be developed in the context of judging historical characters, whereas prediction and conclusion lend themselves to science. The strength of infusion is that it optimises the use of existing classroom time rather than eating into it.

Metacognitive strategies

The teaching strategies used in ACTS are founded on the assumption that thinking skills are 'hidden', and that their development involves making them explicit to learners. This is achieved by a number of strategies. First, learners are taught a thinking vocabulary. In order for learners to perform advanced thinking skills such as problem-solving and creative thinking, they need an age-appropriate language with which to understand these processes. In addition, strategies were developed with which teachers could coach learners in thinking skills. These included the use of thinking diagrams in which processes are broken down, and encouraging reflection on and discussion about thinking.

The effectiveness of ACTS

The effectiveness of the Northern Ireland project was monitored by an open-ended questionnaire administered to participating teachers after one year of infusion lessons. All respondents reported gains in children's thinking skills, particularly improved metacognition, creativity and reasoning ability. Teachers also reported very favourably on the effect of participation in the programme on their own understanding of thinking skills. However, this source of evidence is limited by its reliance on teacher opinion, more so because the teachers were not 'blind' assessors but those involved in the project (Wilson, 2000; McGuinness, 1999). Currently there is a lack of more objective evidence for the effectiveness of ACTS.

Cognitive acceleration

The idea of cognitive acceleration is derived directly from constructivist theory, particularly the work of Piaget and Vygotsky (Chapter 2). Three of Piaget's beliefs are very central to the rationale underlying cognitive acceleration (Adey and Shayer, 2002). First, the functional architecture of the mind includes some general intellectual function, and this general function underlies specific abilities. Second, this general intellectual function increases throughout childhood, and third, both brain maturation and the environment influence its development. Adey and Shayer identify six theoretical foundations of cognitive acceleration:

- *Schemas*: in this context a schema is a general way of thinking that can be applied to a range of situations.
- *Concrete preparation*: before beginning a cognitive task, learners need to understand its aims and context and have the necessary vocabulary.
- *Cognitive conflict*: based on Piaget's idea of disequilibrium and Vygotsky's zone of proximal development, the idea that learning takes place at the limit of a learner's understanding.

- *Social construction*: based on Vygotsky's theory, the idea that cooperative learning facilitates dialogue that in turn enhances learning.
- *Metacognition*: the idea that learning is enhanced by the learner having a conscious awareness of the learning process.
- *Bridging*: Feuerstein's idea that new thinking skills have to be made available to situations beyond the situation where they are learned.

Subject-specific programmes

Like ACTS, cognitive acceleration is integrated into existing lessons and does not exist as a bolt-on to the curriculum. However, rather than being infused into the curriculum across a range of subjects, cognitive acceleration programmes are subject-specific. Thus we have cognitive acceleration in science education (CASE), in maths (CAME) and in technology (CATE).

The three-act model

Cognitive acceleration lessons typically involve three or four 'acts', shown in Figure 5.4. The first is the stage of concrete preparation, designed to make sure that all members of a group can engage in the main task. A problem is introduced to the whole class, sometimes with some 'seeding' questions designed to stimulate interest and initial thinking. Terms are defined at this point to ensure that lack of vocabulary does not hold back individuals. In Act 2 the class is divided into small groups of between two and five learners. These small groups work collaboratively to overcome the cognitive conflict induced by the problem. Where cognitive conflict is not apparent, the teacher can try to induce it by introducing new ideas to small groups. Once small groups have generated enough ideas about how to solve the problem, the teacher can initiate Act 3. Act 3 involves whole-class interactive discussion in which each group in turn quickly demonstrates their responses to the problem. At this point the teacher encourages metacognitive awareness by requiring each learner to describe in their own words the insights they have achieved during the lesson. In some lessons the teacher may prescribe an Act 4, designed to ensure that bridging occurs. This involves a discussion

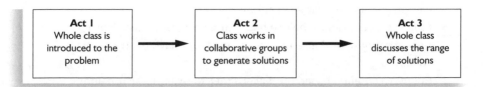

Figure 5.4 **The sequence of acts in a cognitive acceleration lesson**

of how the solutions to the problem and other insights from the lesson could be applied to other areas.

The effectiveness of cognitive acceleration

Perhaps the greatest strength of the cognitive acceleration model in comparison with instrumental enrichment, ACTS and philosophy for children is the rigour with which it has been evaluated. A substantial empirical base now exists to demonstrate beyond question that cognitive acceleration is effective. The most extensively researched programme has been cognitive acceleration in science education (CASE). In the original study, Adey and Shayer (1994) showed that a two-year CASE programme in years 7 and 8 was associated with improved GCSE grades three years later, not only in science but in maths and English. Effect sizes were up to one whole GCSE grade. Figure 5.5 shows the achievement in GCSE science of schools using CASE compared to controls (Shayer, 1999).

At the time of writing, later cognitive acceleration projects have not yet published GCSE data, but comparisons using Key Stage 3 tests suggest a similar pattern of benefits for learners.

Reflection point

What constitutes strong evidence that a programme is effective? How do each of the four programmes outlined here measure up to your standards? How much evidence do you need before you would be convinced to alter your teaching in response to reading about these programmes?

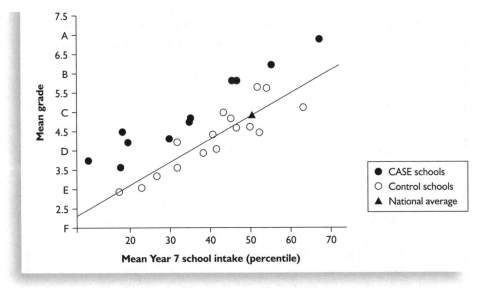

Figure 5.5 **Achievement in GCSE science of CASE and control schools**

Thinking skills in higher education

Although the bulk of research has involved developing the thinking skills of primary and secondary age schoolchildren, advanced thinking skills are very much part of the agenda of higher education, reflected in the current benchmarks issued by the Quality Assurance Agency for Higher Education (QAA), which monitors standards in higher education. Most research at higher-education level has focused on developing skills of critical thinking, predicated on the belief that this is the highest level of thinking and is fostered by study at undergraduate level. Facione and Facione (1997) have set out seven components of critical thinking to be developed by study at higher education:

- *Truth seeking*: objectivity and motivation to discover the truth.
- *Open-mindedness*: tolerance of alternative views.
- *Analyticity*: alertness to consequences and forthcoming problems.
- *Systematicity*: orderly and organised inquiry.
- *Self-confidence*: trust in one's own reasoning.
- *Inquisitiveness*: intellectual curiosity.
- *Maturity*: disposition towards making reflective judgements.

Critical thinking can be assessed by psychometric tests, such as the California Critical Thinking Dispositions Inventory (CCTDI), shown in Box 5.2. This framework and research tool have allowed researchers to investigate the effectiveness of programmes designed to enhance critical thinking.

Using the CCTDI, Rimiene (2002) assessed the effectiveness of a university course in critical thinking comprising three months of four hours per week spent studying the elements of critical thinking and humanistic psychology. Comparisons with a control group revealed a range of effects

Box 5.2

The CCTDI

This has 75 items, measuring seven subscales of critical thinking: truth-seeking, open mindedness, analyticity, systematicity, self-confidence, inquisitiveness and maturity. Answers are obtained using a six-point Likert scale from strongly agree to strongly disagree. Here are some examples:
- Studying new things all my life would be wonderful (assesses inquisitiveness).
- It is impossible to know what standards to apply to most questions (assesses analyticity).
- I believe what I want to believe (assesses open-mindedness).

Source: P. A. Facione (1995)

across the seven subscales of the CCTDI. Open-mindedness, maturity, analyticity and systematicity were significantly improved following the course; self-confidence was unaltered.

The Rimiene study assessed a bolt-on programme analogous to instrumental enrichment or philosophy for children in the school sector. An alternative approach is to embed critical thinking in the existing curriculum, optimising the coverage of existing subject matter. An example of this subject-specific approach comes from Barber (2002), who developed a model specific to undergraduate psychology. The programme involved group evaluation on published studies using original papers. Feedback from participants and staff suggested this was successful in enhancing critical thinking.

Conclusions and personal reflections

Different commentators have arrived at slightly different conclusions regarding the future of thinking skills development. Proponents of thinking skills programmes have enthusiastically promoted their benefits and their impact on future education. Nisbett (1993) proposed that by 2000 no curriculum would be acceptable unless it contributed to the development of thinking skills. Adey and Shayer (2002) have gone so far as to suggest that programmes to develop thinking skills in the context of education may represent a paradigm shift in education, changing entirely the way we think about education and carry it out. Although such a paradigm shift is currently not in evidence and Nisbett's prediction has not yet come to pass, the tremendous optimism of workers in this field is probably largely justified, given the dramatic benefits demonstrated by cognitive acceleration researchers and the warmth shown by teachers surveyed in the ACTS programme. In her influential review, McGuinness (1999) has concluded that there is sufficient evidence to accept that successful thinking skills programmes have a powerful impact on learning.

Although there is a sound basis for enthusiasm about thinking skills development programmes, there are important gaps in our current understanding and further research is needed. As Wilson (2000) points out, most programmes have not been subject to rigorous outcome research; the exception is cognitive acceleration. Therefore we do not know enough about the relative effectiveness of alternative models of intervention or the contexts in which they are most effective. There is also a lack of systematic research into thinking skills in post-16 education, despite the fact that A levels explicitly require the assessment of higher thinking skills.

Self-assessment questions

1. Describe Bloom's taxonomy of thinking skills and outline how it has been applied in curriculum design.

2. Define the term 'metacognition' and explain how it has been developed in one or more programmes for the development of thinking skills.

3. Discuss the major ideas behind Feuerstein's instrumental enrichment.

4. Compare the rationales underlying instrumental enrichment, philosophy for children and cognitive acceleration.

5. Critically compare bolt-on, infusion and subject-specific approaches to thinking skills development.

6. To what extent can thinking skills development programmes be said to be empirically supported?

Further reading

•••••• Fisher, R. (1995) *Teaching Children to Think*. Nelson Thornes, Cheltenham, Glos.

•••••• Fisher, R. (2003) *Teaching Thinking*. Continuum, London.

•••••• McGuinness, C. (1999) *From Thinking Skills to Thinking Classrooms*. Department for Education and Employment, London.

•••••• Sharron, H. and Coulter, M. (1994) *Changing Children's Minds*. Imaginative Minds, Birmingham.

•••••• Shayer, M. and Adey, P. (2002) *Learning Intelligence*. Open University Press, Milton Keynes, Bucks.

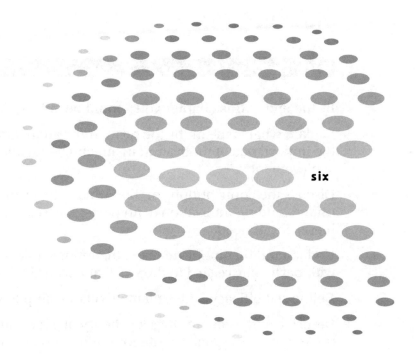

six

Motivation

Motivation

By the end of this chapter you should be able to:

•••••• Explain what is meant by the term 'motivation' and appreciate the importance of motivation in affecting educational achievement.

•••••• Discuss the contributions of the humanistic tradition in understanding motivation, with particular regard to Maslow's hierarchy of needs.

•••••• Understand the importance of attributions in learner motivation with particular regard to the work of Bernard Weiner.

•••••• Define self-efficacy and explain its relationship to motivation.

•••••• Describe and evaluate Dweck's theory of goal orientations and understand how goal orientations affect motivation to learn.

•••••• Explain how teacher expectations can impact on the motivation to learn.

Motivation can be defined as 'the forces that account for the selection, persistence, intensity and continuation of behaviour' (Snowman and Biehler, 2000, p. 371). In other words, it is the sum of the influences that affect why we choose to behave in particular ways. A common lament among teachers is that their students are not motivated. As Snowman and Biehler point out, this represents something of a misunderstanding. We are all motivated all the time – even inactivity requires a motive. What we really mean is that learners do not always share the motivation of educators to learn what we would like them to learn, or at least to learn that particular material on that occasion in the way we envisage. One of the benefits for the teacher of developing a deeper understanding of motivation is that it allows us to take a step back from classroom situations and appreciate the perspective of learners.

If we are to understand the range of motives underlying educational achievement, we need to distinguish between intrinsic and extrinsic motivation. *Intrinsic motives* are those that come from within the individual. We might, for example, relish the pleasure of mastering a new skill or area of expertise, and derive personal satisfaction from improving our performance.

Extrinsic motives are the external rewards that we can gain from learning. These include praise, good grades and qualifications. An unequivocal although perhaps counter-intuitive research finding has been that intrinsic motivation is a much more powerful influence on achievement than extrinsic motivation. Effective strategies to improve the motivation to learn are therefore based not simply on providing rewards for achievement but on meeting the needs of learners and fostering a set of cognitions that predispose them to be motivated to learn. Humanistic approaches address the issue of human needs, whereas cognitive approaches focus more narrowly on patterns of thinking.*

The significance of motivation

As discussed in Chapter 3, we have a dominant cultural belief in Britain that achievement, including educational achievement, is primarily dependent on innate ability. However, there is now a body of evidence to suggest that not only is ability highly malleable, but that for the majority of learners it is a less significant predictor of success than the motivation to learn and to achieve. Cote and Levine (2000) assessed IQ and motivation in 85 incoming students at a Canadian university, and found that motivation on entry was a good predictor of degree class. IQ, by contrast, did not predict academic success. Not all studies have supported the idea that motivation is more important than ability in determining achievement (e.g. Gagne and StPere, 2002), but there is little doubt that motivation is an important causal factor in an individual's progress. As well as accounting for a significant proportion of the variance in achievement, motivation may be one of the more manipulable variables, i.e. it can be altered by pedagogical practice.

Reflection point

Before reading the rest of this chapter, pause to consider this question. How far do you believe that motivation is more important than ability?

The humanistic tradition

Humanistic psychology emerged in the US in the 1930s and assumed particular significance after the Second World War. It is characterised by a positive and holistic view of human nature, seeing humans as fundamentally motivated by a need to achieve and to fulfil their potential. The most influential humanistic model of motivation in the sphere of education comes from Abraham Maslow.

---

* This is not to say that receiving praise and good grades cannot be good motivators, but that they are effective because and only when they foster healthy cognitions about the self and the origins of achievement. This chapter does not cover the now dated behaviourist approaches to motivation that depend on providing extrinsic rewards.

Maslow's hierarchy of needs

Maslow (1954) developed a theory of human motivation that aimed to explain all human needs and place them in a hierarchy representing the order of priority in which people seek to satisfy them. He made a fundamental distinction between D-needs, or *deficiency* needs, which result from requirements for food, rest, safety, etc., and B-needs, *being* needs, which derive from our drive to fulfil our potential. We cannot strive towards our B-needs until our D-needs have been met. Maslow's hierarchy of needs is shown in Figure 6.1.

The idea behind the model is that we ascend the hierarchy, satisfying each motive in turn. Our first priority is to satisfy our *physiological needs* such as food and warmth. Only when these needs have been satisfied do we seek out *safety*. Once satisfied of our safety, we turn to *social needs*, i.e. to belong to a group and relate to others. *Esteem needs* then become paramount, being satisfied by achievement, competence and recognition. Once this has been achieved, our focus will shift to satisfying our *intellectual needs*, including understanding and knowledge. Next come *aesthetic needs*, reflecting the need for beauty, order and balance. The final human need identified by Maslow is for *self-actualisation*, i.e. to find personal fulfilment and achieve one's potential.

Maslow (1970) described self-actualised people as those who were fulfilled and doing all they were capable of. By studying people who he considered to be self-actualised, including American president Abraham Lincoln, physicist Albert Einstein and founder of psychology William James, Maslow identified 15 characteristics of self-actualised people (Box 6.1). It is not necessary to display all these characteristics in order to be self-actualised, and it is not only self-actualised people that display them. Generally, however, those people Maslow considered to be self-actualised displayed rather more of these characteristics than the rest of us.

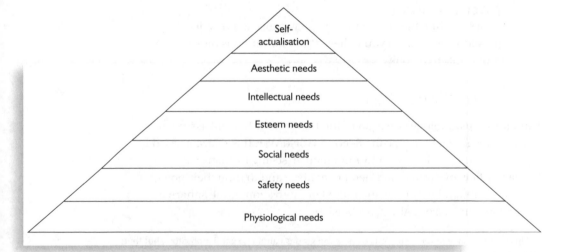

Figure 6.1 **Maslow's hierarchy of needs**

Box 6.1

Features of self-actualised people

- Accurate perception of reality
- Enjoyment of new experiences
- Tendency to have peak experiences
- Clear moral standards
- Sense of humour
- Feeling of kinship with all people
- Close friendships
- Democratic character accepting others
- Need for privacy
- Independence from culture and environment
- Creativity
- Spontaneity
- Problem-centred
- Acceptance of human nature
- Resistance to conformity.

Source: Adapted from Maslow (1970)

The major application of Maslow's ideas has been in helping educators appreciate the sheer range of factors affecting the motivation of the learner. This can be helpful in designing lessons with the needs of all learners in mind. Until learners feel safe and part of a group, they will not have satisfied more basic needs and therefore cannot be expected to focus on higher intellectual interests (Snowman and Biehler, 2000). At an even more basic level, if learners are hungry, cold, etc., their concentration will be affected. Although teachers cannot take full responsibility for all factors influencing a learner's physiological and emotional state, it can be helpful to consider them, such as making sure that new learners have an opportunity to get to know their peers and that groups have regular breaks in which physiological needs can be satisfied. It is instructive to see how many basic needs are frequently not adequately met in educational settings. Following two surveys in 2000 that revealed that only around half of English and Welsh schools provide free drinking water, the *Water is Cool* campaign was launched, with the aim of ensuring that the physiological need for water is met in schools.

On a more philosophical level, Maslow is also helpful in reminding us that we cannot assume that motivation to learn and achieve is a feature of the learner at the moment we encounter them, but is sometimes best thought of as a goal to work towards (Dweck, 2000). Thus counselling and welfare services, which can assist with basic needs, have an important role in education In addition, Maslow has focused our attention on the close relationship between intellectual motivation and our need for self-esteem. If self-esteem is a more basic need than intellectual interest, it follows logically that teachers have an opportunity to stimulate motivation to learn by boosting self-esteem.

Although Maslow's ideas are intuitively appealing and have been applied in a range of contexts, there have been serious criticisms of his work. Maslow's research into self-actualised people was not carried out systematically and the only criterion for identifying a self-actualised person was Maslow's personal appraisal of them. Perhaps most importantly, Maslow's view of people as striving for personal achievement is extremely culture-bound, being firmly located in the individualistic culture of the US (Engler, 1999). Cross-cultural research by Kitayama and Markus (1992) has shown that although positive feelings in American students were associated with personal achievements, Japanese students tended to associate positive feelings with having good relations with others. In addition, while Maslow has been helpful in moulding the way teachers think about learners, the motivational techniques deriving from his work are very limited.

Self-determination theory

Over the past 20 years, humanistic theories of motivation, like Maslow's, have largely been displaced by cognitive approaches (p. 124). However, Edward Deci and colleagues (e.g. Deci *et al.*, 1991) have argued that an understanding of fundamental human needs remains a crucial aspect of our understanding of human motivation. Deci offers a contemporary humanistic theory of motivation in the form of *self-determination theory*. The central idea underlying this approach is that motivation results from self-generated determination to achieve a goal. This determination is a product of three innate human needs:

- *Competence needs*: we have an innate need to believe in our own competence.
- *Relationship needs*: we have an innate need to achieve and maintain satisfactory relationships with those with whom we come into regular contact.
- *Autonomy needs*: we have an innate need to choose our own course of actions.

To Deci, the effective learner is characterised by an attitude of self-determination resulting from the satisfaction of their needs for competence, relationships and autonomy. The effective classroom is one that satisfies these needs and so creates self-determined learners. Teaching that focuses on developing the thinking skills needed to carry out tasks helps foster competence needs, thus constructivist (Chapter 2), metacognitive (Chapter 5) and deep learning (Chapter 4) strategies are all within the spirit of self-determination theory. The need for autonomy is satisfied when learners are in a position to initiate their own goals and make choices about how best to achieve them. From the self-determination perspective, the opportunity for undertaking projects as well as more highly structured teacher-directed activities is an essential element of teaching. Satisfaction of relationship needs involves siting the learner in a social milieu of relationships with peers, professionals and family so that cooperation among peers becomes the norm, and learners can internalise learning strategies, thinking skills and self-regulation from others.

The great strength of self-determination theory lies in its maintenance of the holistic awareness of humanistic psychology combined with a format that lends itself to classroom technique. Box 6.2 is a summary of these applications. On the other hand, all the practical applications of self-determination theory can be understood equally well in terms of other theories. For example, the benefits of cooperative learning are most commonly explained in the light of social constructivist theory (Chapter 2). Moreover, it is difficult to reconcile the emphasis on autonomy with the benefits of goal-setting, which have proved helpful in the light of self-efficacy theory (p. 127). Self-determination theory is helpful in making us reflect on the very purpose of psychological theory in education. It is hard to reconcile with influential and empirically supported cognitive views of motivation, yet it has great heuristic value for professionals who place great personal value on the role of education in satisfying human needs.

Reflection point

Think of a pupil or student you have worked with whose human needs were not being met. What would have helped, and were you or colleagues in a position to do more to help?

Box 6.2

Implications of self-determination theory

- Limit praise to self-initiated tasks, as praise for following instructions undermines autonomy.
- Focus on learning skills to develop competence.
- Stress cooperative learning in order to foster relationships.
- Involve parents in order to place learning relationships in the context of existing relationships.
- Permit choices where possible, and limit deadlines and prescribed tasks to the minimum.
- Acknowledge the unpleasantness of syllabus-driven tasks that do not permit autonomy, cooperation and skill-based competence.

Source: Deci *et al.* (1991)

Cognitive approaches to motivation

Cognitive approaches to motivation take a much narrower view of the person, focusing not on the multiplicity of their needs but on their beliefs and style of information processing. This narrow focus represents something of a trade-off. Although it is a less complete view of the person, so in a sense less valid, the narrow focus of the cognitive approach lends itself to implementing practical techniques to enhance motivation. Three cognitive approaches to motivation have been particularly influential: attribution theory, self-efficacy theory and goal orientations theory.

Attribution theory

Attribution is the cognitive process whereby we explain the causes of events. There are a number of psychological theories aiming to explain the process by which we make attributions. Particularly influential in the field of motivation has been the theory developed by Bernard Weiner (1992). Weiner pointed out that every time learners succeed or fail on a task they attribute this success or failure to a cause. The technical term for this process is *causal inference*. Often we do not have sufficient information to make completely logical causal inferences, but instead rely on general beliefs about the situation and ourselves. These are called *causal schemata*.

Our attributions of success and failure can have a profound effect on motivation to tackle future tasks. Weiner identified three dimensions to the nature of attributions made by learners regarding success and failure. The first dimension is locus of control. *Locus of control* is the extent to which the individual believes they can control events. Generally, an internal locus of control is more adaptive than an external locus; if we believe we can alter events, we tend to be more motivated to tackle them positively. There are now a number of self-rating inventories designed to assess locus of control. One example comes from Pettijohn and items from his scale are shown in Box 6.3.

Box 6.3

Items from Pettijohn's locus of control scale

I usually get what I want in life	○ True	○ False
I need to be kept informed about news events	○ True	○ False
I never know where I stand with other people	○ True	○ False
I do not really believe in luck or chance	○ True	○ False
I think that I could easily win a lottery	○ True	○ False

The second dimension to causality is *stability*. Causes of success and failure may be stable, i.e. they remain constant across situations (e.g. effort, task difficulty), or they may be unstable, i.e. they change from one situation to another (e.g. luck, mood). The final dimension is *controllability*. Table 6.1 shows a matrix of causal attributions resulting from combinations of controllability, locus of control and stability.

The learner with an internal locus of control tends to attribute results to their own actions and characteristics. Where results are judged to be controllable they are attributed to effort. When they are judged to be uncontrollable then ability and mood become the focus of causal inference. The learner with an external locus of control tends to attribute their successes and failures to features of the situation. Stable external causes include task difficulty (uncontrollable) and teacher bias (controllable). Unstable causes include luck and unusual help. Table 6.2 shows a range of learners' responses to success and failure (Craske, 1988).

This range of responses can be explained in terms of Weiner's theory. For example, good and bad 'luck' are external influences, hence these attributions are more likely to be made by those with an external locus of control. Luck is also unstable and uncontrollable in nature. If we believe that luck is the primary factor affecting our success or failure, we will probably not be motivated to make more effort on future occasions. An attribution of 'I am clever' is somewhat more motivating, being internal rather than external. However, it is also uncontrollable, and where we see results as being beyond

Table 6.1 **Factors affecting causal attributions of success and failure**

	Stable control	Unstable control
Internal locus		
Controllable	Typical effort	Atypical effort
Uncontrollable	Ability	Mood
External locus		
Controllable	Teacher bias	Atypical help
Uncontrollable	Task difficulty	Luck

Table 6.2 **Examples of causal inferences about success and failure**

Success	Failure
I had good luck	I had bad luck
It was easy	It was too hard
I tried hard	I didn't try hard enough
I'm clever	I'm not clever enough

our control, there is limited motivation to make greater effort. According to Weiner, the most adaptive type of causal inference involves effort; when we attribute success and failure to the degree of effort committed to the task, we should be maximally motivated to make great effort on future occasions.

Attribution theory has a number of important implications for classroom practice. If teachers and psychologists can identify learners who make unhelpful attributions of their successes and failures and work with them to alter these attributions to be more positive, the learner should in principle be able to improve their motivation. This may be formalised as *attributional therapy* or be carried out more informally in everyday inter-action with learners. Box 6.4 shows examples for the focus of work on attribution.

Box 6.4

Examples of alterations in learner attributions

- Uncontrollable → controllable, e.g. ability → effort
- External → internal, e.g. luck → effort
- Stable → unstable, e.g. potential → mood.

Occasions frequently arise in the classroom when learners make comments such as 'it was easy' in response to success or 'I'm just not up to this' in response to failure. It can be very helpful to challenge these attribu-tions, suggesting that a task was not easy but the learner had put in considerable effort and perhaps demonstrated a talent. Weiner's theory gives us a good basis for understanding how and when to make such challenges. But as with all therapeutic techniques, a degree of caution is needed, and it is important that teachers do not throw out their experience and common sense and embrace techniques like attribution too religiously. The principle underlying all cognitive techniques is that the current beliefs are somehow incorrect, so it is helpful for learners to attribute failure to lack of effort *provided they did not actually make sufficient effort*. However, it is quite possible for learners to make considerable effort and to fall foul of bad luck in exam questions or poor marking, and nothing could be more demotivating than to be told it was a result of lack of effort (Marshall, 1990). In such a case it may be more helpful to agree that the learner was unlucky and focus on the likelihood that next time they will probably have better luck.

Attribution theory can inform classroom practice in a broader sense as well as informing direct response to particular learner attributions (Borich and Tombari, 1997). The teacher can be a *source* of those attributions in the first place. Teachers put across distinct and perhaps unhealthy attributional messages whenever they talk in terms of a learner's ability or intelligence, or when they focus on competitive rather than cooperative learning. Giving excessive help, expressing surprise at success and offering praise for blatantly easy tasks can all reinforce a message that the learner lacks ability (Good and Brophy, 1991; cited in Borich and Tombari, 1997). There is evidence that working with teachers to improve attributional messages is associated with improved educational outcome. In a recent Spanish study, Ramirez and Avila (2002) worked on attributions with 50 teachers and 150 children, taken from a mix of primary and secondary schools. Results showed that teacher and learner attributions were successfully modified and that such modification was associated with reduced teacher burnout (p. 183) and improved school results.

Reflection point

Use the items from Pettijohn's scale to help reflect on your own locus of control. What sort of attributions have you tended to make about your own successes and failures? How might this tendency affect your interactions with learners in response to their successes and failures?

Self-efficacy

Albert Bandura, the key figure in the development of self-efficacy theory, defines self-efficacy as 'people's judgements of their capabilities to organise and execute courses of actions required to attain designated types of perform-ance' (1986, p. 391). Put more simply, it refers to our perceptions of our ability to carry out a task. Self-efficacy is not synonymous with self-esteem, although they may impact on one another. Self-esteem is an emotional experience, describing the extent to which we like ourselves. It is also a global experience – our self-esteem is fairly constant across a range of situations. By contrast, self-efficacy exists within the cognitive domain, describing our *beliefs* rather than feelings, and is specific to particular situations. As educationalists, we are particularly concerned with *academic self-efficacy*, i.e. the beliefs a learner has concerning their abilities to perform educational tasks. Academic self-concept can be extremely context-specific, thus an individual may believe they are highly skilled at maths but not English, and even at algebra but not statistics. Schunk (1991) has suggested four sources of information that we draw on to arrive at our academic self-efficacy.

- *Previous experience*: learners who have previously succeeded in particular tasks will generally tend to have higher self-efficacy for related tasks. Thus the child who has always scored highly in spelling tests will generally believe they have a good ability to spell. By contrast, those who have experienced failure will tend to doubt their abilities in that type of task.

- *Direct persuasion*: just as teachers and other adults can challenge unhealthy attributions of success and failure, so poor self-efficacy beliefs are open to challenge. A persuasive professional can convince learners of their ability to carry out tasks.
- *Observational learning*: we tend to pick up on the self-efficacy of fellow learners. Where peers of previously comparable academic ability or success express their positive beliefs about their ability to perform a task, this suggests that we should also be capable of doing so.
- *Physiological cues*: we constantly experience our physiological state and use this as a source of information about our current emotional state. If we notice the signs of anxiety while carrying out a task, we may attribute them to personal difficulty with the task, leading to reduced self-efficacy. But if we are relaxed while doing a task, we may interpret this in terms of how easily we do that task.

Academic self-efficacy is not static; it is constantly changing in response to these sources of information. One major success or serious failure can exert a considerable effect, at least in the short term. According to Bandura and his colleagues, the motivation to invest effort and persevere with a task largely depends on our beliefs about our competence in that task at that moment. Snowman and Biehler (2000) identify three reasons for this. First, those with high levels of self-efficacy tend to choose more ambitious goals than those with lower levels. They may, for example, set out to master a task rather than merely to attain a minimum acceptable grade. Second, learners with high levels of self-efficacy tend to expect more positive outcomes from a task and therefore see fit to invest more effort in attaining them. Finally, people with high self-efficacy tend to be less discouraged by occasional failure, because they tend to attribute such failure to insufficient effort rather than lack of ability.

There is considerable support for Bandura's fundamental ideas that self-efficacy exists and that it is associated with motivation. The *construct validity* of self-efficacy, i.e. the extent to which it exists as a psychological entity distinct from related constructs such as self-esteem was supported in a recent study by Pietsche *et al.* (2003). Mathematical self-concept was measured using a battery of self-report questions in 416 American high-school students. It emerged that responses clustered into two quite separate scales, one comprising emotional items (self-esteem) and the other comprising beliefs (self-efficacy). Chen (2002) assessed self-efficacy in 107 American secondary school maths students and found it to be strongly predictive of both mathematical performance and self-evaluation of performance.

There are several ways in which self-efficacy can be manipulated to increase learner motivation. As with attributions, the general messages given out by teachers in the form of praise and recognition of achievement can help self-efficacy, but there are more targeted approaches. One such approach involves setting *goals* or *targets*. When learners have concrete, realistic short-term goals to work towards, they can judge their self-efficacy in relation to them. There is clear evidence that, when used appropriately, setting goals or targets can enhance performance (Hallinan and Danaher, 1994; Lee and Gavine, 2003). Highly explicit outcomes are preferable as they provide solid criteria against which the individual can judge their own achievements. Short-term goals are preferable as they are well remembered at the point where outcome is assessed. Figure 6.2 shows an example of an effective goal.

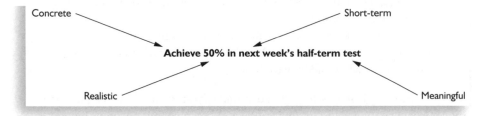

Figure 6.2   **An example of an effective goal according to self-efficacy theory**

129

Given the importance of observational learning in self-efficacy beliefs, another avenue to enhancing self-efficacy involves exposing learners to peer success. This is why it is important to develop a 'culture of achievement' in the learning environment as well as to focus on the individual. It can also be extremely beneficial for teachers to understand the link between buzz phrases like 'culture of achievement' as used in the political domain and psychological theory, because without such a grounding in theory they can appear shallow and serve to encourage a culture of cynicism.

Perhaps the most effective strategy for developing a learner's self-efficacy beliefs is to build on their study skills so as to minimise experience of failure and maximise experience of success. Gaskill and Murphy (2004) demonstrated the effectiveness of this approach by teaching primary school children how to categorise items in order to remember them. When asked to estimate how many words they would be able to remember next time, the children estimated higher following the memory training, suggesting that it had improved their memory self-efficacy. The same principle has been demonstrated with older learners. When library-use self-efficacy was assessed in 49 undergraduates it was found that those who had experienced training in library use had higher self-efficacy and higher library quiz scores.

Goal orientation theory

Arguably the most influential theory of motivation in education, certainly the one currently generating most research, is Carol Dweck's theory of goal orientations. Dweck (1991) distinguished between *learning* goals, also called *mastery* goals, and *performance* goals. When we focus on developing our competence in a task, i.e. mastering it, we set ourselves a learning goal. But when we are focused on obtaining favourable judgements about our ability, we set a performance goal. Although we all set ourselves a combination of performance and learning goals, Dweck suggests that learners can be divided into two categories, based on goal preference:

- *Mastery-oriented* learners have a basic orientation towards adopting learning goals. This leads to seeking out challenge and perseverance in the face of adversity.
- *Helplessness-oriented* learners have a basic orientation towards adopting performance goals. This leads to an attitude of playing safe and giving in when faced with difficulty.

Mastery-oriented learners have an advantage in education because they are more proactive in developing their skills and because they respond better to difficulty. Recall the discussion of beliefs about intelligence in Chapter 3 (p. 45), and Dweck's proposal that learners can be divided into entity and incremental theorists. Entity theorists see intelligence (or academic ability) as essentially unchangeable, whereas incremental theorists see it as malleable, hence worth investing some effort. These patterns of beliefs about ability are closely linked with goal orientations: mastery orientation is associated with incremental beliefs and helplessness orientation with entity beliefs. This follows logically. If we fail in a task and our ability to succeed in that task is unchangeable, then we are indeed helpless. In a study of the relationship between beliefs about intelligence and achievement goals, Mueller and Dweck (1997) identified college students with entity and incremental beliefs about intelligence and gave them a set of statements requiring agreement or disagreement. Three statements were designed to assess goal orientation (Table 6.3).

Table 6.3 **Statements used to assess goal orientation**

Statement	Agreement	Disagreement
Although I hate to admit it, I sometimes would rather do well in a class than learn a lot	Performance goal Helplessness	Learning goal Mastery
If I knew I wasn't going to do well at a task, I probably wouldn't do it even if I might learn a lot from it	Performance goal Helplessness	Learning goal Mastery
It's much more important for me to learn things in my classes than it is to get the best grades	Learning goal Mastery	Performance goal Helplessness

Source: Mueller and Dweck (1997)

In addition, participants were asked whether they would choose a good grade or a productive challenge in class. Most entity theorists (68%) chose the responses indicating performance goals whereas most incremental theorists (65%) opted for the mastery goals. This clearly shows a link between beliefs about ability and achievement orientations, which raises the question, Do implicit theories of intelligence directly influence goal orientations? It was tested in a study by Hong *et al.* (1998) in which students were given a fictitious article either quoting evidence for intelligence being fixed or for its malleability. They were then given feedback on a test and offered the chance of a tutorial before taking a similar test. Most students who had done well opted for the tutorial, but among those who had done poorly, there was a huge disparity between those that had read the article emphasising malleability of ability and those emphasising its immutability. Some 73% of those who had read the malleability article opted to attend the tutorial, compared with 13% of those who had read the immutability article. This strongly suggests that not only is goal orientation a product of beliefs about the nature of academic ability, but also it can be altered by manipulating these beliefs.

There is a large body of research to support the existence of goal orientations and their link to academic motivation and success. For example, in a recent Greek study, Leondari and Gialamas (2002) assessed academic success, goal orientation and implicit theory of intelligence in 451 students aged 10–13 years. In support of Dweck's theory, there was a strong relationship between implicit theory and goal orientation, and between goal orientation and success. Dweck's theory has particular implications for adult returners to education who have already had experience of failure in the education system. Successful return to education is predicated on the belief that previous failure does not equate to inevitable failure on return. A recent French study supports the usefulness of Dweck's theory in understanding the position of adult returners. Dupeyrat and Marine (2001) assessed 142 adult returners aged 20–49 years for implicit theory of intelligence, goal orientation, engagement in learning and self-efficacy. Those with incremental views of ability and a mastery orientation tended to be those who engaged most actively in their learning.

There are clear practical applications of Dweck's theory; crucially, it is important not to reinforce the idea of ability as an entity. Thus, according to Dweck, teachers should never praise learners for their ability; this merely reinforces entity beliefs. Mueller and Dweck (1998) demonstrated the demotivating effect of such praise. Children were given a problem-solving exercise well within their capabilities and were given feedback about their score in three different conditions. All initially received feedback in the form 'Wow, you got x correct. That's a very good score.' A control group received no further comments, but two experimental groups received either intelligence praise, 'You must be really smart at these', or effort praise, 'You must have worked hard'. The children were then offered a choice between a further task that they could comfortably do, a performance goal, and a more challenging one, a mastery goal. The results were dramatic. Over 90% of the effort praise group opted for the challenging task compared with around 30% of the intelligence praise group. In further problem-solving tasks the effort praise group reported most enjoyment and the intelligence praise group the least.

There are other ways of encouraging a mastery orientation. As well as emphasising effort, feedback should as far as possible be referenced to the past accomplishments of the individual rather than relative to the achievements of peers. Comparing to others tends to reinforce entity beliefs whereas comparing results the individual has achieved on different occasions involving different levels of effort and different tasks may have the effect of reinforcing incremental beliefs. Currently a much used phrase in education is 'to celebrate achievement'. From the perspective of goal orientations, it is extremely important to celebrate achievement that results from effort rather than achievement that comes easily. Seeing peers who have not had to work hard and who have marginally outachieved those who have made huge strides by virtue of sheer effort can only reinforce entity beliefs for all concerned.

Dweck's work has further implications for personal and social education (PSE). An important task in education is to challenge the stereotypes held by students of social groups. There is some fascinating evidence that the tendency to stereotype is linked to entity and incremental beliefs. Levy *et al.* (1998) gave college students an article (fictitious) that made a strong case for either entity theory or incremental theory. The students then undertook an apparently unrelated task of assessing the accuracy of stereotypes of ethnic and occupational groups. Those who had read the entity theory article concurred with the stereotypes to a much greater extent than those who had studied the incremental article. This and related studies suggest that successful challenging of entity beliefs in learners can have a direct impact on their social development.

The effect of expectations on motivation

Research into expectations and motivation began with the classic study by Rosenthal and Jacobson (1968) into the 'Pygmalion effect'. The research took place in a primary school in a lower middle-class neighbourhood in an American town. All pupils in the first six years were given an IQ test at the start of the academic year. The 18 teachers at the school were told that the purpose of the test was to identify 'bloomers', children with great academic potential. They were then given a fictitious list of their pupils that scored in the top 20%. The IQ test was administered again at the end of the academic year in order to see whether those identified as bloomers had gained more than their peers. The results were dramatic, particularly with the younger

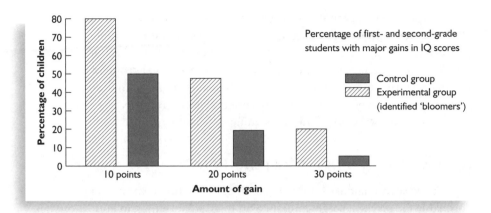

Figure 6.3 **Rosenthal and Jacobson's findings**

children. Over 80% of those identified as bloomers had increased their IQ by 10 points or more, compared with 50% of the controls, and 50% had increased by 20 points or more, compared with around 20% of the controls. Figure 6.3 shows a graph of the results.

These results suggest that teachers must have responded differently to children identified as having high potential. A follow-up study by Chaiken *et al.* (1974) confirmed that this does in fact take place. Teachers in another school were told that certain pupils were especially bright and they were then filmed interacting with their classes. As expected, teachers smiled more frequently, made more eye contact and responded more favourably to comments and questions from these children, who were in fact a random selection of the school population.

A limitation of early research was that teacher impressions were manipulated by false information, and no information was gleaned concerning the sources of teacher expectations in everyday situations free of experimenter manipulation. More contemporary research has continued to support the importance of teacher expectations as an influence on intellectual development, and has given us an insight into the factors affecting teacher expectations. Alvidrez and Weinstein (1999) carried out a longitudinal study of 110 American children from four to 18 years. Socio-economic status (SES), IQ and teacher ratings of academic ability, maturity and assertiveness were recorded and analysed. Low SES and perceived immaturity were associated with low estimates of ability. High SES, maturity and assertiveness were associated with high teacher ratings. When IQ was controlled, teacher ratings at four years were predictive of grade averages and Scholastic Aptitude Test (SAT) scores at 18, suggesting that teacher beliefs were an influence on academic progress.

There is some evidence to suggest that stereotyping of the abilities of different ethnic groups contributes to differential achievement, known as

133

stereotype threat, and that it is possible to counteract these disparities by tackling stereotypes. Influenced by Dweck's work on entity and incremental beliefs in intelligence, Aronson *et al.* (2002) set out to tackle Black American students' stereotypes of their own ability. An experimental group of college students were taught that intelligence is malleable rather than fixed in order to reduce stereotype threat. This experimental group reported greater enjoyment of college and achieved significantly higher grades.

Conclusions and personal reflections

Special educational needs notwithstanding, motivation is for most learners probably the greatest single influence on their achievement in education. It is therefore of vital importance that teachers and other professionals working with learners have an understanding of how to enhance motivation. The best-known theory of motivation, which dominates most textbook accounts, comes from Maslow. However, while Maslow is useful in reminding us of the breadth of human needs, his work does not readily lend itself to devising motivational techniques. For this we need to draw on more modern cognitive theories, such as attribution theory, self-efficacy and goal orientations. These have clear implications on how to use goal-setting and feedback in everyday classroom situations, and how to challenge and manipulate maladaptive beliefs, such as beliefs about the origins of success and failure and the nature of academic ability.

Taking a step back and thinking about education policy and its relationship to classroom practice, a good understanding of theory and research into motivation can illuminate the messages teachers receive from policy-makers. Thus terms like 'celebrating achievement' and 'culture of success', and policies demanding target-setting and challenging learners are not merely political invention, although they are undoubtedly perceived as such by many teachers, but are in fact founded on sound motivational principles. However, although an understanding of learner motivation should help prevent such cynicism, it also points to the dangers of oversimplifying these potentially useful techniques. Targets are effective in enhancing self-efficacy only under particular circumstances, and when using goal orientation it is much more productive to 'celebrate' some forms of achievement than others.

Self-assessment questions

1. Define motivation and explain its significance to the process of learning.

2. Critically discuss the contribution of humanistic theory to understanding motivation.

3. Explain how either attribution theory or self-efficacy can be applied to enhancing learner motivation.

4. Discuss the importance of beliefs about the origins of success and failure and beliefs about the nature of academic ability in motivation.

5. With reference to cognitive theories of motivation, evaluate the importance of celebrating achievement and achieving a culture of success.

Further reading

•••••• Bandura, A. (1986) *Social Foundations of Thought and Action*. Prentice Hall, Englewood Cliffs NJ.

•••••• Chaplain, R. (2000) Helping children to persevere and be well-motivated. In *The Psychology of Teaching and Learning in the Primary School* (ed. Whitebread, D.). Routledge Falmer, London.

•••••• Dweck, C. S. (2000) *Self-theories: Their Role in Motivation, Personality and Development*. Psychology Press, Philadelphia PA.

•••••• Dweck, C. S. (2002) Messages that motivate: how praise moulds students' beliefs, motivation and performance (in surprising ways). In *Improving Academic Achievement* (ed. Aronson, J.). Academic Press, San Diego CA.

•••••• Maslow, A. H. (1943) A theory of human motivation. *Psychological Review*, 50, 370–386.

•••••• Weiner, B. (1992) *Human Motivation: Metaphors, Theories and Research*. Sage, Thousand Oaks CA.

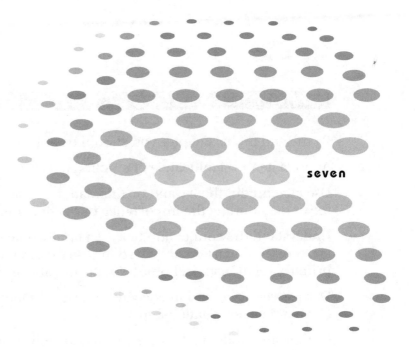

seven

Emotional
Factors in
Learning

Emotional Factors in Learning

learning objectives

By the end of this chapter you should be able to:

•••••• Appreciate the significance of emotional factors in learning.

•••••• Use attachment theory and/or Kleinian psychoanalysis as a basis for understanding the importance of relationships.

•••••• Understand the connection between family relationships and learning, with particular regard to research into quality of primary relationships, home climate and abuse.

•••••• Discuss research into the origins and significance of the teacher–learner relationship.

•••••• Outline and evaluate the practice of educational therapy as a means to aid learning in emotionally damaged individuals.

•••••• Describe research into peer relationships and appreciate their influence on learning.

•••••• Define bullying and appreciate the range of factors influencing bullying.

•••••• Examine strategies to tackle bullying behaviour with particular regard to the Olweus programme.

•••••• Critically discuss the concept of emotional intelligence and consider its application in education.

For some time education policy has tended to treat learning and the social-emotional development of learners as separate issues, albeit both of paramount importance. This is reflected in the functional separateness of pastoral systems and teaching systems within institutions. However, the everyday experience of practitioners suggests strongly that learning is closely bound up with a range of social and emotional factors (Greenhalgh, 1994). This is in line with research findings. In a Brazilian study, Jacob *et al.* (1999) assessed 8–12-year-olds of average and below average academic achievement on a range of emotional and intellectual measures.

When IQ was accounted for, emotional factors, including self-esteem and emotional competence, were significantly associated with educational achievement. More recently Aluja and Blanch (2002) investigated the relationship between a range of personality traits, IQ and emotional maladjustment and educational achievement. Emotional maladjustment was the factor most strongly associated with underachievement. So there is ample empirical support for the importance of emotional factors in learning. Consider the scenarios in Box 7.1.

We can explain each of these scenarios with reference to psychological theory. Alex is showing the classic signs of an insecure attachment. We might wonder whether this relationship with her primary carer has shaped her later relationships, and is now reflected in her ambivalent relationship with her teacher. This case illustrates the importance of the quality of relationships in learning. John's psychological development appears to have been knocked off kilter by the experience of trauma, in this case childhood sexual abuse (CSA). What is particularly interesting about the case is the apparent effect of trauma, most obviously *emotionally* salient, on his *cognitive* development. This illustrates the interdependent nature of emotional and intellectual development. Julian's problems are his poor *sociometric* or popularity status and the apparent tolerance of bullying in his school. There are several factors

---

Box 7.1

Case examples

- *Alex*, six years old, has had a disrupted home life due to her mother's chronic mental health problems. At school she exhibits clingy behaviour towards her teacher, accompanied by periodic tantrums, particularly when the teacher cannot pay her as much attention as she would like. Alex's language development is lagging behind her age norms.
- *John* suffered sexual abuse while in primary school. Some years later, he is still suspicious of adults and exhibits little interest in his work. Although his IQ was above average on entry to primary school, it has slipped down to below average.
- *Julian* has a large facial birthmark and bright ginger hair. Although on starting school he was cheerful and socially skilled, he has never been popular. At the age of 11 he has few friends and is regularly a victim of unchecked bullying.
- *Amy*, despite any record of childhood trauma or obviously dysfunctional relationships, has poor self-esteem and has difficulty getting on with her peers. She finds it hard to work cooperatively with others and tends to be insensitive to their needs.

affecting sociometric status, but with ginger hair and a disfigurement, Julian was always at a disadvantage in the popularity stakes. We might speculate that Amy, like Alex, has attachment problems and, like Julian, her sociometric status is probably poor. However, speculation aside, we can safely identify her as having a problem with emotional intelligence. In other words, she lacks the skills needed to interact meaningfully with others on an emotional level.

Learning and relationships

All the scenarios in Box 7.1 involve children who have problems with relationships – with family, peers or professionals, sometimes all three. It is these relationship problems that are affecting their experience of education and probably their ability to learn. The connection between relationships, emotional development and learning is complex, and many psychologists and teachers have found it helpful to use overarching theories as heuristic devices to help think about these issues. Here the psychodynamic approach to psychology, with its emphasis on emotion and relationships, has proved especially helpful, so we briefly review two particularly relevant psychodynamic theories, Kleinian psychoanalysis and attachment theory.

Kleinian psychoanalysis

Melanie Klein was a student of Sigmund Freud, and her ideas concerning the importance of instinct and early relationships ultimately come from his influence. Unlike earlier psychodynamic theorists, however, Klein placed her emphasis very much on the developmental significance of the first year of life. One of Klein's innovations was the concept of *phantasy*, the mental representation of instincts. She described phantasy as 'an activity of the mind that occurs on deep unconscious levels and accompanies every impulse experienced by the infant' (Klein, 1959, p. 21). For example, on one level hunger is experienced as a phantasy of suckling a 'good breast', but simultaneously on another level it is experienced as the persecutory phantasy of denial of nurture by a 'bad breast'. The infant cannot initially distinguish between phantasy and reality, thus bodily needs are experienced as real persecution.

According to Klein, our capacity to enter into relationships and our tendency to experience persecution, hence to hate, are rooted in these early phantasies. Even when cognitive development allows us a more logical understanding of relationships, they are always coloured by phantasy. Thus the learner who expresses an apparently unwarranted sense of being persecuted by their teacher may be influenced by persecutory phantasy derived from their first interactions with another person. Coren (1997) suggests that learning is represented in phantasy as an *oral* process in which knowledge represents nurturance. Popular metaphors such as 'thirst for knowledge' illustrate the oral nature of the learning experience. Wittenberg *et al.* (1983)

suggest that the passivity of many learners can be explained in terms of reversion to an infantile state in which knowledge is taken in with the passivity of a suckling baby.

Introjection and the inner world

The *inner* (or internal) *world* is Klein's term for our mental representations of our social world and is 'peopled' with *internal objects*, the mental representations of people with whom we have a relationship. From a few months of age the infant can introject a complete representation of the primary carer. If she has been kind and reliable, then she will be introjected as a 'good object'. As the developing child forms new relationships, these are also introjected to form part of the inner world. Because we project our internal objects on to all new people we meet, having good internal objects is essential in forming successful relationships. This process of perceiving new people and relationships in the light of previous significant relationships is known as *transference* or *parataxic distortion*.

Developmental positions

Instead of thinking in terms of developmental stages, Klein (1945) saw the major qualitative change in psychological development as being between two basic orientations towards internal and external objects. For the first few months the infant spends most of its time in the *paranoid-schizoid* position. The paranoid-schizoid position is characterised by persecutory anxiety and the tendency for *splitting*, the tendency to see the world in simple terms of good and bad. The tendency for splitting remains within us to adulthood, and stress can lead to a reversion to the paranoid-schizoid position, whereupon one of our likely responses is to begin to see complex situations in highly 'black and white' terms, splitting elements of the situation into good and bad.

From around three months of age the infant becomes capable of adopting the more mature *depressive* position. By six months the child typically spends most of its time in the depressive position. In the depressive position, the experience of persecutory anxiety and the use of splitting decline, but the child does begin to experience low self-esteem, guilt and sadness, as adult carers become the target of an ambivalent combination of love and hate. Wittenberg *et al.* (1983) describe a range of expectations students are likely to hold of the teacher, based on infantile modes of thinking. Learners are in a vulnerable position, and may respond to stress by reversion to a paranoid-schizoid state. They may thus envy and idealise teachers, or split them into the good providing teacher and the bad withholding teacher. Splitting is particularly apparent when students are taught by a team of teachers. Learners in the depressive position are generally those who appear most 'together', but may require different intervention to compensate for their reluctance to make demands of their teacher or express difficulty to them.

Containment and thinking

Klein's student and colleague Wilfred Bion developed her ideas further; their ideas are often known as the Klein–Bion school of psychoanalysis. Bion (1962) proposed that the primary carer has a major role in helping the infant think (initially thinking for them), so the ability to think is always rooted in social interaction. This is strongly reminiscent of Vygotsky's idea of the intermental plane (p. 28), Mercer's concept of 'interthinking' (p. 32) and Feuerstein's mediation (p. 103). To Bion, because of the function of 'thinking for' a learner, it is essential that the teacher keep their students 'in mind'. Thus the tendency of the teacher to think regularly about their learners is not merely a matter of professionalism or humanity but is actually an essential part of the learning process. The teacher who keeps their learners in mind is helping them to think and learn. Anxiety, like information, is processed for the infant by their primary container. This process is called *containment*. According to Bion, the professional who contains anxiety, perhaps by setting clear boundaries and demonstrably tolerating difficult feelings on the part of learners, is aiding the learner in the same way as a primary carer aids their infant (Kalu, 2002).

Attachment theory

John Bowlby originally developed attachment theory, integrating psycho-analysis and ethology, the study of animal behaviour. His aim in devising attachment theory was to reintroduce a scientific ethos to psychodynamic theory, Klein and Bion having shifted psychoanalysis into the realms of a philosophical rather than psychological understanding of the person. Like the psychoanalytic theories of Klein and Bion, attachment theory places tremen-dous significance on the infant's primary relationship. However, both the precursors and processes of this relationship are explained in rather different terms. Like Klein, Bowlby believed that neonates are born predisposed to form relationships. However, to Bowlby, the mechanism of relationship seeking and formation is best explained in terms of a *behavioural system*, i.e. an instinctive set of interactive behaviours such as smiling, sucking, gesturing and crying. Babies also have a tendency to orient themselves towards adult faces in prefer-ence to other stimuli. These innate behaviours were termed *social releasers* because their function is to elicit instinctive social responses from adults. These instinctive responses are also organised into a behavioural system. The interplay between the infant and parental behavioural systems is the process that builds the attachment between infant and carer. The importance of the interplay between social releasers and parenting responses, as postulated by Bowlby, is firmly supported by contemporary research (Koulomzin *et al.*, 2002).

Internal working models

Bowlby (1969) proposed that the developing child formed a mental represen-tation of their first attachment relationship and that the nature of this representation has profound effects on later relationships. This is very much consistent with Klein's inner world construct; however, in keeping with his greater emphasis on scientific rigour, Bowlby regarded the psychoanalytic idea of the inner world as somewhat woolly. His own concept of the mental representation of the primary relationship was the *internal working model*. The developing child internalises a working model of relationships from their early interactions, in particular those with the primary carer. If the internalised working model is of a positive relationship with a carer, then future relationships will be interpreted in the light of these qualities. But if the child is neglected or abused, there is a strong probability they will reproduce these patterns in future relationships. This phenomenon is clearly demonstrable (van Ijzendoorn, 1995; Zhang and Hazan, 2002) and is clearly relevant in understanding how learners respond to teachers. A learner that has positive experiences of relationships will have positive working models and thus positive expectations. They will tend to bring that expectation to their relationship with their teacher, whereas an individual whose primary relationship has been unsuccessful will have poor internal working models and will probably have more difficulty in building a positive relationship with a teacher or other professionals.

Attachment types

Bowlby's student and colleague Mary Ainsworth developed and expanded on his basic ideas. Ainsworth's particular contributions lay in operationalising Bowlby's ideas and setting them out in a more empirically testable form. In particular, Ainsworth developed a classification of attachment types and empirical tests for their assessment. This in turn has allowed systematic research into the sequelae of infant attachment type. Based on children's behaviour on separation from and reuniting with their primary carer, Ainsworth *et al.* (1978) proposed that the vast majority of infant attachments fell into three distinct categories:

- *Type A, avoidant*: children classified as avoidant tend to play independently and do not show significant anxiety at being separated from their primary carer. They make little effort to make contact when the primary carer returns. Between 20% and 25% of British 12–18-month-olds are classified as type A (van Ijzendoorn and Kroonenberg, 1988).
- *Type B, securely attached*: these children play fairly independently and typically show mild distress when separated from the primary carer. However, they enthusiastically greet the primary carer on her return, and are easily comforted. Between 60% and 75% of British 12–18-month-olds are classified as type B.
- *Type C, resistant (or ambivalent)*: resistant children explore their environment less than the other attachment categories. They become

highly distressed on separation from the primary carer, but they do not readily accept comfort on her return. Around 3% of British babies and toddlers are classified as type C.

A minority of children with atypical attachments fall outside this normal range. Main and Solomon (1986) have termed this pattern disorganised or *type D* attachment. Type D children may alternate between avoidant and resistant behaviour or they may combine them, maintaining proximity but avoiding contact and resisting when cuddled. Typically they appear afraid of the primary carer and may prefer the company of strangers.

If we accept the major tenet of attachment theory that the quality of the primary relationship tends to be generalised to other relationships, we would expect type A, B, C and D individuals to respond differently towards both teacher and peers. Type As, who are characterised by detachment, would be expected to have a small number of friends and a distant relationship with their teacher. Type Bs would be expected to have the closest relationships with peers and teachers, and the ambivalent and angry type Cs would be expected to have difficulty in all relationships. It would be expected that the type D classification is associated with generally dysfunctional relationships.

Sensitive responsiveness

Ainsworth believed, like Bowlby, that the major determinant of the quality of a child–parent relationship was the quality of care provided by the primary carer. However, Ainsworth went further in operationalising the quality of care. She identified the key variable in the quality of parenting as *sensitive responsiveness*, defined as the success with which the parent picks up the child's non-verbal signals. There is ample evidence to support a role for sensitive responsiveness in the development of secure attachment, although modern research suggests important roles for the temperament of the child and a range of external factors such as poverty (Atkinson *et al.*, 2000). If sensitive responsiveness is the key to building mother–infant attachment, then it follows that teachers who are sensitive to the unvoiced needs of their learners should be more successful in building relationships with them.

Comparing the two theories

Although the details of both theories are open to criticism (Jarvis, 2004a), there is little doubt that the emphasis placed on the relationship with the primary carer in both Kleinian psychoanalysis and attachment theory is justified. There is a wealth of research supporting the notion that the quality of the primary relationship is powerfully predictive of future relationships, and that this impacts on a number of developmental domains, including learning and educational achievement. Both approaches are helpful in allowing the professional to think clearly about the apparently irrational responses exhibited by learners towards peers, adults and learning itself, i.e. they serve as heuristic devices. The chief difference between the two theories lies in their *epistemological* basis, i.e. the theory of knowledge on which they are based. Kleinian theory is philosophical in nature, using rich and imaginative concepts like 'inner world' and 'containment', which are often highly meaningful to the individual, capturing their experience of working, in particular with vulnerable learners. Its usefulness is thus primarily phenomenological (experiential). Attachment theory, by contrast, is highly scientific, using precisely defined terminology and generating testable hypotheses. Which theory the professional finds a more useful heuristic device will be largely influenced by their preference for scientific precision or discursive exploration of ideas. Such preferences are probably a result of learning style (Chapter 4).

Reflection point

Consider your responses to these two theories. Which makes more sense to you? How intuitively appealing do you find them in comparison to the more cognitive theories discussed in the preceding chapters? To what extent do you find that overarching theories like these are helpful in understanding a complex issue like the relationship between emotion and learning?

Research into relationships and education

There is a wealth of research investigating the significance of parental and teacher relationships in the learning process. Research has revealed that the quality of family and teacher relationships is profoundly important in successful education.

Family relationships

Research has supported the importance of attachment status, parenting style and the broader home environment in determining academic motivation and success and quality of peer relationships. Vondra *et al.* (1999) carried out a longitudinal study on 156 children. Attachment to primary carer and siblings was assessed, and data about classroom behaviour was gathered in the form of teacher reports. Secure attachments to primary carer and positive relations with siblings were both positively related to the quality of relationship with the teacher and with the teacher's perception of social competence in the classroom. Howes (1997) assessed attachment security in 107 children aged from birth to five years and looked for associations with their play at nursery. Securely attached children engaged in more complex play with peers. Interestingly, given Ainsworth's sensitive responsiveness hypothesis, adult carer behaviour predicted both attachment status and complexity of play.

Similar findings have emerged in studies of older children and adults. Wong *et al.* (2002) examined the relationship between learner perceptions of their attachment to primary carers and academic motivation and test performance in 135 American high-school children. Secure attachment was associated with high levels of motivation and achievement. Perrine (1999) further found that responses to teacher intervention varied as a function of attachment type. A total of 151 undergraduate students were assessed on their response to a 'please see me' note from a professor. Students showing insecure attachments (types A and C) exhibited significantly more negative emotional responses to receiving the note, tended to attribute the note to more negative reasons (i.e. they were in trouble) and went to less effort to make contact with the professor. There is additional evidence to suggest that attachment status has a role in response to exam stress. Horppu and Ikonen-Varila (2001) assessed attachment type in 231 candidates for Finnish teacher training and their response to entrance exams and interviews. Insecure attachment was associated with greater exam stress, particularly with more anxiety and more negative self-appraisal. Interviewers were more likely to approve securely attached interviewees.

Levels of family support

Other studies have looked at the family environment in a broader sense, particularly the role of family support. Baharudin and Luster (1998) looked at 898 families with 6–8-year-old children, and assessed the relationships between predictors of the quality of family environment, including parental educational level, IQ and self-esteem, and academic achievement. Clear relationships emerged between the predictor variables and the levels of support provided in the home, and between levels of support and success at school. Bacete and Remirez (2001) collected teacher estimates of family support and socio-economic status as defined by the mother's educational level and profession. Academic achievement was rated based on mark books. Statistical analysis revealed that achievement was closely related to parental involvement, which in turn was a product of socio-economic status. In other words, more highly educated mothers took a more active role in children's education and this was reflected in their children's achievements.

Child abuse

There are a range of situations that might be classified as child abuse, and the interested reader is advised to pursue more specialist literature. Put simply, child abuse occurs when a child is subjected to systematic traumatic experience, which may include physical chastisement, premature sexual activity or emotional attack, such as verbal denigration. Individuals who have suffered abuse or trauma in childhood typically have lower IQ than their peers, and there are numerous cases in the literature of children who have been wrongly identified as having pervasive learning difficulties when in fact their symptoms were emotional responses to abuse (Alvarez, 1992; Sinason, 1992). Carrey *et al.* (1996) compared the IQ as measured by the Wechsler test (p. 48) of 18 people aged between seven and 23 who had been abused as children and 18 matched participants who had not suffered abuse. The abused group had significantly lower IQ than the control group and were particularly disadvantaged in verbal abilities. In a larger study, Lane (1998) assessed 53 sexually abused boys aged 11–18 and compared them to a control group of non-abused boys. No overall difference in IQ was found between the two groups, but the abused group did emerge as significantly lower in verbal ability. Cahill *et al.* (1999) reviewed studies of the relationship between several types of early maltreatment of children and concluded there is ample evidence to say that neglect, physical abuse and sexual abuse are all associated with reduced intelligence.

The link between emotional trauma and impaired cognitive development is counter-intuitive and requires explanation. From a psychoanalytic perspective, Alvarez (1992) suggests that the disrupted process of introjection of relationship figures into the internal world in turn disrupts the taking in of information. In other words, the quality of *receptiveness* generalises from early relationship experiences to learning experiences. Wittenberg *et al.* (1983) suggests that, to the deprived or abused child, the sense of helplessness engendered by not knowing or understanding something is intolerable and can only be coped with by defence mechanisms such as detachment or aggression. Attachment theorists operate on a different level of explanation, and rather than speculating on the nature of the internal world, they look at the impact of attachment-related behaviour on learning activity. Abuse is strongly associated with the highly dysfunctional type D attachment pattern. Type D individuals find it very difficult to develop the quality of relationships with peers and teachers that facilitate the kind of interactions associated with successful learning.

Teacher relationships

Teaching and learning are interactive processes and take place in the context of a socially prescribed teacher–learner relationship. Everyday experience tells us that whether we are in the role of teacher or learner we spend considerable time thinking about our relationships with our learners or teachers. Sigmund Freud once remarked, 'It is hard to decide whether what affects us more and was of greater importance to us was our concern with the sciences that we were taught or with the personalities of our teachers' (Freud, 1914; cited in Coren, 1997, p. 52).

A number of studies have highlighted the importance placed by teachers and learners on the quality of their relationship. A straightforward and effective protocol for investigating learner perceptions of good teachers was developed by Kutnick and Jules (1993). This involves writing an essay entitled

'What Makes a Good Teacher'. Research using this approach has uncovered age and gender effects. Jules and Kutnick (1997) compared the answers of boys and girls aged between eight and 16 years from Trinidad and Tobago, looking for information on the personal characteristics, pupil–teacher relationship, control strategies, teaching methods and pupil progress and results. Both sexes placed considerable value on pupil–teacher relationships, although boys showed more concern over the control strategies used by teachers.

Using a similar methodology, Beishuizen *et al.* (2001) looked at the responses of 198 Dutch children aged seven, 10, 13 and 16 years, comparing their responses to those of their teachers. Responses were analysed using two dimensions: the extent to which learners saw good teachers in terms of knowledge transmission as opposed to establishment of good relationships, and the extent of attachment or detachment towards school and teachers. Among secondary school teachers and pupils there was considerable agreement; both parties said that the major element of good teaching is the establishment of a good teacher–learner relationship. Primary teachers also held this view, but primary school pupils focused more in their responses on the subject knowledge and teaching skills.

Using a slightly different approach, Reid and Johnson (1999) compared the perceptions of university lecturers and students about effective teaching in higher education. Forty-eight participants ranked the characteristics of approachability, clarity, depth of knowledge, interaction, interest and organisation. Based on this pilot, a larger sample of 102 lecturers and 102 students rated a range of characteristics. Both groups agreed that interest, clarity and organisation were important attributes of good teachers, but approachability and quality of interactions were rated much higher by the students than by the teachers. Overall, a clear message emerges from research into learner perceptions; the most important factor identified by learners across a wide range of ages and learning contexts is the teacher's capacity for successful relationships with learners.

Compensation hypothesis

An interesting question with important practical applications concerns the extent to which the development of a good teacher relationship can compensate for poor family relationships. We know, for example, that good levels of sensitive responsiveness on the part of teachers are associated with attachment-related behaviour and sophistication of play (Howes, 1997). Copeland-Mitchell *et al.* (1997) set out to directly test the compensation hypothesis. Sixty-two children aged 2–4 years were assessed for attachment to primary carer and teacher and their social competence and popularity with peers. It was found that secure attachment to the primary carer and the teacher was associated with popularity and social competence. Where the primary carer relationship was insecure and the teacher relationship was secure, popularity and social competence were significantly better than cases where both attachments were insecure, but generally not as good as where both relationships were secure. This suggests that a secure teacher attachment partially compensates for an insecure attachment with the primary carer. This is highly significant as it suggests that the effort expended in building a good relationship with a difficult learner is in fact a good investment.

Educational therapy

Although good relationships with education professionals can partially compensate for the disadvantages of insecure attachment, experience of abuse and generally poor home environments, a minority of emotionally damaged learners require specialist individual attention. Generic counselling of a variety of forms is now widely available in educational institutions. Most counselling is time-limited and aimed at resolving acute life problems rather than chronic problems such as emotional resistance to learning (this is not to suggest that it is not helpful). There is, however, a specialist form of psychotherapy specifically for such cases. Irene Caspari, a psychotherapist, developed educational therapy in the 1970s. It is based on psychodynamic principles and combines psychoanalytic therapy with teaching. The theoretical background to educational therapy is a blend of attachment theory and psychoanalysis. Particularly important is the development of a relationship such that the therapist becomes an 'educational attachment figure' (Barrett and Trevitt, 1991). The Caspari Foundation, which trains and accredits educational therapists, recommends educational therapy when the following scenarios affect a learner's ability to concentrate or learn:

- Learning and communication difficulty
- Poor social behaviour and relationships
- Experience of bereavement and separation
- Accidents
- Family mental health problems
- Deprivation and/or abuse.

Educational therapy takes place in once-weekly sessions of 50 minutes, typically lasting three to four terms. The aim of therapy is exploratory, aiming to help learners gain insight into the emotional blocks to their learning and then work through them; this allows the learner to overcome anxieties about learning and develop meaningful relationships in the context of education. The content of sessions varies according to the age of the learner and their particular problems, but typically it consists of educational activities such as writing, and more overtly therapeutic techniques such as drawing and play.

Box 7.2

Two examples of educational therapy

- *Nina*, a six-year-old girl, presented with extreme anxiety related to schoolwork and an inability to play. She was referred by an educational psychologist. The therapist used drawing as a way to explore and work through her anxiety. Initially her drawings were poor, inhibited by her anxiety, but after nine months of therapy they improved and she regained the capacity for play.
- *Omar* was an eight-year-old boy referred for language difficulties. He had recently come to Norway and did not speak Norwegian. This left him socially isolated and he had unusual difficulty in picking up the language. The therapy focused on teaching him Norwegian in the context of a therapeutic relationship.

Source: Marstrander (1996)

Marstrander (1996) provides two illustrative cases (Box 7.2). Evidence for the effectiveness of educational therapy comes almost exclusively in the form of published case studies, and there is a lack of systematic outcomes research. However, the results of case studies are encouraging and there is a body of research supporting the effectiveness of psychoanalytic therapy in other contexts (Jarvis, 2004a).

Reflection point

How much importance have you accorded to your relationship with learners? In developing your professional practice, has this been a primary focus or have you been more concerned with the cognitive aspects of learning?

Peer relationships

Learners do not merely maintain relationships with family and teachers. Learning takes place in a social milieu. Our daily interactions with friends have traditionally been taken for granted (Pellegrini and Blatchford, 2000), yet we invest in them considerable time and energy, and experience considerable distress and distraction as a result of discord. In a study of children's perceptions of school, Blatchford (1996) discovered that seven-, 11- and 16-year-olds consistently identified their peer relationships as one of the two main factors affecting their experience of school; the other factor is schoolwork. In spite of this acknowledged importance, there is a dearth of research into the relationship between educational systems and peer relations. What we do know is

that successful peer relations and friendships convey a range of developmental advantages on children (Hartup, 1992), and probably continue to do so
for all learners regardless of age.

Worryingly, given the importance of peer interaction, recent
educational policy has not been helpful in fostering peer relations, because
the increasingly crowded curriculum has led to a reduction in the time
given over to breaks in the school day. Blatchford and Sumpner (1998)
surveyed primary and secondary schools about changes in break and lunch
times in the period 1990–96. Some 38% of junior schools and 35% of
secondary schools reported that in the period 1990–96 they had reduced
the lunch break, and 27% of junior schools and 14% of secondaries had
abolished the afternoon break. The most common reasons cited for this were
to increase teaching time and to reduce the opportunity for inappropriate
behaviour.

Sociometric status

Individual differences in popularity may be important in affecting learning. An
important classification system comes from Coie and Dodge (1983), who
identified five categories of *sociometric status* or popularity type. The categories arise from a study in which children were asked to categorise their
peers as 'liked most' or 'liked least'. Children in the sample were categorised
according to their tendency to be identified as liked most or least. The five
categories are shown in Box 7.3.

Box 7.3

Coie and Dodge's classifications of sociometric status

- *Popular children* were identified as those who tended to be categorised by peers often as 'liked most' and seldom as 'liked least'.
- *Average children* were identified as moderately liked and equally
  likely to be categorised by peers as 'liked most' or 'liked least'.
  Children tended not to have strong opinions for or against them.
- *Controversial children* were identified as being frequently categorised as both 'liked most' and 'liked least'. They were therefore
  very popular with some peers and very unpopular with others.
- *Neglected children* were identified as those rarely categorised as
  'liked most' or 'liked least'. They appeared to be little noticed by
  their peers.
- *Rejected children* were identified as those frequently categorised as
  'liked least' and rarely as 'liked most'. They were therefore the
  most unpopular group.

Factors affecting sociometric status

Physical attractiveness

Physical attractiveness appears to be one factor affecting sociometric status. Coie *et al.* (1982) rated children for attractiveness, then asked members of peer groups to rate each other as 'most liked' and 'most disliked'. A strong relationship emerged, with the most attractive children being those most likely to be categorised as 'most liked' and the least attractive children as those most likely to be categorised as 'least liked'. Langlois *et al.* (1995) examined parental attitudes towards physically unattractive children from infancy and discovered that premature and disfigured babies tended to receive less attention and lower expectations from adults. There may thus be a *self-fulfilling prophecy* at work, in which physically unattractive children are not less popular with peers merely because they are unattractive to them, but because their development has already been adversely affected by adult attitudes.

Social skills

There is little doubt that some children are more socially skilled than others or that highly skilled children are more likely to have successful relationships with their peers. However, the precise nature of social skills has proved much more difficult to pin down. Coie and Dodge (1988) had 6–9-year-old American boys rate each other as 'most liked' and 'most disliked' then observed classroom behaviour and questioned teachers about the strengths and weaknesses of each child. It emerged that three social factors were associated with high popularity: sporting prowess, skilful use of humour and pro-social (generous) behaviour. It appears that different competences are valued in boys and girls. A study of peer perceptions of anger and distress in 56 children (average age four years), found that in girls, high levels of anger but not distress were associated with peer rejection. In boys, expressions of anger and distress led to peer rejection.

Quality of early relationships

Securely attached children (type Bs) tend to have better peer relationships than insecurely attached children. Remember that type A attachment is characterised by *avoidant*, i.e. distant and unemotional, behaviour and type C by *resistant*, i.e. ambivalent and bad-tempered, behaviour. If these patterns of relating to others persist through childhood and characterise all relationships, it is unsurprising that they would cause problems for children. Research has found that type A children tend to have the lowest social status among peers (La Freniere and Sroufe, 1985) and to be most likely to be bullied (Troy and Sroufe, 1987). A study by Myron-Wilson and Smith (1998) confirmed this and further suggested that type C children are the most likely to be bullies. A total of 196 primary school children aged between seven and 11 years from a south-east London primary school took part in the study. All children were assessed for attachment type using standard questionnaires. Involvement with bullying was examined by a test called the Participant Roles Scale, in which each child identifies their peers as either a bully, a victim of bullying or uninvolved in bullying. It was found that securely attached children were assessed by their peers as very unlikely to be involved in bullying, either as bully or victim. Type A children were the most likely to be identified by peers as victims of bullying, and type C children were the most likely to be rated by peers as bullies.

Attachment type is not merely associated with popularity and positive patterns of social interaction with peers, but also with the formation of friendships. Kerns (1994) studied interactions between pairs of four-year-old friends with secure and insecure attachments. It emerged that pairs of securely attached friends had more successful and positive interactions than pairs where one had an insecure attachment. The implication of this is that securely attached children will find it more rewarding to interact with each other, whereas insecurely attached children, who would benefit most from interacting with securely attached peers, are likely to find themselves isolated (Erwin, 1998). There is some evidence that the relationship between attachment, popularity and friendship is different in adolescents than in younger children. Kerns and Stevens (1996) found that securely attached adolescents had more frequent and successful interactions with peers than insecurely attached individuals, but they were no more likely to have close friendships.

Benefits of popularity and friendship

There is a clear link between sociometric status and educational achievement. In a recent Portuguese study, Lopes *et al.* (2002) took 173 students aged 10–14 years and followed them for two years, looking at their sociometric classification, grades and teacher assessments. Rejected and controversial children accounted for a disproportionate percentage of low achievers and they were more likely to be rated by teachers as disruptive. Risi *et al.* (2003) carried out a 10-year study of 524 American children looking at the long-term results of low sociometric status in primary school. Interestingly, cultural differences emerged, with low sociometric status predicting underachievement in white middle-class children but not in working-class children or those from minority ethnic groups. There is some evidence to suggest that language development and social cognition may be enhanced by sociometric status and in turn impact on learning.

In a recent study by Pellegrini and Melhuish (1998), 28 pairs of children were observed in tasks of *literate language*. Literate language can be defined as children's talk about their own mental processes. It was found that pairs of friends were more likely to use literate language than pairs of non-friends. It was also found that the use of literate language predicted good performance in school-based tests. This has an important implication: children who have friends are advantaged in school work, and friendship may be one thing that could improve the performance of children who are not doing well at school work. This is addressed later in the chapter. In terms of social benefits, having friends is, unsurprisingly, associated with lower levels of loneliness (Zettergren, 2003). In adolescence, when peer relationships become increasingly important and friends replace family as major sources of social support, loneliness for friendless individuals becomes an increasing problem, and loneliness is one of the most frequently reported problems in adolescence (Shultz and Moore, 1989).

Bullying

There has been considerable concern in recent years over the impact of bullying on learning (DfEE, 2000). Bullying can be defined as existing when 'a student is being bullied or victimized when he or she is exposed, repeatedly and over time, to negative actions on the part of one or more other students' (Olweus, 1993, p. 9). Childline receives 20 000 calls per year about bullying, and in 2003 it is believed that up to 16 children committed suicide as a direct result of bullying. Since 1999 schools are required to have an anti-bullying policy, and since 2003 bullying has been a focus of Ofsted inspections. In a recent survey of UK children and young people (Oliver and Candappa, 2003) 51% of primary and 54% of secondary school pupils thought that bullying was a problem at their school and a significant number (51% of primary and 28% of secondary school children) reported that they had suffered bullying in the previous term. Gender had little impact, but minority ethnic groups were at elevated risk (33% of black and Asian children). There was considerable variation between schools, and percentages were significantly higher in the worst institutions. The most commonly reported forms of bullying were verbal, although physical aggression was also common. Some 20% of primary and 6% of secondary school children had been racially abused and 11% had been called anti-gay names. Interestingly there was evidence of an emerging trend for e-bullying, with 4% of secondary pupils having received unpleasant text messages and 2% unpleasant emails.

Assessing bullying

There are several ways to gather data about bullying. The most common method of assessing bullying behaviour is by peer nomination. A good example of a peer nomination scale comes from Björkqvist *et al.* (1992), in the form of the Direct and Indirect Aggression Scales (DIAS). This contains 24 general items and subscales to assess physical, verbal and indirect aggression. Example items are shown in Box 7.4.

Effects of bullying

The effects of bullying are significant. In a study of the effects of exposure to violence, D. Schwartz and Gorman (2003) found that bullying, in common

Box 7.4

Items from the DIAS

Name of classmate ....
Answer the questions by circling the number which seems to tell
about his/her behavior in the closest way: 0 = never, 1 = seldom,
2 = sometimes, 3 = quite often, 4 = very often

1. Hits the other one	0	1	2	3	4
2. Shuts the other one out of the group	0	1	2	3	4
3. Yells at or argues with the other one	0	1	2	3	4
4. Becomes friends with another as a kind of revenge	0	1	2	3	4
5. Kicks the other one	0	1	2	3	4

with several other forms of exposure to violence, was associated with
academic difficulties in urban children (average age nine years). More
seriously, being the victim of bullying is associated with psychosomatic
(stress-related) and mental health problems. In a large-scale study, Bond *et al.*
(2001) surveyed 2680 students aged 13–14 years for bullying and symptoms of
anxiety and depression. A feature of this study was *cross-lagging*. This means
that the young people were surveyed three times, and correlations were
calculated between early bullying and later symptoms, and between early
symptoms and later bullying. This design allows the direction of causality to
be teased out. If bullying at 13 were associated with symptoms at 14 rather
than the reverse, this would indicate that the bullying led to the symptoms
rather than the reverse. This was in fact the case, and there was no relationship between symptoms at 13 and later bullying. Karin *et al.* (2001) examined
the psychosomatic effects of bullying on 856 Norwegian adolescents aged
13–15 years. A range of symptoms were noted, including irritability,
headache, backache, nervousness and insomnia. Nervousness and
insomnia were particularly associated with bullying in girls; irritability,
headache and backache were particularly associated with bullying in boys.
Occasionally the victims of bullying may react extremely violently with tragic
consequences. Although this line of research is highly controversial, and
statistics cannot be taken as solid evidence of causal relationships, Leary *et al.*
(2003) have noted that of the 15 high-profile school shootings that took place
in the US between 1995 and 2001, the perpetrators of 13 (87%) were socially
rejected and had suffered either chronic or intensive short-term bullying
before the attacks.

Factors affecting bullying

There has been a wealth of research into the factors associated with bullying behaviour. A Finnish study (Kumpulainen *et al.*, 2001) of 420 primary school children revealed that male bullies were nearly 10 times as likely to have psychiatric problems as those not involved in bullying. Female bullies were four times as likely as non-bullies to exhibit mental health problems. Victims were also likely to show symptoms, but recall the cross-lagged study by Bond *et al.* (2001), showing that symptoms are more likely to be results rather than causes of bullying. Type C attachment (Myron-Wilson and Smith, 1998), a developmental history of abuse by caregivers (Shields and Cicchetti, 2001) and low self-esteem – though not as low as victims (Karatzias *et al.*, 2001) – are also reliably associated with bullying. Being a victim of bullying is also associated with low self-esteem (O'Moore and Kirkham, 2001), experiences of child abuse (Duncan, 1999) and being in a minority ethnic or sexual group (Oliver and Candappa, 2003).

However, bullying is a social process and cannot be entirely explained by individual characteristics of bullies and victims. Bullying is more common in schools where there is a low level of learner satisfaction and educational achievement (D. I. Miller *et al.*, 2000) and less common where there are high levels of social support (Naylor and Cowie, 1999). Natvig *et al.* (2001) investigated the relationship between stress and bullying in 885 Dutch 13–15-year-olds and found that high stress levels predict bullying. These findings suggest that bullying is systemic in nature, resulting from the effect of the environment on the individual bully. There are particular situations where bullying is more common, such as when a new group member wishes to assert their position (Pellegrini and Blatchford, 2000). Social processes operating between learners may also affect the development of bullying. O'Connell *et al.* (1999) investigated the role of imitation and reinforcement in bullying behaviour. A total of 120 primary school children were classified as bullies, victims or controls (no involvement). They were videotaped in the playground engaged in bullying and the episodes were analysed for imitation and reinforcement. In 21% of cases the bullying was imitated and in 54% it was watched without intervention – this was inter-preted as passive reinforcement, making repetition of the behaviour more likely.

Anti-bullying strategies

Bullying, like any behaviour manifested by individuals within an institution, can be addressed at the level of the individual or the institution. Individualised intervention comes in the form of counselling and social skills training. Results of individualised programmes are somewhat inconsistent. Baldry and Farrington (2004) investigated the effectiveness of an Italian programme involving videos and booklets designed to increase awareness of the consequences of bullying, aimed at 10–16-year-olds. Although there was some reduction in bullying in older adolescents, rates actually increased in younger children. Peer counselling and befriending schemes have been demonstrably more effective (Menesini *et al.*, 2003), although there are a range of practical problems to overcome (Price and Jones, 2001).

It is well established that there are wide differences in the prevalence of bullying in different institutions, and that a range of systemic factors affect bullying. It follows that systems can be designed to reduce the incidence of bullying. The best-known anti-bullying programme was developed by Dan Olweus (2001). The rationale underlying Olweus' work is that bullying reflects multiple problems and has to be tackled on several levels. Box 7.5 shows the major components of the programme. Studies of the effectiveness of the Olweus programme have revealed impressive results. Olweus (1991) evaluated the effects in 42 schools in Bergen from 1983 to 1985. Reported bullying fell by over 50% and spin-off benefits included a reduction in other antisocial behaviour such as vandalism, shoplifting and truancy. These findings have since been replicated in the UK (P. K. Smith and Sharpe, 1994) and Norway (Olweus, 2001).

Box 7.5

Components of the Olweus programme

Institutional level
- Forming a bullying prevention committee
- Auditing current levels of bullying by anonymous questionnaire
- Training for staff
- Coordination of supervision
- Adoption of strict anti-bullying rules
- Establishing systematic consequences of bullying behaviour
- Staff discussion groups
- Parental involvement.

Classroom level
- Reinforcement of school policy
- Regular classroom meetings
- Meetings with parents.

Individual level
- Interventions with bullies
- Interventions with victims
- Discussion with parents of bullies and victims.

Reflection point

Recall your own experiences of sociometric status and, if applicable, bullying at school. How might these experiences influence your perceptions of the learners you work with? Consider, for example, whether you have a tendency to resent or appease particular individuals.

Emotional intelligence

Much of the recent work on developing the emotional aspects of learning has centred on the idea of emotional intelligence and a range of closely related concepts, including emotional literacy, emotional competence and emotional well-being. One of the problems in dealing with the literature in this area is in reconciling the subtly different definitions used by the different research groups who favour each term (Weare and Gray, 2003). The term 'emotional intelligence' was first used by Salovey and Mayer (1990), referring to the cognitive processes involved in perceiving, regulating and expressing emotion. The journalist Daniel Goleman popularised the concept (Goleman, 1996), using a much broader definition including social skills. Although the concept of emotional intelligence has proved helpful in drawing attention to the link between emotion and learning, the word 'intelligence' has unfortunate connotations, making emotional intelligence appear measurable, fixed and innate.

Many psychologists question whether the cognitive ability or abilities involved in emotional 'intelligence' can strictly be described as intelligence. According to Weare and Gray, most UK practitioners prefer a range of other terms, although they still have their problems. The term 'emotional literacy' is popular, although the link between emotion and literacy is not intuitively obvious and can cause confusion. The term 'emotional well-being' describes a state rather than a quality of the individual, and can be a product of any number of situational variables as well as individual variables. Arguably the most precise term, describing the current ability of the individual to meet the standards of skill in their cultural context, is 'emotional competence' (Topping, 1998). Nonetheless, because of its popularity, the term 'emotional intelligence' is used predominantly in this chapter.

Programmes to develop emotional intelligence

There have been many attempts at developing programmes to systematically improve emotional intelligence. In the UK there is no single widely used programme, although off-the-shelf systems are available from the US. These may focus on a wide variety of skills and situations, including stress management, drug abstinence and the reduction of aggression, truancy and pregnancy. Some programmes focus on developing empathy and encourage peaceful, conflict resolution, and assertive expressions of feelings and needs. Table 7.1 shows a taxonomy of generic emotional competences (Weare and Gray, 2003).

Table 7.1 **A taxonomy of emotional competences**

Area of competence	Subcategory of competence
Self-esteem	Self-value and self-respect
	Acknowledgement of right to be valued by others
Accurate self-concept	Identify strengths
	Identify weaknesses
	Accurate perception of personality
Autonomy	Independence of thinking
	Makes sense of self
Experience of emotion	Experiencing and recognising a full range of emotion
	Awareness of the effects of different emotions
	Talking about a full range of emotions
Expression of emotion	Use of language, expression, etc., to communicate emotion
	Developing a language to describe complex emotions
	Expressing emotion through other media, e.g. writing, music, art
Contextual awareness	Taking into account other people in expressing emotions
Emotional regulation	Recognise the factors affecting emotion
	Self-soothe when upset or angry
	Think clearly despite powerful emotion
	Avoid sulking
	Use strategies such as distraction, self-talk and relaxation
Increasing positive emotion	Experience happiness
	Experience amusement
	Experience calm and relaxation
	Live in the moment
Resilience	Survive and learn from negative experiences
Emotional problem-solving	Delay gratification
	Anticipate consequences of actions
	Solve problems in spite of emotional strain
	Appraise chances of success realistically
Attachment	Have affection for others
	Trust in their affection
Empathy	Recognise emotions in others
	Have compassion for others
	Refrain from harming others
	Tolerate difference

In addition to these generic competences, specific programmes may focus on particular issues. For example, Southampton LEA has focused on anger management whereas Cumbria has a particular focus on loss and bereavement. Weare and Gray (2003) suggest that successful programmes share the following features:

- *Behaviours are explicitly taught*: programmes focusing on attitudes alone do not generally make a significant impact.
- *Skills are taught in empowering ways*: where learners contribute to the programmes, their sense of ownership aids the learning.
- *A step-by-step approach is taken*: new ways of thinking are being taught, and these need to be broken down to their components, such as clarifying a problem, evaluating alternative solutions and reflecting on the success of the choice.
- *Generic skills are generalised to real life*: it is more effective to teach generic skills, such as assertiveness, problem-solving and empathy, and to then apply them to real life rather than to use programmes aimed specifically at a single situation such as resisting drugs or sex.
- *Programmes are positive and active*: there is full learner participation and the emphasis is on developing skills rather than singling out or punishing lack of skills.
- *Programmes make use of interactions*: teacher–learner and learner–learner interactions may be achieved in whole-class interactive methods, cooperative group work, and peer teaching, etc.
- *Programmes are congruent with the wider system*: work in emotional intelligence programmes can be reinforced by a system where teachers demonstrate the necessary competencies and can be undermined by a system where they do not.

Evidence for the benefits of emotional intelligence programmes

Effectiveness reviews of programmes designed to develop emotional intelligence (e.g. Catalano *et al.*, 2002; J. Wells *et al.*, 2003) have concluded that although only a minority of programmes rigorously evaluated their success, the majority of those showed very good results. Because the links between emotion and learning are not intuitively obvious, it is worth looking at how improvements in emotional intelligence affect learning. Several reviews have concluded that programmes are associated with improved attendance, motivation and morale (e.g. Durlak and Wells, 1997). These in turn contribute to achievement. Moreover, emotional intelligence training generalises to the modern workplace with its emphasis on teamwork and communication, thus enhancing learners' employability. Some reviews have suggested that developing emotional competencies has more impact on achievement than cognitive intervention (Goleman, 1996), although this is controversial and should be taken as opinion rather than fact.

Reflection point

In spite of the evidence supporting the effectiveness of emotional intelligence programmes, there has been some resistance from UK teachers, on the basis that the idea is overly American and incompatible with the British 'stiff upper lip' culture. How do you feel towards emotional intelligence?

Conclusions and personal reflections

There is no doubt that emotional factors have a profound effect on learning, or that many emotional problems are rooted in relationships. Many teachers and psychologists have found Kleinian psychoanalysis and attachment theory particularly helpful in understanding the significance of relationships in emotional development and its link to learning, but not everyone likes to use theory in this way. Yet regardless of how we respond to psychological theory, we should recognise that the importance of the quality of relationship with family and teacher is firmly supported by research. Peer relationships are also of profound importance to learners, and the importance of sociometric status should be acknowledged. Bullying is a serious problem, but one that can be tackled effectively once it is acknowledged.

There are several interventions that can help the emotional well-being of learners. Individuals who are emotionally damaged and suffer emotional blocks to their learning can benefit from counselling, particularly educational therapy, although there is cause for concern over lack of systematic evaluation of educational therapy's effectiveness. Although some individuals are particularly vulnerable as a result of their developmental history, for most learners it is important not to overly individualise emotional problems, and systems can be a focus of intervention. Anti-bullying and emotional intelligence programmes have proved highly effective in improving well-being and academic achievement.

Self-assessment questions

1. Critically compare Kleinian psychoanalysis and attachment theory as ways of understanding the significance of family relationships in emotional development and learning.

2. Discuss research into the importance of relationships with the primary carer and the teacher in learning. How important is the concept of the 'educational attachment figure'?

3. Explain what is meant by sociometric status. How important is it in affecting educational achievement?

4. What individual and systemic factors affect bullying behaviour? How can it be tackled?

5. Critically discuss the concept of emotional intelligence. How useful has it been in aiding learning?

Further reading

Barrett, M. and Varma, V. (1996) *Educational Therapy in Clinic and Classroom*. Whurr, London.

Coren, A. (1997) *A Psychodynamic Approach to Education*. Sheldon Press, London.

Greenhalgh, P. (1994) *Emotional Growth and Learning*. Routledge, London.

Pellegrini, A. D. and Blatchford, P. (2000) *The Child at School: Interactions with Peers and Teachers*. Edward Arnold, London.

Urquhart, I. (2000) Teaching children with emotional difficulties. In: *The Psychology of Teaching and Learning in the Primary School* (ed. Whitebread, D.). Routledge Falmer, London.

Weare, K. and Gray, G. (2003) *What Works in Developing Children's Emotional and Social Competence and Well-being?* Department for Education and Employment, London.

Wittenberg, I., Henry, G. and Osborne, E. (1983) *The Emotional Experience of Learning and Teaching*. Routledge, London.

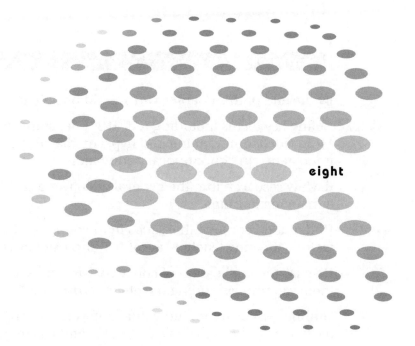

eight

ICT and
Learning

ICT and Learning

learning objectives

By the end of this chapter you should be able to:

●●●●● Define key terms including ICT, ILT, e-learning, intranet, VLE, MLE, videoconferencing and hypermedia, and appreciate their importance in contemporary education.

●●●●●● Review research into the general effectiveness of ILT in enhancing learning.

●●●●● Understand some of the issues in introducing ICT, including factors affecting teacher use of ILT and teacher resistance.

●●●●●● Discuss the application of constructivist and social constructivist theory to understanding the effective use of ICT.

●●●●● Outline research into individual differences in ILT use, particularly about the role of gender and learning styles.

One of the greatest social changes in the early twenty-first century has been the rapid development of computer-related technology. The importance of information and communication technology (ICT) is growing rapidly and many millions of pounds have been invested in bringing information technology to education. The rationale for this is not merely that learners should acquire a working knowledge of ICT to prepare them for the workplace, but also that the proper use of ICT can enhance the quality of learning itself. Education Secretary Charles Clark put it this way: 'ICT can make a significant contribution to teaching and learning at all stages and across all areas of the curriculum. ICT should be embedded in all our education institutions and in all the teaching that takes place there' (Clark, 2004).

The main purpose of this chapter is not to review the field of ICT research as a whole – it is an enormous body of literature – but to examine how a psychological understanding can help us realise how and when ICT can enhance the quality of learning. This requires a broad application of the psychological theory reviewed in previous chapters, ranging from the use of social constructionist theory to understand teacher resistance to technology, to the use of constructivist and social constructivist theory to understand the cognitive benefits of using ICT in particular ways.

Explanations of some basic terms

One of the systemic problems in developing the role of information technology in education has concerned the complex and esoteric nature of the
concepts and language used by specialist practitioners. A particular implication of this specialist nature of educational ICT has meant that the overlap
between those with a grasp of the technology and those with a good understanding of its pedagogical applications has been relatively small. This in turn
meant that often during the initial introduction of ICT to education, it was
driven by the technically minded rather than the pedagogically wise, leading
to expensive failures and a degree of teacher cynicism. It is important for
teachers to have at least a basic understanding of ICT and its educational
applications if they are to take a role in shaping the role of ICT in future
education. With that in mind, the early part of this chapter is devoted to a
brief overview of some of the major concepts.

ICT, ILT and e-learning

There is an important distinction to be made between information and
communication technology (ICT), information and learning technology (ILT)
and e-learning. As with many other modern technical terms, bear in mind
that none has been used entirely consistently in the literature (Taggart, 2004).
Nonetheless, in principle each has a distinct meaning. *ICT* is a generic term
used to describe computing hardware and related communication technology such as telephone systems and networked computers. *ILT* is a fairly
broad term that denotes 'the application of IT skills to learning situations
using ICT' (National Learning Network, 2004). In other words, the focus in ILT
is on efficient ways of using ICT to enhance learning. As well as the obvious
uses of personal computers (PCs), this includes the use of other devices such
as interactive whiteboards. *E-learning* has been defined as 'Internet or
Intranet based training that enables users to access training courses and
learning materials on a desktop computer' (Training Press Releases, 2001).
This then has a narrower meaning, referring to the delivery of whole courses
or course elements using internet technology.

Intranets, VLEs and MLEs

Delivery of ILT requires that information is organised and presented to the
learner in a user-friendly manner. The most common way in which this is
achieved is by using an intranet. Leafe defines an intranet as 'a web or
network-based system open to approved users' (Leafe, 2001, p. 182). It is now
the norm for computers in schools and colleges to be networked. This has
considerable advantage over individual PCs, allowing 'many users access to
the same materials at the same time and enabling knowledge, concepts and
understandings to be communicated between many users. A teacher can
display content as many times as there are machines available, enabling many

pupils to access a single resource without huge photocopying costs. Content can be immediately updated, with updates available to all users' (ibid., p. 185).

The other principal method of delivering ILT is by virtual learning environments (VLEs[1]). A VLE is an integrated system of software that performs several educational functions, including delivery, assessment and tracking. This is a more sophisticated and ambitious approach than a simple intranet. According to the Joint Information Systems Committee (JISC), a virtual learning environment has the following components:

- Controlled access to curriculum that has been mapped to elements (or chunks) that can be separately assessed and recorded.
- Tracking student activity and achievement against these elements using simple processes for course administration and student tracking that make it possible for tutors to define and set up a course with accompanying materials and activities to direct, guide and monitor learner progress.
- Support of online learning, including access to learning resources, assessment and guidance. The learning resources may be self-developed items or professionally authored and purchased materials that can be imported and made available for use by learners.
- Communication between the learner, the tutor and other learning support specialists to provide direct support and feedback for learners, as well as peer-group communications that build a sense of group identity and community of interest.
- Links to other administrative systems, internally and externally.

VLEs are a component of a managed learning environment (MLE). An MLE is 'the whole range of information systems and processes of an institution (including its VLE if it has one) that contribute directly or indirectly to learning and the management of that learning' (JISC, 2003). Figure 8.1 shows the systems relationship between an MLE and a VLE.

Multimedia and hypermedia

A *medium* is the way that information is brought to the user. Multimedia simply means the use of multiple ways of storing and transferring information. When we speak of multimedia we are really speaking about accessing educational software via CD-ROMs and the internet. *Hypermedia* describes the format of the learning material delivered by multimedia. Bruntlett (2001) defines hypermedia as 'text, animation, video, sound and images presented in high quality digital resources'. The simplest form of hypermedia is hypertext. This is essentially text presented on multimedia, but with all the advantages this can bring over printed text. Material can be instantly cross-referenced

---

[1] Alternative in the sense that ILT can be delivered via either system, not in the sense that an institution will use only one or the other.

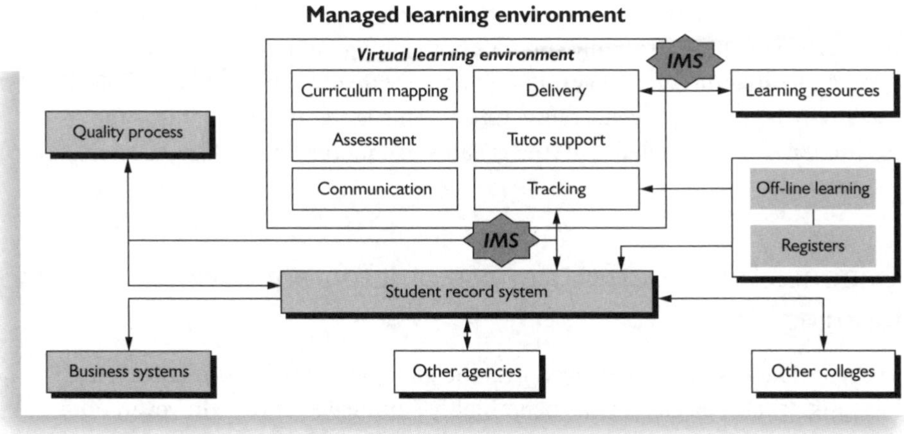

Managed learning environment

Figure 8.1 **The relationship between a VLE and an MLE**

from one source to another and several texts can be viewed simultaneously. Links can direct the reader to further sources, which may be differentiated according to level of understanding and the requirements of the particular task.

Videoconferencing

Videoconferencing allows learners and teachers to communicate from different locations. The varying bandwidths of the internet make it unreliable and videoconferencing is thus usually supported by an ISDN line. This mode of communication has multiple applications. Learners working on similar projects in different parts of the world can collaborate irrespective of geographical considerations (Cifuentes and Murphy, 2000). Specialist teachers can teach groups studying more esoteric subjects by videoconference, allowing schools and colleges to support small groups without the financial burden and practical difficulties of maintaining a teacher at the institution (Gilbert, 1999). Students who cannot easily attend institutions due to geographical remoteness or disability can be included in education (Donegan, 2002).

Interactive whiteboards

An interactive whiteboard has been defined by the British Educational Communications and Technology Agency (Becta) as 'a large, touch-sensitive board, which is connected to a digital projector and a computer' (Becta, 2003). The board can display information from the computer, including internet searches, video clips, hypertext and student presentations, or handwritten information put directly on to the board. As well as being tremendously versatile in the range of data they can present, interactive whiteboards have specific pedagogical advantages; a simple example is that board notes can be printed, saving time normally spent in note taking. An internet search can be brought to an entire group simultaneously. Critically, the teacher can use ILT in whole-class interactive teaching (p. 33). This is significant as this is the teaching mode associated with the greatest frequency of teacher–learner interactions.

Evidence for the effectiveness of ILT in enhancing learning

There is a large body of research into the effectiveness of ILT in enhancing learning. By and large this has been highly supportive of ILT. However, note that an unusually high percentage of references in this literature are from sources other than peer-reviewed journals and conference proceedings, thus there may be questions regarding its quality. For example, of the 14 references cited in the 2003 Becta research review on interactive whiteboards, only two were from conferences and four from journals. Note also that ILT enthusiasts are likely to be over-represented among researchers in this field.

Even with these provisos in mind, there is still overwhelming support for the appropriateness of ILT. Rehbein *et al.* (2002) tested the effect of hypermedia use on learning in 96 Chilean 9–11-year-olds. Participants studied human biology using an interactive hypermedia package, an e-book, a printed booklet or unsupported lectures. When assessed, the two groups that studied the material electronically showed a more advanced understanding than those using more conventional approaches to studying. Research also suggests that students enjoy using electronic resources. Simon (2002) surveyed 22 American college-level biology students during a semester in which they used e-books. Respondents were very positive about the technology and were eager to use e-books in further courses.

Even where hypermedia has an interactive element, there is a limit to how active the learner can be when locating information. A different approach to using interactive software that places the learner in a more active position involves carrying out experiments in virtual reality. Triona and Klahr (2003) compared 9–11-year-old children studying science in two conditions. In the standard condition they carried out science practicals using real equipment and in an experimental condition they carried out identical experiments in virtual reality. They were assessed for skills of experimental design and hypothesis generation; no difference emerged between the conditions.

The internet has numerous applications in education, ranging from a medium for doing homework to complete e-learning packages. Dufresne *et al.* (2002) compared the effectiveness of web-based and pen and paper homework for physics students. Marks for groups doing web-based homework were found to be modestly but consistently superior to those of the traditional groups. More mixed results were found in a study of social-work students who had completed a master's degree in social work by e-learning. Compared with a control group of campus-based students, the e-learners were more satisfied with academic staff and, paradoxically, more likely to socialise with fellow students. However, in spite of greater satisfaction with their research ability, the e-learners were less likely to have had their research published. In another study of social-work e-learning (MacFadden *et al.*, 2002), 19 learners evaluated a six-week online course in multicultural awareness. Again results were mixed, with some learners relishing the freedom to plan their time and work online at their convenience, and others disliking the lack of structure.

Research paints a very mixed picture of other uses of ICT, including videoconferencing. In an American study, Furst-Bowe (1997) found that students who had done courses by videoconferencing were satisfied with the experience. However, the social psychology of the situation has to be taken into account in devising effective lessons. Tyler (1999) reports that videoconferencing between two classes resulted in reduced on-task interaction between learners, intergroup conflict and domination of between-group interactions by a minority of learners.

Reflection point

Consider the evidence presented here and elsewhere about the effectiveness of ILT. How strong do you think the case is that ILT enhances learning is? Based on your experience, what factors might affect the success of ILT, and independent of these, what factors do you think might influence professional attitudes?

Factors affecting the uptake of ICT and ILT

Existing research paints a positive picture of the benefits of using ILT, so why is it not used more? Some factors are related to individual differences in teachers. Van Braak (2001) assessed the relationship between computer use and a range of variables in 236 Belgian secondary school teachers. Being male, teaching a technology-based subject, general attitudes to computers, attitudes to ILT and innovativeness all predicted greater computer use. Contrary to predictions, age was not associated with ILT use.

In addition to individual teacher characteristics, some systemic factors have worked to slow the introduction of ICT and ILT to education. The 1997 Stevenson Report concluded that the use of ICT in education was 'primitive', and recommended that teachers have access to training and up-to-date machines of their own. Since then there has been a rapid increase in funding for training and access to technology, and teacher use of ICT has improved, although not to the extent envisioned by technologists and government.

Box 8.1

Factors inhibiting the uptake of ICT in education

- Lack of time
- Lack of equipment
- Lack of training

- Lack of sense of purpose
- Resistance to change
- Initiative overload.

Source: Dawes (2000), Butler (2001) and Taggart (2004)

A number of studies have identified key factors slowing the uptake of ICT; some are shown in Box 8.1.

There are some signs that these problems are being overcome. In 2000 the UK government allocated £20 million to subsidise teachers' purchase of their own machines, resulting in a huge increase in the number of teachers with a PC at home (Dawes, 2001). In the most recent of the above studies, Taggart (2004) notes that there was relatively little evidence of resistance to ILT in his survey and that access to equipment was better than indicated by earlier studies. This is not to suggest, however, that there are no ongoing issues. Two particularly thorny issues that mediate teacher attitudes to ILT are the relationship between teachers and technologists and concerns over the future role of the teacher.

The teacher–technologist relationship

Historically there has been little love lost between teachers and purveyors of ICT. As Dawes puts it, 'Teachers have long been seen by educational technologists to exhibit a range of obstructive behaviours from incompetence to sheer bloody-mindedness, resisting change' (2001, p. 61). This has led to a highly negative image for teachers in the ICT advertising literature. Adopting a social constructionist approach (p. 6), Selwyn *et al.* (2000) deconstructed representations of teachers and ICT in advertising and found ICT to be constructed in four ways:

- *As a new form of education*: the teacher is associated with old-fashioned ideas and positioned as a hindrance to progress.
- *As a traditional form of education*: a familiar and comforting tool.
- *As a problem for teachers*: the only honourable path for teachers is to step aside and allow experts, i.e. ICT purveyors, to take over.
- *As a solution to educational problems*: teachers are positioned as struggling and failing to cope with their jobs because of their traditional pre-ICT approaches.

These social constructions of teachers are unhelpful and probably encourage resistance to change among teachers who may come to perceive ICT as at best a threat to their own worth and at worst a commercial exploitation of their learners.

Fears of the teacherless classroom

Fears of the teacherless classroom are connected with the teacher–technologist relationship. As Dawes (2001) points out, the discourse in which technology is positioned as modern and a solution for problems and teachers are presented as old-fashioned and obstructive, carries with it the implication that technology will replace the teacher. Since the inception of ILT there has been a degree of tension between those who see technology as a tool to be incorporated into classroom teaching (computer-aided learning) and those who see it in the long term as a substitute for our current popular under-standing of the nature of the classroom (computer-based learning). Some teacher concerns have centred around the anxiety that in actively supporting the development of computer-based learning they are effectively turkeys voting for Christmas. Such fears may not be entirely unfounded. As one technologist suggested, 'You wouldn't really want to pay for several teachers when we achieve the same with a computer suite and a technician would you?' (anon., personal communication). However, in terms of current research and policy, computer-aided learning has emerged as significantly more important than computer-based learning, and the recent emphasis on tools such as interactive whiteboards and data projectors, which clearly support conventional teaching, have gone some way to alleviate fears of teacher obsolescence.

171

A helpful way of thinking about future developments in the classroom comes from Cuban (1993). Cuban distinguishes between the technophile vision of the future classroom in which learners have sufficient access to software of such good quality that the role of the teacher becomes more that of coach and mentor, and a preservationist vision in which the teacher maintains their existing role but simply uses technology to achieve more efficient transfer of knowledge. This is a healthy discourse because it positions enthusiasts and the more cautious users of ILT in a positive light, encouraging dialogue. Currently, it seems that both the preservationist and technophile visions are to some extent being realised, and that the tension between them is a healthy one, although some debates have become highly polarised, Papert (1996) has coined the term 'cyberostriches' for proponents of the preserva-tionist vision. In any case there is little evidence that technology can replace teachers, although it may come to modify their role (Selinger, 2001a). Certainly there is no evidence to suggest that it is currently doing so. Estimates (e.g. Passey, 1999) suggest that, on average, learners spend less than 10% of their time in the classroom using ILT.

⊗Reflection point

Consider the above issues. Where do you stand on ILT? Would you consider yourself enthusiastic, cautious or threatened? To what extent might your feelings be influenced by political factors, fear of obsolescence and more practical factors such as access to equipment and training?

Benefits of ILT: the constructivist understanding

Recall from Chapter 2 the constructivist view of education. This derives from the work of Jean Piaget and has as its central tenet the principle that cognitive development and learning are closely linked. As the developing child explores the world, they construct successively more sophisticated representations of it and so develop cognitively, becoming capable of more advanced reasoning. Application of this principle to ILT has involved emphasising the role of exploring the world and emphasising the developing cognitive abilities by interaction with computers. The use of web browsers such as Internet Explorer has provided an unprecedented opportunity for learners to explore the world, asking their own questions and seeking their own sources of information (Churach and Fisher, 2001). However, much of the exploration using the net tends to be superficial (Selinger, 2001b), and from a constructivist perspective there is an important role for teachers in setting the sort of search tasks that push learners to make decisions and select lines of research, constructing individual understandings as opposed to simply locating and re-presenting existing materials.

The constructivist understanding of ILT and its role in developing thinking owes much to the work of Seymour Papert. In keeping with the constructivist principle that knowledge cannot be passively absorbed from transmission but has to be constructed through an active process of learning, Papert is a stern critic of much existing educational software that presents information to learners in a didactic format. Specifically, Papert (1996) criticises software for giving agency to the machine rather than the learner by posing and answering specific questions rather than letting the learner set their own agenda and solve problems imaginatively. In his seminal work, Papert (1980) suggested that children acquire new thinking skills when they learn to program computers. Papert was one of a team that developed the child-friendly programming language Logo. An example of a child-friendly feature of Logo is a turtle graphic that can be directed to draw lines by typed commands. For example, the command FORWARD 50, LEFT 90 would direct the turtle graphic to draw a 50 mm straight line then turn 90° to the left. Papert proposed that using Logo helped children's thinking by developing their ability to use formal operational reasoning as opposed to concrete operational thought. Research attempting to validate this claim has produced mixed results. Children exposed to Logo have generally not been found to be more capable of formal operational thinking, but there is evidence (e.g. Kramarski and Mevarech, 1997) that when accompanied by metacognitive training, Logo use is associated with improved metacognition, i.e. awareness of one's own mental processes and problem-solving strategies (p. 101). In addition, Subhi (1999) showed in a study of 217 Jordanian primary school children given either Logo or standard computer-assisted learning that the use of Logo was associated with increased mathematical and creative ability.

Benefits of ILT: the social constructivist understanding

More in keeping with most current educational thinking is the social constructivist theory of Lev Vygotsky (p. 27). The central tenet of social constructivism is that the active construction of understanding takes place during interaction with more knowledgeable or experienced tutors or co-learners, hence effective education depends principally on the quality of interaction that characterises learning activities. From a social constructivist perspective, early attempts to introduce ILT failed to enhance learning because they positioned the learner in a passive rather than active role, failing to involve sufficient interaction with a machine or with other learners. Early visions of classrooms full of students working independently and silently on computers are a far cry from the interactive learning supported by current research. Our current understanding of the effective use of ILT is much more in line with social constructivist theory, and recent developments in ILT have made it more interactive.

An example of the application of social constructivist theory to ILT comes from Leafe (2001), who proposes three ways in which learners can use an intranet, distinguished by the level of interaction with other users and the technology:

- *Browsing*: use of the intranet to locate and access existing information.
- *Interaction*: use of the intranet to narrow down and access specific information by interacting with the system.
- *Collaboration*: use of the intranet to communicate with other users to obtain and generate information.

Browsing for information is the most *passive* way of using an intranet. Here passivity is defined by the degree of interaction with the computer, either with the system or with other users. A student might follow a set of links until they reach a particular page of subject-related information then print it and add it to their notes. *Interaction* is a more active learning process. An example would be the use of an online database, in which the learner is required to enter details and make choices to narrow down what information they want to retrieve. *Collaboration* involves online interaction with other learners.

This is the most active type of learning using the intranet in the sense that it involves the greatest degree of cognitive effort to interact with other users via the machine. An example of a collaborative task takes place when learners divide up a project and each takes responsibility for generating a part of the project, which is then assembled from these components.

Interactions with software

If interaction is the key element of learning, there are several ways this can be achieved using computers. One form is interaction with software. Whenever we use educational software, there are a series of on-screen prompts that help us progress through the task at hand. Crook (1994) has suggested these prompts constitute a form of scaffolding that moves learners through a zone of proximal development (ZPD). The learner can normally make choices about how much detail they require from prompts. This means that, just as a teacher will reduce the amount of help they give as the learner moves through the ZPD, the computer-aided learner can select a declining level of detail in their on-screen prompts. There are now educational programs designed on this principle. Bornas and Llabres (2001) developed interactive software for teaching maths and reading. This had options for three levels of scaffolding throughout. After 10 weeks (15 hours), children working on this program were assessed for achievement and style of reasoning in the subjects. Although the group using the interactive program showed no more achievement than controls, they were significantly more advanced in their thinking strategies. In another study, comparing the effectiveness of hyper-media software with and without an online assistant (OLA), Garcia (2002) taught design to 45 American primary school children. Independent raters consistently scored the resulting projects higher in the experimental group that received the OLA.

Interactions with peers

Interaction in computer-aided tasks can also be by peer interaction. Studies comparing individual and collaborative working generally suggest that peer interaction during computer-aided tasks enhances learning and that appro-priate computer-aided tasks enhance the quality of interaction. In a recent Spanish study, Pifarre and Sanuy (2002) looked at interactions between 13–14-year-old dyads ($n = 92$) when carrying out a joint problem-solving task, either using spreadsheet software or manual calculation. In the spreadsheet condition, better-quality dyadic interactions and better outcomes were recorded. This suggests that the computer provided a helpful medium for effective interactions. In a similar vein, Svensson (2000) looked at the interac-tions between 33 students aged eight years engaged in a variety of learning activities, both conventional and computer-aided. Children interacted with peers around twice as often during computer-based tasks as in conventional activities, and a greater proportion of interactions were on-task. In a meta-analysis of 122 studies involving a total of over 11 000 participants, Lou *et al.* (2001) concluded that small groups learning by working collaboratively using technology did better than those working alone.

Reflection point

Consider your own experience of using ILT and your understanding of social constructivist theory. To what extent do you think interaction enhances learning with computers? If the level of interaction is increased, what are the potential problems for teachers?

Individual differences in ILT use

Suppose we adopt an understanding of ILT based entirely on constructivist and social constructivist principles, then we can easily underestimate the importance of qualitative individual differences that characterise learners in their ability to use technology and their preference for using it. Most research into individual differences has focused on two areas: learning styles and gender.

Learning styles, multiple intelligences and ILT

The concept of multiple intelligences helps us understand why some students do better than others using computers. In the Lou *et al.* (2001) meta-analysis, a minority of students did not benefit from cooperative learning. This can be understood in terms of Gardner's multiple intelligences theory (p. 51) as being a result of these students having a low interpersonal intelligence and therefore having interaction with other people as their least preferred method of study.

There is some evidence to suggest that using computers is most benefi-cial to students with a visual learning style. S. M. Smith and Woody (2000) assessed learning styles in a college; they followed up a psychology class using a predominantly computer-based approach and a control class receiving conventional teaching for one term. They found that at first the class using computers did worse but by the end of the term they exceeded the achieve-ments of the conventional group. Interestingly, the students that benefited most from the use of computer-based learning were those with a visual learning style. This makes sense as looking at a computer screen is a very visual experience.

In keeping with previous findings from studies conducted in the more traditional classroom, it seems that field independence (p. 77) conveys an advantage to learners taking exams using ILT. Childress and Overbaugh (2001) assessed 204 trainee teachers using the group embedded figures test and assessed their performance on an ICT course. Although cognitive style did not predict overall grade, field independence was associated with higher exam marks.

There is also a small body of research suggesting that learning style affects the way learners use hypermedia. Ford and Chen (2000) studied the behaviour and performance of 65 postgraduate students in a hypermedia-based tutorial. Cognitive and learning style was assessed in terms of field dependence (p. 77) and wholism (p. 81). How participants navigated their way through the hypermedia environment was predicted by their cognitive style. Serialists progressed in linear steps whereas wholists were more likely to leap from one area to another unpredictably.

Gender

Women are currently under-represented on ICT-related courses (Millar and Jagger, 2001). In addition, and perhaps related to this, some evidence suggests there are gender differences in attitudes to computers that may affect the abilities of male and female learners to make effective use of ILT. Brosnan (1999) assessed attitudes using a drawing task. A total of 395 English primary school children aged 5–11 years were asked to draw a computer. Some 30% of girls drew a male using the computer whereas only 4% of boys drew a female user. Girls were also significantly less likely to draw smiling faces. Interestingly, these differences were more pronounced with older children, suggesting that girls acquire more negative attitudes to ICT while at school. Males also tend to score more highly on the computer use self-efficacy (CUSE) scale (Cassidy and Eachus, 2002). Objective measures also show that girls tend to be less involved with computers in the classroom. Mucherach (2003) used teacher interviews and classroom observations of 306 students aged 12–13 years to examine boys' and girls' use of computers in three schools. Boys were significantly more likely to use computers and their use was characterised by a greater degree of competition.

There is a limited body of literature aiming to explain such findings. Bhargava (2002) explains the discrepancies between male and female attitudes to ILT in terms of gender bias in software. A range of existing software was studied and evidence emerged that characters, content and reward systems were biased towards a male orientation. Thinking more broadly, L. Miller *et al.* (2000) point out that advertisements for technology, to which girls are exposed from an early age, tend to portray women in decorative or submissive secre-tarial roles, and that girls therefore do not have access to role models making effective use of ICT. It seems likely that the greater use of ILT by male teachers (van Braak, 2001) may compound this role-modelling problem.

Conclusions and personal reflections

ILT is a broad church, ranging from the delivery of entire courses by e-learning to the use of interactive whiteboards in whole-class interactive teaching. In between these extremes there are a plethora of strategies for the use of ICT to enhance learning. The empirical base for believing that ILT does indeed enhance learning is fairly strong, although be aware that there are some mixed findings and that, because the bulk of researchers are ILT enthusiasts, there may be a pro-ILT bias in the published literature. There is clear evidence to support the effectiveness of hypermedia and internet-based tasks. Some ILT applications, for example videoconferencing, are not well validated by research. Teacher attitudes to ILT are mixed but appear to be growing more positive, partly because of practical considerations such as access to equipment and training, but perhaps also because of the direction of recent developments, with computer-aided learning in a fairly conventional classroom becoming the dominant and less threatening vision of ILT in the future.

In keeping with its influence on contemporary education in general, the social constructivist approach has dominated our current understanding of the potential benefits of ILT and the most effective ways of putting ICT to use in education. Research has firmly supported the social constructivist princi- ples that effective learning involves active interaction and that this interaction can be achieved via or around computers. However, bear in mind that there are substantial individual differences in learning, thus a minority of learners may not benefit from a high level of interactivity and indeed some learners are better suited than others to the highly visual nature of ILT. There are also currently gender differences in ILT proficiency, and this is likely to be a product of gender bias in software and the tasks set. This should be addressed as a matter of urgency.

Self-assessment questions

1. Distinguish between ICT and ILT.

2. Explain the features of intranets, VLEs and MLEs.

3. Which ILT applications are best suited to whole-class learning and which are designed for individual use?

4. To what extent does research validate the use of ILT?

5. Compare and contrast constructivist and social constructivist approaches to understanding the benefits of ILT.

6. What individual differences are there in learners' ability to use ILT?

Further reading

•••••• Bhargava, A. (2002) Gender bias in computer software programmes: a checklist for teachers. *Information Technology in Childhood Education Annual*, 14, 205–218.

•••••● Chang, N. (2001) Is it developmentally inappropriate to have children work alone at the computer? *Information Technology in Childhood Education Annual*, 13, 247–265.

•••••● Leask, M. (ed.) (2001) *Issues in Teaching Using ICT*. Routledge Falmer, London.

•••••● Roschelle, J. M., Pea, R. D., Hoadley, C. M., Gordin, D. N. and Means, B. M. (2000) Changing how and what children learn in school with computer-based technologies. *Future of Children*, 10, 76–101.

Website

•••••● www.becta.org.uk/research/index.cfm

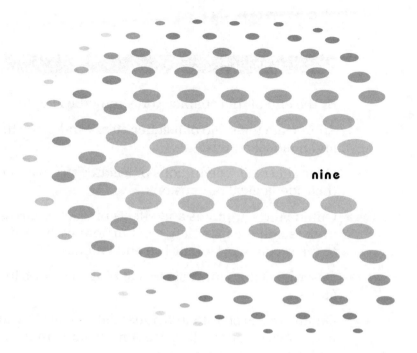

nine

Teacher
Stress

Teacher Stress

By the end of this chapter you should be able to:

- Appreciate the scale of teacher stress and place the issue in legal and political context.

- Offer alternative definitions of teacher stress and understand their ideological dimensions.

- Outline the symptoms and effects of teacher stress, and understand the experience of burnout with particular reference to the recent work of Carlyle and Woods.

- Describe factors intrinsic to teaching that contribute to teacher stress.

- Outline research into individual differences in vulnerability to teacher stress, including cognitive factors, motivation to teach and use of coping strategies.

- Explain how systemic factors affect teacher stress, with particular reference to social status, communication, bullying and inspection.

- Outline and evaluate individual and organisational approaches to tackling teacher stress, and appreciate the limitations of current evidence for effective practice.

It is widely acknowledged that the UK is currently experiencing an epidemic of work-related stress. Health and Safety Executive (HSE) figures suggest that the annual number of days taken off work due to stress in 2001 was around 13 500 000, double the figure recorded in 1996. Even by these standards, teaching emerges as a particularly stressful occupation. Teaching and nursing are the occupations associated with the highest rates of stress, depression and anxiety (HSE, 2002). In a survey of 488 Scottish teachers, Dunlop (2004) found that 44% of respondents identified their job as either very stressful or extremely stressful. Only 14% reported teaching to be mildly stressful or not stressful, and 78% believed they had suffered health problems as a result of work-related stress. In a survey of head teachers by the National Association of Head Teachers (NAHT) in May 2000, 40% of respondents reported having visited their doctor with a stress-related problem in the previous year, 20% considered that they drank too much and 15% believed they were alcoholics. Some 25% suffered from serious stress-related health problems, including hypertension, insomnia, depression and gastrointestinal disorders.

Stress impacts greatly on teacher retention, recruitment and retirement, contributing to a national shortage of teachers. Currently, only around 35% of trainees remain in teaching for more than three years, and 49% of early retirement on health grounds is attributable to issues of mental health (Nash, 2004). A study conducted for the *Times Educational Supplement* in 1997 found that 37% of secondary vacancies and 19% of primary vacancies were due to ill-health, as compared to 9% of nursing vacancies and 5% in banking and the pharmaceutical industry. Recruitment also appears to be affected by repre-sentations of stress. A MORI poll of 2017 British adults conducted in April 2001 revealed that teaching is seen as difficult, poorly paid and held in low public esteem. Graduates had significantly more negative beliefs about teaching than non-graduates. Between 1986 and 1996 the numbers taking early retirement increased by 50%, leading the government to alter pension rules to make it much more difficult to take early retirement (Rafferty, 1997).

The legal context

All employers, including schools and colleges, have legal obligations under the Health and Safety at Work Act 1974 and the Management of Health and Safety at Work Regulations 1995. In addition, the HSE (2003) has recently issued benchmarks to which all employers are expected to conform (Box 9.1).

Box 9.1

Benchmarks for stress at work

- *Demands*: greater than 85% of employees indicate that they are able to cope with the demands of their jobs.
- *Control*: greater than 85% of employees indicate that they are able to have a say about how they do their jobs.
- *Support*: greater than 85% of employees indicate that they receive adequate information and support.
- *Relationships*: greater than 65% of employees indicate that they are not subjected to unacceptable behaviour at work.
- *Role*: greater than 65% of employees indicate that they understand their role and responsibilities.
- *Change*: greater than 65% of employees indicate that they are frequently engaged during periods of organisational change.

Source: HSE (2003)

A standard questionnaire for an organisation-wide stress vulnerability audit can now be obtained from the HSE. The HSE guidelines are designed to protect the rights of the employee, and there have been vigorous objections from some bodies, notably the Confederation of British Industry, which argues that the complex overlap between work and lifestyle do not lend themselves to legislation.

The legal ante of teacher stress was upped in 2000 when a Welsh teacher won a landmark victory against Newport County Borough Council for failing to respond to her suffering stress in the classroom and was awarded substantial compensation. Subsequent decisions and appeals have muddied the waters, but in April 2004 the House of Lords ruled on a test case firmly establishing that schools are responsible for the psychological well-being of employees. Teacher stress is now firmly on the political agenda, and representations of the nature of stress have become polarised between unions and employers. Unions see stress as an organisational issue whereas employers see it as an individual issue.

Defining teacher stress: where psychology meets politics

We can think of stress in three ways:
- As a vulnerability in the individual
- As excessive demands in the environment
- As a transaction between the individual and their environment.

It is now generally acknowledged among psychologists that all stress involves a transaction between the individual and their environment. However, there are several working definitions of stress, and they vary considerably in the emphasis placed on individual vulnerability and environmental pressures. Leading stress management expert Stephen Palmer suggests that 'stress occurs when perceived pressure exceeds your ability to cope' (2001, p. 1). This definition emphasises the role of the individual in terms of their perceptual processes and their ability to cope with pressure. At the opposite extreme, a conference resolution from the National Union of Teachers (NUT) has defined stress as follows: 'Conference reaffirms the Union's longstanding view that stress at work is an organisational problem which employers are required by law to take steps to remove or reduce, and the chief causes of which are inappropriate working patterns, excessive or unnecessary demands on employees and inappropriate or bullying management styles' (NUT, 2000). This approach does not take any account of individual vulnerability.

The decision to define stress at the individual or organisational level is not politically neutral (Handy, 1995; Jarvis, 2003, 2004b). Definitions that emphasise stress in the environment locate responsibility for stress in the organisation; this is essentially a left-wing ideological position. Individual definitions, on the other hand, attribute responsibility to the employee, and this can be seen as absolving employers of responsibility, a right-wing position. Generally, in response to organisational stress, managers have opted for individually based stress management interventions, at least partly in the belief that stress is the responsibility of the individual rather than the organisation (Daniels, 1996). Newton (1995) points out that such individualised approaches are rooted in the discourse of traditional managerialism so that what is at stake is not stress as such but the fitness of the individual to keep their job. Discourses of stress have certainly shifted emphasis over the past 100 years from the external environment to internal factors (Hepburn and Brown, 2002). The HSE offers a transactional definition of work-related stress as 'the adverse reaction people have to excessive pressure or other types of demand placed upon them' (HSE, 2003). This is a transactional definition, taking account of the individual and the environment, but its emphasis is on the environment, and this is in line with the HSE approach of attributing responsibility for stress to employers.

Reflection point

Reflect on your personal view about the best definition of stress. How might this be affected by ideological factors such as your identification with trade unionism or your party politics?

The experience of teacher stress

Stress is likely to lead to a blend of physiological and psychological symptoms. Individual teachers vary in their particular responses, partly in response to their coping strategies. For example, in a study by Kyriacou and Pratt (1985) it emerged that those teachers who experienced high levels of anxiety tended to cope by very detailed preparation. Box 9.2 shows a range of common physiological and psychological stress symptoms.

Individual physiological characteristics may also affect the stress response. Teachers who are unfit or overweight are more vulnerable to the impact of stress on their blood pressure, whereas those with unhealthy diets may be particularly sensitive to gastrointestinal problems. There are several indicators that can be used to assess teacher stress. A common 'objective' measure is sickness rates. However, sickness can be affected by a number of factors, and it is not easy to isolate stress as a causal factor. Most researchers have relied on self-reports. Box 9.3 shows one such measure (Kyriacou, 2000).

Burnout

A particularly serious consequence of prolonged work-related stress is burnout. Burnout is such an issue in teaching that nearly a quarter of all

Box 9.2

Common stress symptoms

Physiological	Psychological
Insomnia or hypersomnia	Irritability
Irritable bowel and other gastrointestinal problems	Depressed mood
Back and other muscular aches	Tension
Mouth ulcers	Compulsive thoughts of work
Loss of appetite or increased appetite	Repetitive images of humiliation
Raised heart rate and blood pressure	Tearfulness
Fatigue	General dissatisfaction
Panic attacks	Inflexible or bolshy attitudes
Eczema	

burnout research has involved teachers (Schaufeli, 1998). Maslach and Schaufeli (1993) have identified three elements to burnout:

- *Depersonalisation*: the burnt-out individual distances themselves from others. This leads to reduced quality of contact with learners and colleagues.
- *Reduced personal accomplishment*: the burnt-out individual devalues their work.
- *Emotional exhaustion*: the burnt-out individual spends considerably less time than normal in an emotionally positive state and is dominated by a sense of weary resignation.

Depersonalisation may be a particular issue for teachers for two reasons. First, they spend much time in the classroom isolated from the supportive presence of colleagues. Second, because teaching is such an interactive process, loss of personal relationships with learners quickly leads to a decline in performance and thus in satisfaction. Although depersonalisation may be a coping mechanism that allows teachers to 'survive' in the profession, in the long term it is maladaptive because of the resultant loss in job satisfaction.

Experiences of teacher burnout

Numerous studies have looked at the symptomatology of teacher stress. Much more unusual and highly illuminating has been a study by Carlyle and Woods (2002) in which 21 teachers who suffered burnout and were diagnosed with a

Box 9.3

A measure of teacher stress

Rating scale
0 = never
1 = sometimes
2 = often
3 = almost every day.
Rate how often you feel in the following ways using the above response scale (circle one of the numbers 0 to 3 for each item) then add up your score.

I find myself worrying a lot about problems at work	0	1	2	3
I feel work is affecting my home life	0	1	2	3
At the end of a school day I feel emotionally exhausted	0	1	2	3
Work seems to be one hassle after another	0	1	2	3
I get very upset by problems during the school day	0	1	2	3
I wake up at night thinking about problems at work	0	1	2	3
I feel overloaded with the work that needs to be done	0	1	2	3
I get tense and frustrated by events at school	0	1	2	3
I feel my work is affecting my health	0	1	2	3
I feel I am unable to cope with the demands made on me	0	1	2	3

Score
0–4 = low level of stress at work
5–15 = moderate level of stress
16 = high level of stress.

Source: Kyriacou (2000)

stress-related condition were periodically interviewed throughout the following year. Based on these interviews the authors suggest that teacher burnout follows a set process, in which the individual's sense of personal identity changes.

1. *Organisational stress*: stress originating from societal factors manifesting in management practices, including increased accountability, bullying, poor communication, blame and disrespect, cascades through the organisation, so that stress is effectively 'caught' from colleagues. Learners are 'infected' by stressed teachers and respond by transmitting this stress back to other teachers.

2. *Stress in the family*: competing demands of work and family life interact and exacerbate work-related stress so that the family becomes an additional stressor rather than a support mechanism to buffer the effects of work-related stress.

3. *Identity loss*: a downward spiral results in which teachers lose their prior identity and experience loss of ability to self-regulate emotions and loss of *ontological security*, the sense that one remains the same person over time. At this point, coping mechanisms come into play, including the use of psychological defences and the seeking of stress management.

4. *Liminality*: this describes the transition from one state or stage to another, in which the characteristics of the person in the previous state or stage are lost and have not been replaced. Teachers who have lost their identity through stress go through a liminal stage, including substages of 'hitting rock bottom' followed by 'cocooning', in which teachers seek a safe environment in which to experience grief at the loss of their old identity and seek a new identity, perhaps through religion or political activity. Following cocooning, teachers enter a substage of 'bridging', in which they begin to make contact with teaching or a new career or lifestyle.

5. *Reconstruction of identity*: not all burnt-out teachers reach this stage. However, the majority of Carlyle and Woods' sample did re-engage successfully with employment, having reappraised their goals and attitudes. A minority of teachers return to their old jobs following burnout. Around half return to teaching and most of the remainder find new careers. A significant minority take early retirement on health grounds.

Causal factors in teacher stress

There are unquestionably a number of causal factors in teacher stress. Stress always involves a transaction between the individual and their environment (Cox, 1978), therefore it is the exception rather than the rule to be able to pinpoint a single cause of stress, although particular events may be the catalyst for the appearance of stress-related symptoms. When thinking of the causes of teacher stress, it can be helpful (Jarvis, 2002) to think of potential causal factors as falling into three broad areas: factors intrinsic to teaching, cognitive factors affecting the individual vulnerability of teachers, and systemic factors operating at the institutional and political level.

A common argument is that teaching is inherently stressful, so those who cannot take the heat should get out of the kitchen. However, the existence of factors other than those intrinsic to teaching can be demonstrated by cross-national comparisons of teacher stress. Travers and Cooper (1997) surveyed 800 teachers in England and France about stress and found substantially different responses: 22% of sick leave in England was attributed to stress, but 1% in France; 55% in England reported recently considering leaving teaching, but it was 20% in France. Interestingly, there was substantial agreement between teachers in England and France over the sources of pressure; both groups cited classroom discipline, low social status and lack of parental support. However, teachers in England reported more problems with long hours, overwork and political interference.

The commonality of reported sources of pressure between teachers in England and France could lead us to a social representations interpretation of teacher stress in Britain, in which teachers experience stress because they take on a consensual belief about teaching as stressful. However, there are also notable differences in the reported experiences of the English and French groups, which could lead us to the more 'common sense' interpretation that teachers in Britain operate in particularly stressful conditions, in particular with regard to workload and political intervention.

Factors intrinsic to teaching

Research has suggested that a number of stressors are intrinsic to teaching. In the Travers and Cooper study, workload and long working hours emerged as particular issues for English teachers as opposed to colleagues in France (Travers and Cooper, 1997). When Travers and Cooper questioned British teachers across all educational sectors, high workload, poor status and poor pay emerged as three of the seven major sources of stress; the others were systemic in origin. Similarly, in a recent Scottish survey, Dunlop (2004) reported that excessive workload was reported as the single greatest source of teacher stress, named by 25% of respondents.

A study by Male and May (1998) of learning support coordinators in further education (FE) colleges illustrates the importance of these factors. Thirty-five coordinators were assessed for burnout, stress and health. Overall, mixed evidence for heightened stress in this group emerged, but there was strong evidence for work overload and excessive working hours, associated with emotional exhaustion. A study in 2000 by the Teachers Benevolent Fund identified 93 000 UK teachers as experiencing severe stress as a direct consequence of overwork. Much of the research into workload has been concerned with teachers' perceptions of their workload, but a recent government-commissioned report by auditors PricewaterhouseCoopers took objective measures of workload as well as self-report measures and concluded that teachers work more intensive weeks than any comparable profession, were not supported in implementing change and were not accorded professional trust.

Some research has identified a cyclical pattern in the effects of overwork, contingent on the academic year. Kinnunen and Leskinen (1989) assessed 142 teachers by repeated self-report during the autumn and spring terms of an academic year. It was found that recovery from stress occurred each weekend during the spring term, but that by the end of the longer autumn term, weekend recovery no longer took place.

A factor related to workload is *role overload*, which takes place when an employee has to cope with a number of competing roles within their job. A study by R. T. Pithers and Soden (1998) has highlighted role overload as a significant stressor in teachers. They assessed levels of strain, organisational roles and stress in 322 Australian and Scottish vocational and FE lecturers. Strain was average in both national groups, but there were high levels of stress, with role overload emerging as the major cause.

Classroom discipline is inevitably a significant source of potential stress, being named in the Dunlop survey as the second greatest source of teacher stress, named by 20% of respondents. R. Lewis (1999) examined teachers' estimations of stress arising from being unable to discipline pupils in the way they would prefer. Overall, maintaining discipline emerged as a stressor, with those worst affected being teachers who placed particular emphasis on pupil empowerment. A study of 1000 student teachers (Morton *et al.*, 1997) revealed that classroom management was their second greatest source of anxiety, the greatest being evaluation apprehension. Of all the stressors reported, classroom management anxiety was the only one that did not decline following teaching practice. Interestingly, it seems that although discipline is a potential source of stress to all teachers, there is actually considerable variation in what individual teachers consider to be a discipline problem. Greene *et al.* (1997) suggest there are compatibility problems with particular teachers and learners; one teacher might emphasise quiet and experience considerable stress in response to a noisy pupil, whereas another might be particularly sensitive to challenges to their authority and become stressed in response to a learner that frequently asks searching questions.

Evaluation apprehension is an issue of increasing import, as quality assurance procedures increasingly demand lesson observation. The phenomenon is currently under-researched in qualified teachers, although there is a modest body of research on student teachers. Capel (1997) questioned student physical education (PE) teachers following first and second teaching practices on their levels and sources of anxiety. Evaluation apprehension emerged as the stressor in both practices. Similarly, the Morton *et al.* study found that of all the sources of stress for student teachers, evaluation apprehension was the greatest, although it declined following teaching practice, suggesting that it is reduced by exposure and positive experiences of observation feedback. The moderating effects of exposure to lesson observation are an area requiring further research.

Interestingly, surveys of quality of working life in teachers have found mixed results, with high ratings of stress being balanced against positives. Sturman (2002) surveyed 285 teachers in 53 secondary schools and 389 in 129 primary schools, using a standard quality of life measure. This assessed satisfaction, challenge, autonomy, communication, colleague and management support, stress, salary and responsibility. Respondents scored highly as compared with other occupational groups in general job satisfaction, job security, colleague support and assessment of communications. However, they were dissatisfied with salary, stress levels and role overload. A survey of staff in higher education (HE) institutions (Tytherleigh, 2003) revealed that working in higher education was associated with rather different stressors. In contrast to school and college teachers, HE teachers did not experience overwork and role conflict as significant stressors, but they reported serious problems of job insecurity and quality of relationships with colleagues.

Reflection point

What aspects of your job do you find cause you the most stress? To what extent are these inevitable aspects of teaching and to what extent could they be alleviated? If you are a trainee teacher, think about your experience of teaching practice or a previous job.

Individual differences in vulnerability to teacher stress

Although teachers tend to identify stress as the direct consequence of their environment, there is now a substantial body of research examining the cognitive factors affecting individual susceptibility to stress among teachers. The term 'cognitive factors' covers a range of beliefs, and other mental processes such as attribution and self-efficacy (Chapter 6). Chorney (1998) investigated the role of self-defeating beliefs in stress by asking 41 teachers to identify what they needed to do to be a good teacher, and 92% of responses were couched in absolute terms, such as 'must' and 'need'. Endorsement of these beliefs was widespread in the sample and significantly associated with high levels of stress. In another study by Bibou-Nakou *et al.* (1999) the role of attributions was examined. Two hundred primary school teachers were presented with four hypothetical class management situations and they were questioned about their attributions in each case. There was a significant association between internal attributions (i.e. attributing problems to themselves) and symptoms of burnout, suggesting that teachers who blame themselves for difficulties are more vulnerable to stress.

Self-efficacy has also been researched as a cognitive vulnerability factor. Friedman examined the self-reports of newly qualified teachers and described his findings as the 'shattered dreams of idealistic performance' (2000, p. 595). Respondents revealed sharp declines in self-efficacy as they found that they could not live up to their ideal performances. Brouwers and Tomic (2000) analysed the relationships between self-efficacy and burnout in 243 secondary school teachers. It emerged that self-efficacy had an immediate effect on personal accomplishment and emotional exhaustion and a long-term effect on depersonalisation.

The greatest volume of contemporary research concerning cognitive vulnerability to teacher stress relates specifically to individual differences in coping style. Griffith *et al.* (1999) questioned 780 primary and secondary school teachers, aiming to assess the associations between stress, coping responses and social support. High levels of stress were associated with low social support and the use of disengagement and suppression of competing activities as coping strategies. Interestingly, statistical analysis revealed that coping style not only mediated the effects of environmental stressors, but also influenced teachers' perceptions of their environment as stressful. This is important as it suggests that some of the stressors associated with teaching may not be inherently stressful but act as stressors only in transaction with coping style. A different approach to assessing the relationship between coping strategies and teacher stress was employed by Admiraal *et al.* (2000); they looked at active versus passive responses to disruptive behaviour in the classroom. A group of 27 student teachers gave a total of 300 responses to indicate their coping responses to everyday stressful classroom situations. A strong relationship emerged between a coping style involving active behavioural intervention and teacher satisfaction, and there was a weaker relationship with pupil time on task.

Although the study of individual differences and teacher stress has been dominated by the cognitive approach, psychodynamic factors may also be important. Freudenberger, the originator of the term 'burnout', believed that vulnerability to burnout resulted from overdedication to work resulting from its use as a substitute for a social life. Pines (2000, 2002) has suggested that career choice is influenced by unconscious factors and that people choose an occupation that is capable of replicating childhood experiences, gratifying their unmet childhood needs and allowing identification with parents through following their career paths. Pines (2002) investigated possible psychodynamic factors in teacher burnout in a study of 700 American and Israeli teachers, including those from the primary, secondary and college sectors. Participants were administered a measure of burnout and asked questions concerning their childhood experiences, motives for and expectations of teaching and what they believed to be the most important factors in teacher burnout. They were also questioned about the personal importance they placed on teaching. As hypothesised, the greater the personal importance of teaching, the higher the scores on the burnout measure, showing that a deep commitment to teaching is associated with stress. Identification with a role model was the second most frequently reported influence on choice of career (23%). There was some tentative support for the idea that goals in teaching are related to childhood trauma. Participants reported a high level of separation, anxiety and helplessness in childhood and these were associated with discipline problems as a source of stress; in other words, discipline was an issue because discipline-related incidents brought to mind childhood trauma.

Despite the sound research base of the individual approach to teacher stress, there have been objections to this line of research on ideological grounds. Handy (1995) has suggested that the individualisation of stress has served to depoliticise the concept, shifting the emphasis from organisations and society at large to the individual, with the result that the individual assumes responsibility for their own stress.

Coping strategies

One of the ways in which stress affects job performance and health-related behaviour is by triggering coping strategies, and one reason some individuals are more vulnerable to stress than others is because of their coping strategies. A common distinction is between problem-focused (or direct action) coping, aimed at alleviating the problem causing stress, and emotion-focused (or palliative) coping, aimed at alleviating the negative emotions associated with stress (Lazarus and Folkman, 1984). Coping strategies can also be classified as adaptive or maladaptive. Adaptive strategies are effective in tackling stress; maladaptive strategies may provide momentary relief, but they are associated with negative longer-term effects (Cooper *et al.*, 1988). Research has given us quite a good understanding of the direct action and palliative coping strategies used by teachers. Box 9.4 shows some commonly used strategies.

The relationship between problem/emotion focus and the adaptive nature of coping strategies is complex and depends on a set of individual and situational variables. It is tempting to say that dealing with a problem directly is adaptive whereas retrospectively making oneself feel better is maladaptive, and in many cases this is true. However, making effective use of social support

Box 9.4

Commonly used teacher coping strategies

Problem-focused strategies (Benmansour, 1998)	Emotion-focused strategies (Salo, 1995)
Advance planning	Avoidance of thinking about problems
Strategies to improve learner performance	Problem-solving
Adaptation to circumstances	Social support
Increase effort	Thinking about work alone
Use more motivational techniques in class	Focusing on leisure activities
Get used to problems	Use of food, alcohol and tobacco
Talk to colleagues about problems	
Avoid exaggerating problems	
Talk about problems during meetings	

networks and drinking alcohol in moderation are associated with health benefits, whereas increasing effort and accepting injustice are likely to be maladaptive in the long term. Note, for example, that submission (i.e. giving up a struggle and accepting the inevitable) is associated with a decrease in arousal levels, hence the immediate physiological experience of stress, but also with an *increase* in levels of cortisol, the hormone responsible for many of the long-term health effects of stress (Looker and Gregson, 1996).

Reflection point

How stress-proof are you? Consider your cognitions, your motives for entering teaching and your coping strategies.

Systemic factors

In this context the term 'systemic' is used to describe a broad cluster of organisational factors that are not intrinsic to the nature of teaching, but which depend on the climate of the educational institution and the wider context of education, including the political domain. There is a complex relationship between society, institutions and individuals, and the emotional state of an individual at any moment is largely a product of social and political forces (Blackmore, 1996). Nias (1996) suggests there has been something of a shift in the emphasis teachers place on systemic factors as opposed to those intrinsic to the profession, so that where teachers at one time attributed most stress to problems with learners, they now report that most negative emotions arise in response to contact with other adults and from policies.

Travers and Cooper (1997) found that teachers named lack of government support, lack of information about changes, constant change and the demands of the National Curriculum as among their greatest sources of stress. These 'trickle-down' systemic factors act in addition to and feed into the dynamics of individual organisations (Jennings and Kennedy, 1996). At the level of the institution, factors such as social support among colleagues and leadership style appear to be important in affecting stress levels. Dussault *et al.* (1999) assessed isolation and stress in 1110 Canadian teachers and, as hypothesised, found a strong positive correlation. Van Dick *et al.* (1999) questioned 424 teachers from across all German sectors about their work stress, social support and physical illnesses. It was found that social support had a direct positive effect on health and a buffering effect on work stress.

Leadership style has also emerged as a significant organisational factor. Harris (1999) assessed teacher stress and leadership style in three American primary schools, using the Wilson Stress Profile for Teachers. The principal in each school was classified differently, and teachers had significantly lower stress in the school where the principal was classified as high in both task and relationship focus; this leadership style is associated with strategic vision and a close personal relationship with staff. Leadership style appears in part to be a response to trickle-down stressors. Hoel *et al.* (1999) surveyed English teachers and found that 35% reported having been bullied by a manager in the past five years, as opposed to an average of 24% across all occupational sectors. More recently, an analysis of the issues brought by teachers to the telephone counselling service Teacher Support Line (Nash, 2004) revealed that conflict with colleagues was the most common problem leading teachers to seek counselling (24% of cases), and that 66% of these conflicts were with a manager. One interpretation of these findings is that managers failing to cope with workloads and experiencing stress themselves are resorting to bullying as a maladaptive coping strategy. Although evidence is currently anecdotal, it has been suggested (Jarvis, 2004b) that middle managers are particularly at risk from systemic stress as their role combines high levels of accountability with low levels of control.

Many writers have cited the inspection regime to which schools and colleges are currently subjected as a systemic cause of teacher stress. Jeffrey and Woods (1998) have identified a clash of values between the education and inspection systems. Examples of these disparities are shown in Box 9.5. In fairness, this should not be to suggest that the inspection regime is without merit, and criticisms need to be balanced against the measured gains in standards that have arisen following and perhaps in response to the inception of Ofsted. However, there is little doubt that the climate and character of inspection contributes to teacher stress.

Box 9.5

Disparities in the values of education and inspection systems

Inspection	Education
PEDAGOGY	
Transmissional	Creative
Behaviourist	Constructivist
Formal	Informal
Examination	Support
Instant performance	Long-term benefits
CULTURE	
Competition	Collegiality
Blame	Support
Managerialism	Professionalism
Control	Self-regulation
Consumer	Producer

A transactional picture

It has been firmly established that occupational, individual and systemic factors are all important in the origins of stress. Chris Kyriacou (Kyriacou and Sutcliffe, 1978; Kyriacou, 2000) has offered a model for understanding the relationship between environmental stressors, individual vulnerability and resulting teacher stress (Figure 9.1).

This approach reconciles the conflict between stress in the environment and in the individual by seeing environmental pressures as *potential* stressors. Whether or not they actually induce stress is influenced by the interpretations of the individual teacher. If the teaching environment is sufficiently stressful, virtually any teacher would perceive events as threatening and experience actual stress. However, more vulnerable teachers may perceive threats in a much more benevolent environment and so experience stress in the absence of significant external stressors. This raises the question of what makes an event threatening. According to Kyriacou, stress occurs when self-esteem or well-being is threatened. An increase in workload is likely to induce stress, because it will be perceived as a threat to the well-being of the individual; however, a perceived insult or the frustration of a wish can also induce stress, because it can be interpreted as a threat to self-esteem.

There have been attempts based on Kyriacou's model to compare the importance of potential stressors and individual teacher characteristics, but results can vary wildly as a result of precisely what internal and external factors are input into the equation. Adams (2001) assessed potential stressors in the form of student variables and systemic factors and internal factors, including locus of control, self-esteem and job satisfaction in 235 American vocational teachers. Internal factors emerged in this study as four times as important as environmental variables, but there are important provisos to the usefulness of this study. Job satisfaction, life satisfaction and illness were taken as internal causal factors. In fact, they are likely to be effects rather than causes of stress, so their importance becomes greatly exaggerated in the analysis. Moreover, a very limited range of systemic factors operating at the organisational level were included in the analysis, so the influence of internal factors is exaggerated. Studies like this are interesting, but without an agreed set of causal factors to study they cannot be said to provide a definitive answer to the relative importance of internal and external factors.

Managing teacher stress

Several strategies can be used to attempt to tackle the problem of teacher stress. Approaches can be pitched at the level of the organisation or the individual, with all the ideological baggage this entails. Conyne (1991) distinguishes between three levels of stress management intervention:

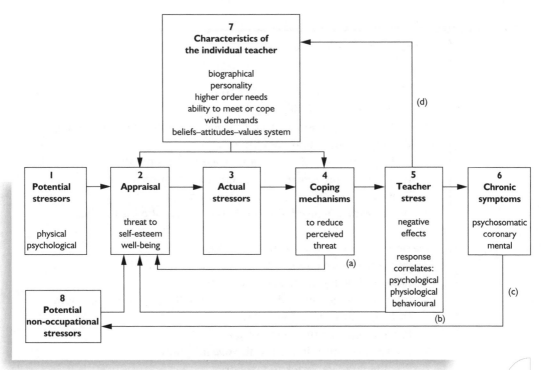

Figure 9.1 **Kyriacou and Sutcliffe's model of teacher stress**

- *Primary prevention*: approaches that prevent teachers becoming stressed; they can include organisational changes and stress training for individuals.
- *Secondary prevention*: approaches to detecting signs of stress in teachers before they develop clinical conditions.
- *Tertiary prevention*: approaches to dealing with teachers when they have developed stress-related conditions.

It is better to tackle the roots of teacher stress rather than to ameliorate the damage once teachers are suffering stress-related illness. As Albee says, 'No disease or disorder has ever been treated out of existence' (2000, p. 847). Preventative strategies can take the form of stress-proofing the organisation, the individual or both.

Organisational interventions

Given the number of intrinsic and systemic factors in the environment that contribute to teacher stress, it follows logically that positive changes in organisational procedures and climate should have a positive impact on teacher stress. The National Union of Teachers (NUT, 1990; cited in Kyriacou, 2000) has issued an action plan for education managers setting out three areas of

Box 9.6

Items from the NUT action plan

The task environment
- Design jobs and allocate duties so that teachers' skills are matched to their responsibilities.
- Reduce time pressure and introduce time management training.
- Provide more non-contact time.
- Make greater use of admin and learning support staff.
- Improve the physical environment and resources.
- Provide behaviour management training.
- Work towards shared aims and objectives of the institution.

The problem-solving and social environment
- Develop a more cooperative and supportive culture.
- Provide time for staff to relax together.
- Improve the quality and cohesiveness of the social environment.
- Develop team problem-solving.
- Provide time for problem-solving.
- Improve communication in the organisation.
- Provide good feedback to teachers.
- Share information in the hands of senior staff.

The developmental environment
- Develop better person management in the organisation.
- Improve management style.
- Demonstrate appreciation of teacher effort and achievement.
- Improve in-service training.
- Provide support facilities for staff, including counselling, leisure and occupational health.
- Make efforts to improve the public perception of teachers.

change: the task environment, the problem-solving and social environment, and the development environment. Box 9.6 shows some recommendations from each environment.

Kyriacou (2001) suggests that it is important to consult with teachers on matters such as curriculum development, which directly affect them. In addition, role overload can be addressed through clear job descriptions and communication problems can be addressed by establishing clear lines of two-way contact. Mentoring and staff development management can enhance professional identity and sense of accomplishment.

Certain situations arising in teaching can prove particularly stressful, and it is important that organisations can cope with this. For example, arriving as a newly qualified teacher (NQT) is a stressful time. Surveys of NQTs (e.g. Cains and Brown, 1998) suggest that NQTs find informal support from colleagues the single most important factor in buffering stress. Provision of a mentor for all new staff and for staff taking on new roles can be an important factor in tackling stress, although it is not clear whether formal mentoring provides exactly the same type of support as informal social contact. Appraisal is another period of potentially high stress, although it can be a positive experience for many teachers (Kyriacou, 1995). Positioning appraisal in a discourse of staff development rather than one of accountability may make it less threatening.

Large-scale empirical studies demonstrating the effectiveness of organisational development in reducing teacher stress are non-existent in the research literature. This is for methodological reasons; to establish such an experiment would require that all other conditions remain constant while a range of institutions experience a standard organisational intervention. In reality there is no way to isolate institutions from a range of other changes during the period of organisational intervention, and of course there is no single 'fits all' intervention that could be applied to a range of institutions. What we do have are case studies of what appear to be stress-proof organisations and of instances where a management strategy was associated with reduced stress (Carlyle and Woods, 2002).

Weller and Hartley (1994) offer a case study of the US state of Georgia's introduction of total quality management (TQM) in schools. TQM is a management ethos characterised by participatory planning and a culture of listening that aims to create a positive emotional climate in the workplace. According to Weller and Hartley, the introduction of TQM significantly reduced teacher stress in Georgia. Troman and Woods (2001) have described a low-stress school characterised by trust, participation and humour – attributed to management style. But case studies like this have clear limitations. Without detailed information on the characteristics of the individual staff, it is premature to conclude that the happy school is a direct result of management. Moreover, we cannot know how the management strategies used in that case might interact with situations in a different school environment. In short, case studies are unrepresentative and non-generalisable one-offs, and one must conclude that the empirical base for organisational interventions is currently fairly weak.

Individual interventions: stress management for teachers

Individual interventions in stress management can be undertaken on the initiative of the individual or provided by the organisation. For example, training can be used to enhance the effectiveness of the coping strategies on which teachers normally rely. In a discussion of what the individual teacher can do to cope with stress, Kyriacou (2000) identifies three broad approaches: pre-empting stress, direct coping strategies and palliative coping strategies. Teachers skilled in time management and assertiveness and who are physically fit are likely to be relatively resistant to the effects of stress. It may in principle be possible to pre-empt stress by providing training in these areas. Similarly, direct action (or problem-focused) approaches, including planning and preparation, relaxation, confrontation management, social support and maintaining a healthy work–life balance can benefit from training. Palliative (or emotion-focused) approaches tackle the emotional experience of stress and include exercise, self-medication, pampering and formal relaxation procedures such as meditation.

Organisations may choose to provide formal stress management training. Stress management training is aimed at the individual, raising ideological issues as it can be interpreted as placing blame for stress with individuals and absolving organisations of responsibility. Most stress management is multimodal (Palmer, 1996), involving relaxation procedures, time management and some form of cognitive restructuring to help the teacher reinterpret their working environment as less stressful. Although stress management training is based on empirically validated procedures and is demonstrably effective in some settings, there is little direct evidence for its effectiveness in reducing teacher stress. In a review by Jarvis (2002) an electronic search revealed only two recent studies published in 'quality' journals in the previous five years supporting stress management for teachers.

Considering the vast extent of literature on generic stress management and the origins of teacher stress, the tiny volume of research into interventions to combat teacher stress is of grave concern. In one of these studies, Hall *et al.* (1997) examined the effect of human relations training on teacher stress. Thirty-two participants took part in a two-year humanistic-experiential master's degree programme and were interviewed at the end of the course. Stress was reported as having been reduced as a result of the course. The other published study, by V. L. Anderson *et al.* (1999), concerned the effectiveness of meditation as a stress management strategy. Ninety-one teachers took part in a five-week course of meditation; levels of stress were compared before and after. As hypothesised, levels of stress were lower following the course. A larger-scale systematic review reported by Dunlop (2004) located 17 studies of individualised teacher stress interventions, out of a total of 23 studies including studies at the organisational level, but the quality of measures across these studies was so poor that it was impossible to do meaningful analysis of alternative strategies.

Cognitive interventions

Cognitive restructuring is a standard procedure in stress management training, but raises particular issues for teachers. A common approach to cognitive restructuring is rational emotive behaviour therapy (REBT). Here is how Abrams and Ellis (1996) describe the assumption underlying REBT-based stress management: 'Stress does not exist. There is no iconoclasm intended here. We mean it quite literally. Stress does not exist in itself. Stress is like good or evil: it exists only in the perceptions and reactions of the beholder' (ibid., p. 62). This is an extreme position difficult to reconcile with research into intrinsic and systemic factors underlying teacher stress. Jarvis (2003) has explored the effects of REBT on teacher stress through a case analysis of teacher responses to a stress management training based on REBT, in which 'maladaptive' beliefs concerning stress were identified and challenged. One belief common to most teachers concerned the role of the organisation in creating stress and the trainer duly challenged this, attempting to shift attributions towards individual responsibility. Questionnaires and interviews administered two years later to participants in the training showed that this challenge had led to distress and offence. Responses included 'it made me feel like shit to be honest' and '[stress management is] blaming people to make them feel inadequate'. Jarvis explains these responses in terms of social representations theory. Participants appeared to have anchored their understanding of the experience of stress management in a political rather than a psychological understanding and they experienced *ideologic strain*. In other words, what had been challenged was not simply a maladaptive belief in individuals but rather their whole ideology, something central to their self-concept. In line with previous social representations research, this study showed that challenges to ideology resulted in a hardening of attitudes, and Jarvis concluded that, on this basis, cognitive techniques are probably inappropriate for stress management training in teachers.

Counselling services

The Teacher Support Network (2004) outlines the rationale for counselling: 'Talking with a counsellor can help teachers to deal with the underlying reasons for stress, review their perspective and establish strategies for dealing with stressful situations in the long term' (Teacher Support Network, 2004, p. 11). Although there are problems in relying on counselling alone to tackle teacher stress, there is no doubt that counselling can be very helpful for many people. Accurate figures for the total use of counselling services by teachers are impossible to gather, but in 2002–03 some 6% of the teaching profession used the Teacher Support Line (Nash, 2004). The Teacher Support Network (2001) carried out a clinical audit on the effectiveness of its telephone counselling: 77% of respondents reported that counselling had improved their personal insight; 70% believed it had been helpful in exploring coping strategies; 45% believed it had helped their daily functioning and work performance. These figures are encouraging, but social policy analysts do not universally accept this type of audit as firm evidence. The gold standard in outcome research of this type is widely agreed to be the random control trial

(RCT), in which clients are randomly allocated to treatment and no-treatment groups and their outcomes compared. This approach raises ethical as well as practical problems, so there is a dearth of such evidence for teacher counselling.

Combined interventions

A good example of an integrated programme to tackle teacher stress is reported by Coalter (2002). With the endorsement of the teaching unions, York City Council and Businesshealth plc worked collaboratively to tackle stress in five primary schools. A total of 164 staff (88%) completed confidential assessments of their health and their experience of work-related pressure. Individuals were offered counselling, workshops on stress management and health checks. Each school was audited for its individual pattern of stressors and strategies were developed to tackle institutional problems in each school. Head teachers were provided with mentoring to help with organisational development. After a year, 55% of staff reported improved health and 57% attributed this to the programme. Mean absence was reduced from 10.5 days per year to 8.9.

A major project currently being rolled out nationally is the well-being programme, devised by the Teacher Support Network. Like the York project, this involves an audit of the organisation, based on the HSE criteria (p. 181). Each institution then receives customised assistance, which can include streamlining of bureaucracy, improvement of social support through staff social activities, provision of better facilities and stress management techniques such as t'ai chi. Following the original project, which ran for two years in Norfolk from 1999 to 2000, 89% of head teachers reported improvements in school culture and 70% reported improvements in staff retention and recruitment; 88% rated staff performance as improved. This integrated approach is in its infancy and more systematic research is needed, but these early results are extremely promising. One factor underlying its success may be the fact that teachers respond more positively to individual interventions when they are clear that organisational factors are a simultaneous focus of attention, thus there is not the same potential for ideologic strain.

Conclusions and personal reflections

Occupational stress is a major national problem and the teaching profession has been particularly hard hit. There are a range of definitions for stress, bringing with them important ideological baggage, and representations of stress vary between different professional groups. Stress is associated with a decline in performance and health, so there are important pragmatic and ethical reasons to take its management seriously. Causal factors in teacher stress include factors intrinsic to teaching, such as heavy workload, long working hours, discipline and evaluation apprehension. Individual teachers vary in their vulnerability according to their coping strategies, self-efficacy, attributions, commitment and resolution of childhood trauma. Systemic factors, including management style, communications and the clash of values experienced in inspection are of further importance.

Jarvis (2002) has concluded that although the total volume of research into teacher stress is substantial and although we have a fairly sophisticated understanding of its origins, there are still some important limitations and gaps in our understanding. We understand intrinsic stressors in teaching, but there has been little or no research into the effects of reducing or mediating them, in part because they are largely determined at a national level and are not easily open to experimental manipulation. It is well established that cognitive factors mediate the effects of stressors in teachers, and that in other contexts cognitive therapy can alter maladaptive cognitions. However, the small body of research into cognitive restructuring in teachers shows negative results. The body of research concerning other individual interventions is minuscule. Systemic factors are clearly important in the origins of stress but do not easily lend themselves to manipulation for stress reduction. Other than case studies, there is little empirical support for the effectiveness of organisational development in stress management. The limitations of using the existing research base to plan stress management in British education are compounded by other factors. Studies may not generalise well across education sectors and the base of cross-national and cross-sector comparisons is inadequate to make judgements about when generalisation is justified. Much of the published research concerns student and newly qualified teachers. Although this is clearly important in its own right, we should be wary of generalising from students to qualified teachers and from NQTs to experienced teachers.

Self-assessment questions

1. Referring to national statistics and the law, explain why teacher stress is considered to be such a problem.

2. Compare a range of definitions of stress, with reference to their ideological implications.

3. Explain what is meant by teacher burnout. How might burnout affect responses to learners?

4. Distinguish between intrinsic, individual and systemic factors affecting teacher stress and explain how they might operate in conjunction.

5. Critically compare organisational and individual approaches to stress management with reference to empirical studies and ideological implications.

Further reading

•••••● Carlyle, D. and Woods, P. (2002) *Emotions of Teacher Stress*. Trentham Books, Stoke-on-Trent, Staffs.

•••••● Dunlop, C. (2004) Report of the Healthy Working Lives Research Group. Paper presented at the Improving Employee Effectiveness in the Public Sector Conference, University of Stirling, September 2004.

•••••● Jarvis, M. (2002) Teacher stress: a critical review of recent findings and suggestions for future research directions. *Stress News*, 14, 12–16.

•••••● Kyriacou, C. (2000) *Stress-Busting for Teachers*. Nelson Thornes, Cheltenham, Glos.

•••••● Kyriacou, C. (2001) Teacher stress: directions for future research. *Educational Review*, 53, 28–35.

•••••● Wilson, V. (2002) *Feeling the Strain*. Scottish Council for Research in Education, Glasgow, Report 109.

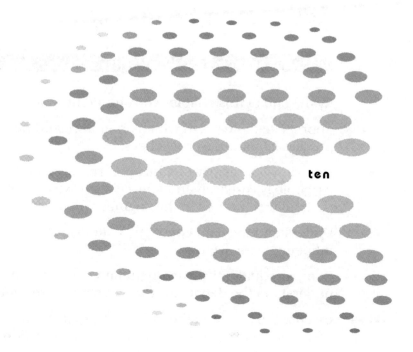

ten

Education
Research

Education Research

learning objectives

By the end of this chapter you should be able to:

- Appreciate the ways in which an understanding of the research process can empower teachers.

- Overview the history of education research and educational psychology research and appreciate its visions of purpose, with particular reference to the engineering model.

- Understand the concept of epistemology and how epistemology influences research.

- Compare qualitative and quantitative research methods and understand the debate over their relative usefulness.

- Discuss the uses and limitations of experiments, correlation and regression, case studies and surveys in education research.

- Describe and evaluate the use of action research.

- Outline systematic review and meta-analysis as ways to derive conclusions from multiple studies.

- Critically evaluate the education and educational psychology research for its rigour and relevance to practice.

Education differs from comparable professions, such as medicine and psychology, in that although there is a thriving field of professional research, it takes place largely in isolation from professional practice. It is a rare doctor that does not peruse the medical research literature at least occasionally, and it would be unusual for a psychologist not to at least dip into current psychological literature – this is a requirement if they have chartered status and a practising certificate – but teachers largely ignore education research. As we shall see throughout this chapter, there are a range of sound practical and political reasons why this should have become the case. Given the extent of divorce between educational practice and research, why have this chapter at all?

Actually there are good reasons why an understanding of education research can empower practitioners. First, teachers and other education professionals are subject to policy decisions that are based on research findings, or at least justified using research findings. These decisions can only be challenged by understanding the limitations of research. In other words, even if we ultimately reject the usefulness of education research, we should at least do so for good reason. Second, professionals that do wish to use research as part of the reflective approach to their practice benefit from the critical tools to select and evaluate appropriate research. Third, if practitioners have a good understanding of the research process, they can actively participate in it and influence the research agenda. The top-down national agenda of evidence-based practice can therefore be supplemented by a complementary agenda of bottom-up practice-based evidence. Finally, and perhaps most obviously, teachers may wish to use research to evaluate aspects of their own practice. Action research, the tradition in which this sort of self-evaluation takes place, is discussed on p. 216.

The historical context

The idea of researching education appeared in the late nineteenth century, at the same time as psychology was emerging as a discipline distinct from biology and philosophy. Perhaps the first piece of education research was conducted in 1870, when 2000 children were surveyed on entry to primary school in order to discover the 'content of their mind'. In the 1880s Ebbinghaus' pioneering work on memory drew attention to the possibility of enhancing the retention of information in education and at the same time Binet began researching into intelligence in French schools. By the early twentieth century there were experimental comparisons of the effectiveness of different pedagogical techniques (e.g. Rice, 1913).

   Educational psychology proper has its roots in the development of IQ tests by Binet and Simon (1905). This early area of intelligence research illustrates neatly the disparity between the intentions of education research and *post facto* ideological objections. The stated intention of the Binet and Simon test was the identification of children who would benefit from special schooling, and IQ tests still have such practical applications. However, to contemporary critical psychologists and many educational academics, the legacy of this psychometric tradition is not so much the targeting of resources to vulnerable individuals, but rather the inappropriate application of culture-bound tests to effect a perpetuation of racial and socio-economic divisions (Burman, 1994).

   For the first half of the twentieth century, education research was essentially psychological. By the 1950s, however, the discipline of sociology had become the dominant influence in educational academia and the role of socio-economic status in educational opportunity became the central focus of education research. It was at this time that educational psychology emerged as a distinct discipline, with Cyril Burt being the first person in the UK to use the title 'educational psychologist'. Since then there has been an explosion in the scale and sophistication of research in education and educational psychology. Computerisation of statistical analysis has meant that numerical information can be handled on a larger scale. Also, since the 1970s there has been a steady growth in the acceptance of qualitative methods (p. 208).

In England by the late 1990s there were around 3000 people based in approximately 100 institutions engaged in education research, with an annual budget of over £50 million (Hillage *et al.*, 1998). Findings are disseminated in a range of journals of educational psychology and education research, the latter influenced by both psychological and sociological traditions. There are a number of important debates concerning education research, the most fundamental concerning its purpose.

The aims and purpose of education research

Bassey (1995) defined education research as something that 'aims critically to inform educational judgements and decisions in order to improve educational action'. The attempt to identify the most successful curricula and the most effective pedagogical techniques can be traced back to 1892 (De Landsheere, 1988), when Rice questioned 1200 teachers about curriculum content and teaching methods. Rice's research led to some interesting findings, such as the then surprisingly low correlation between spelling ability and the time spent in learning spellings by rote (Rice, 1913). Rice's approach of looking for relation-ships between particular pedagogical devices and educational outcomes (outcome research) is an important influence on education policy. This type of outcome research has been explained in terms of an *engineering model* of education research inspired by the relationship between developments in the natural sciences and technological developments in the twentieth century. According to the engineering model, increases in our understanding of the processes of learning should be accompanied by improvements in pedagogical technique. Thus the purpose of education research is simple – to produce facts that can be directly applied in classroom practice.

Rice's engineering approach to education research has become popular with policy-makers but tends to be less popular with practitioners. There are sound reasons for this. Firstly, practitioners tend to have a detailed under-standing, albeit often implicit rather than explicit, of the subtleties of the classroom, including the complex interactions between teacher characteris-tics, pupil characteristics and technical effectiveness. This means that they quickly recognise the 'facts' identified by engineering model research as oversimple, perhaps holding true only for a specific subject, age group, socio-economic group, etc. Teachers thus tend towards cynicism when presented with simplistic advice based on research findings purporting to demonstrate the superiority of one pedagogical approach or technique over another. In addition, it has become part of teachers' folk beliefs that policy-makers either selectively fund or selectively draw from academic research when looking for support for those approaches currently in political favour, and that inconsistencies are glossed over.

Other commentators have taken a broader vision of education research. For example, Foster (1997) defined education research as the 'set of activities which involves the systematic collection and analysis of data with a view to producing valid knowledge about teaching, learning and the institutional frameworks in which they occur'. Indeed only a minority of published studies are directly concerned with classroom practice. In 1997 the National Foundation for Education Research (NFER) produced a breakdown of the subject matter of published research. A summary is shown in Table 10.1.

Table 10.1 The top 10 research topics by key word search

Rank	Topic	Percentage by key word
1	Education policy	47%
2	Subject based	31%
3	Teaching methods	28%
4	Education management	26%
5	Non-specific, including ILT	24%
6	Approaches to learning	24%
7	Key skills	15%
8	Assessment	12%
9	Institutional effectiveness	8%
10	Family and cultural issues	7%

Source: NFER (1997)

The tension between research for understanding and for policy development is perhaps a healthy one. The engineering model can be mechanistic and prescriptive, and is associated with a simplistic relationship between research, policy and practice. However, the academic ideal of 'knowledge for its own sake' can lead to the establishment of an esoteric body of findings of little relevance to practitioners (Sutherland, 1997). In a survey of education academics, the majority thought that the proportion of funded research devoted to policy issues was too high and favoured more 'blue skies research', defined as 'research where the notion of application of the findings is secondary to the contribution to, and accumulation of, knowledge' (Hillage *et al.*, 1998, p. 13).

Reflection point

Consider your attitude to the education research you have come across in this book and elsewhere. To what extent is it 'blue skies' research and to what extent can it be easily applied in real-life contexts? Do you see blue skies research as an indulgence or policy-related research as unduly restrictive and prescriptive?

Epistemological foundations

Regardless of where one stands on the engineering model and the relevance of blue skies research, the agreed purpose of research in general is the furtherance of knowledge. However, there is surprisingly little consensus about what actually comprises knowledge. *Epistemology* is the name given to the branch of philosophy devoted to understanding the nature of knowledge. The tension over the nature of knowledge centres around two epistemological positions, the positivist and the hermeneutic. The *positivist* tradition dominated the social sciences throughout most of the twentieth century. The positivists were a group of Viennese philosophers who held that knowledge could only be based on sensory experience and that knowledge advances only through the description of empirical facts. Research that conforms to the criteria of positivism focuses on observable or otherwise testable phenomena, often but not exclusively seeking to establish cause-and-effect relationships (Mautner, 1998). The traditional research methods of experiment, correlation, survey and observation are founded on the positivist epistemology.

With the advent of postmodernity in the late twentieth century, the whole existence of the empirical fact has been called into question. Social scientists have explored an alternative epistemological position, the hermeneutic. The term 'hermeneutic' was first used in the seventeenth century by Dannhauer, who proposed that the reading of religious, legal and classical texts required not merely a literal reading but *interpretation* (Mautner, 1998). The hermeneutic or interpretative approach posits that truth can be gleaned not merely by observation but by the subjective interpretation of narrative. With the recent advent of postmodernism and the concomitant rise of hermeneutic epistemology in social science, a new range of interpretative qualitative methods have been devised. These include discourse analysis, narrative analysis and grounded theoretical research.

Qualitative and quantitative methods

Hayes defines quantitative methods as those 'which involve the manipulation of numerical data' (2000, p. 239). This frequently but not exclusively involves null hypothesis significance testing. Qualitative approaches, by contrast, attempt to draw out the *meanings* of data. Some modes of research such as experimentation and correlation are explicitly quantitative in that their aim is to generate and manipulate numerical data, whereas others such as discourse analysis and psychoanalytic interpretation are entirely interpretive and by definition qualitative. There is, however, more overlap between quantitative and qualitative analysis than this simple distinction suggests. For example, interview and other narrative data are most commonly subjected to qualitative analysis; the aim is to draw out the common themes in the narrative of respondents. However, there is often no reason why quantitative data cannot be drawn from the same transcripts. An example of a study extracting quantitative and qualitative data from pupil narratives comes from Jules and Kutnick (1997), who investigated the perceptions of 1756 children from Trinidad and Tobago about 'what makes a good teacher' by the analysis of interviews and essays. Qualitative analysis was necessary to draw out the themes identified by children and appreciate the importance accorded to similarity to parents, feelings of security and boundaries. However, quantitative analysis was further useful in demonstrating statistically significant age and sex differences in the frequency with which pupils cited particular teacher characteristics. This information has clear practitioner relevance and would not have been readily available from qualitative analysis alone.

Strong views on the merits of quantitative and qualitative research abound, and the dichotomy has led to some rather stereotyped representations of quantitative research as crude and clumsy, and of qualitative methods as informal and lacking in rigour. The field of education research has escaped the worst excesses of enmity between qualitative and quantitative researchers that has dogged some academic domains, such as social psychology, where qualitative researchers (e.g. Doherty and Anderson, 1998) who have cited statistics in introductions to their papers have found it necessary to apologise for this and to publicly reaffirm their qualitative position. However, it is fairly clear that, epistemological and political debates aside, in practical terms there is an important place for both quantitative and qualitative research in education. It can be helpful to think of qualitative methods being more subtle and thus often more helpful in understanding the subtleties of a phenomenon. However, numerical data is often more helpful for demonstration and empirical validation, revealing the strength of relationships and effects.

Major research methods

This section is devoted to basic description and evaluation of the usefulness of some of the major research methods used in education and educational psychology research. Table 10.2 compares the frequency with which research methods were used in 2003 in the *British Journal of Educational Psychology*, published by the British Psychological Society and *Educational Research*, published by Routledge.

Table 10.2 illustrates the differences in the emphasis on different research methods apparent between the educational psychology tradition and the education research tradition. There is more experimental and correlational work in the educational psychology tradition. Education research papers are more often theoretical or commentary-based rather than empirical studies. Education researchers are more likely than psychologists to rely on qualitative methods. These differences probably reflect the sociological influence on education research. In fairness to education research, it should be acknowledged that there are subject-specific journals, notably the *International Journal for Science Education*, which do contain more empirical studies and a high proportion using quantitative methods (Grace, personal communication).

Table 10.2   **Research methods in published papers in 2003**

	British Journal of Educational Psychology		Educational Research	
	Number of papers	Percentage*	Number of papers	Percentage*
Experiment (including pre-experiment)	10	30%	2	10%
Natural experiment	5	15%	4	20%
Correlation or regression	10	30%	1	5%
Interview	0	0%	4	20%
Questionnaire	4	12%	3	15%
Longitudinal	2	6%	0	0%
Content analysis	2	6%	0	0%
Discourse analysis	0	0%	1	5%
Commentary/theoretical	1	3%	6	30%
Case study	0	0%	0	0%

*Some studies employed a combination of techniques, so the percentages add up to more than 100%. In addition, the total number of studies appears to exceed the number published in 2003.

Experimental research

The aim of an experiment is the establishment of a cause-and-effect relationship. The effect of an independent variable is assessed on a dependent variable. This involves comparison of two or more conditions. According to Cohen and Manion (1994), there are three variations of the experimental method commonly used in education: the pre-experiment, the true experiment and the quasi-experiment. *Pre-experiments*, also known as pre-test/post-test comparisons, involve measuring the dependent variable before and after manipulating the independent variable in a single group of participants. For example, we might assess thinking skills (see Chapter 5), undertake a thinking skills course then reassess the same skills. This allows us to infer that any improvements in thinking skills are a result of the course. The limitation of the pre-test/post-test design is that we can only *infer* that any change is the result of the course. In a real-life educational setting, numerous other variables also exert a constant effect on learners over time. If pre-test/post-test comparison indicates that an ability is measurably superior at post-test, then we cannot be sure this is attributable to the independent variable.

An alternative to the pre-test/post-test comparison is the *true experiment*, which involves the random allocation of participants to conditions, including a control condition. This randomisation is important in fairly apportioning all relevant variables to the experimental and control group, meaning that the experimental and control groups are truly equivalent. When this has been achieved, it is possible to attribute differences at post-test to the manipulated independent variable. In practice we can only be certain that experimental and control groups are equivalent if group size is large. Returning to the example of the thinking skills course, if two randomly allocated groups are tested for thinking skills then one group is subjected to the thinking skills course and both groups are reassessed, any difference in the post-test scores of the two groups will indicate the effect of the course.

True experiments are superior in principle, because of the greater certainty that results can be attributed to the independent variable, but there are several circumstances in which they are not possible for practical or ethical reasons. A simple practical problem arises when a whole-class technique comes to be tested. In many circumstances it would simply be too disruptive for the teaching to randomly divide classes into experimental and control groups and give them different learning activities. If different existing classes were to be used, then random allocation would not be possible. In addition, were we to restrict the availability of an efficacious technique to only an experimental group and deprive a random selection of learners of its benefits, this would raise ethical issues and be unacceptable to many practitioners. In these circumstances, pre-test/post-test comparison may be preferable.

The third experimental design identified by Cohen and Manion is the *natural experiment* or *quasi-experiment*. This involves the use of a non-equivalent control group. In some studies, such as gender comparisons, the independent variable is defined by group membership and *any* comparison is by definition quasi-experimental. Quasi-experimental designs are also used when two pre-existing groups such as classes or schools take the role of experimental and control groups. Post-test comparison is still possible, but it is much less certain that differences between groups are attributable to the manipulated independent variable.

Experiments are of greatest value when researchers are interested in outcomes associated with a particular pedagogical technique or approach. A teacher or researcher can fairly easily demonstrate the potential of a technique with a simple pre-test/post-test comparison or quasi-experimental design. Yet despite their usefulness, there are a range of problems that limit the validity of experimental findings and it is important to be aware of these problems in order to appraise the results of one's own research and any on which we might be tempted to base a policy change. One particular problem in education experiments is the *Hawthorne effect*. This occurs when partici-pants realise they are the subjects of study and accordingly perform better regardless of the efficacy of the procedure. This may be particularly the case when a novel experience and a break from routine in an experimental condition imbue participants with an enthusiasm not shared by the control group. The Hawthorne effect may lead researchers to attribute more signifi-cance to the experimental condition than is justified. This problem can be compounded by a statistical phenomenon known as *regression to the mean*. This means that low pre-test scores have a general tendency to become higher in post-test assessment, further exaggerating the significance of pre-test/post-test differences.

Correlational research

The feature of correlational research is the establishment of relationships between measured variables. Wherever a psychological variable felt to have a bearing on achievement is measurable, such as IQ, learning style, learning strategy, motivational style and thinking skills, it becomes possible to assess its relationship to other variables, most obviously measures of outcome such as GCSE score or grade point average (GPA). We might also look for relationships between these apparently independent variables, to see for example whether high IQ is associated with a particular learning style.

In addition to the obvious interest engendered by understanding the relationships between educational outcome and other variables, it can also be highly instructive to look at the relationships between what appear to be independent variables and *process* variables. For example, we know that deep learning strategies are associated with higher grades. However, this raises the question of 'why'? Is a deep learning strategy associated with time spent on independent study? If so, such a finding would suggest that time spent on independent study may be the crucial factor in understanding the link between learning strategy and educational outcome.

Another important purpose of correlational techniques is in testing the psychometric properties of the assessment tools used in research and in the practice of educational psychology. Recall the figures in Table 10.2 on the frequency of use of correlational research in educational psychology and education research. The greater figure for educational psychology (30% compared to 5%) is largely accounted for by the assessment of psychometric tests. For example, in Chapter 4 a range of learning styles assessments were discussed. These assessments to which psychometric tests are subjected include internal reliability, the extent to which each question or statement in a scale or subscale measures the same thing. This is assessed by correlating responses to each item with those of the other items. Recall the internal reliability of each of the four dimensions of Honey and Mumford's Learning Styles Questionnaire (LSQ). Table 10.3 shows the internal reliability of the LSQ.

There are several variations on the basic procedure of correlation. *Partial correlation* can be used to assess the relationship between two variables while controlling for a third. For example, we might be interested in the relationships between IQ, socio-economic status (SES) and GCSE score. We know that there is a modest positive correlation between IQ and SES. Using partial correlation it is

Table 10.3 **Internal reliability of the LSQ**

Dimension	Reliability
Activist	0.74
Pragmatist	0.59

212

possible to establish the relationship between IQ and GCSE score, controlling for SES, or between SES and GCSE score, controlling for IQ. This allows us to see relationships independent of confounding variables.

Multiple correlation, more commonly called *multiple regression*, is a further variation on the basic correlational procedure. In multiple regression, a set of variables are all intercorrelated. For example, we might be interested in a range of factors underlying A level success. Possible independent variables affecting A level success might include IQ, learning style, gender, SES and motivational style. Using multiple regression, it is possible in one calculation to compare the strength of the relationship between each of these variables and A level. Moreover, multiple regression also allows us to see the relationships between each of these variables, for example, whether SES is associated with a particular motivational style.

Correlational techniques are extremely useful, in particular where several variables are involved (e.g. factors predicting academic success), making it impractical to establish a range of quasi-experimental groups. In such a case, multiple regression analysis can be helpful in teasing out the subtle relationships between variables. But caution is needed when using correlational techniques to tease out cause-and-effect relationships. Although we can establish the relationship of an apparent independent variable such as achievement motivation and an apparent dependent variable such as SAT scores, it can be unclear whether one is the product of the other, or whether a third variable underlies both. It is quite possible that SAT scores impact on achievement motivation, and that both are influenced by some additional variable such as thinking skills (Chapter 5) or strategic learning (Chapter 4). Where measurements are taken over time, one way to establish cause and effect is cross-lagging. This essentially means that each variable measured at the start is correlated with the other variables later on. Suppose achievement motivation measured before SATs is more strongly correlated to SAT score than achievement motivation measured after it, this suggests that achievement motivation is the independent variable. If the strength of the correlation increases following the SATs, then this suggests that SAT scores affect achievement motivation.

Survey research

Surveys by questionnaire, interview or focus group have a specific purpose in education research – to establish people's personal responses to an issue. These responses might be in the form of knowledge, opinion, feelings, attitudes or experiences, assessed by written questionnaire, individual verbal interview or focus group. Surveys have numerous applications, ranging from student questionnaires for departmental quality assurance purposes to focus groups designed to uncover teacher concerns about policy change and interviews to establish the course of identity change during teacher burnout.

The relative merit of questionnaires, interviews and focus groups depends on the situation. Questionnaires can be quickly and easily distributed to large samples and are suited to gathering large volumes of quantitative data. Their limitations are in the form of poor response rates and limited opportunities for additional questioning based on initial responses and for gathering qualitative data. Interviews allow for more qualitative data to be gathered and for respondents to make salient points not anticipated by the researchers. They typically have better response rates, but sample sizes tend to be limited by the time required for each interview. Reliability – the extent to which each interview assesses the same variables in different respondents – tends to be lower than for questionnaires because of the introduction of additional variables in the form of the interviewer.

Cohen and Manion (1994) distinguish between four types of interview. In *structured interviews* the exact format has been decided in advance, and all respondents are asked the same questions in the same sequence using the same wording. *Unstructured interviews*, by contrast, are more open; respondents are cued with the same questions but are then allowed to diverge considerably from these questions in their responses. In *non-directive* or *clinical interviews*, there are no set questions and respondents are encouraged to explore the issues according to their own agenda. The interviewer's role becomes one of clarifying rather than directing the discourse. *Focused interviews* have a specific purpose to assess responses to a particular experience. As far as possible they are non-directive, but the interviewer formulates hypotheses in advance and aims to address them by analysing respondents' answers.

Focus groups are group interviews where the interactions between group members stimulate the generation of ideas and opinions and add to the information gathered (Wilson, 1997). They derive from the psychodynamic tradition, being developed by Ed Bernays, Freud's nephew. The rationale behind the original focus groups was that people jointly free-associating in a group setting would arrive at a consensus about their unconscious motives and wishes. Nowadays, the discourse generated in focus groups is widely interpreted as the result of the social processes of the group, although very few published studies have provided us with information about these processes (Kitzinger, 1994). There are advantages to the use of focus groups over traditional interviews. Participants speak in a group of peers and are thus more inclined to speak freely. This was noted by A. Lewis (1992) in a study of 10-year-olds' attitudes to special educational needs, in which the children picked up on and expanded each others' points. The usual power dynamic of the researcher-participant dyad is broken down in focus groups, probably reducing inhibitions. This richer data from focus groups is balanced, however, by some limitations to the group situation. Participants may be influenced in their expressed opinions and emotions by social acceptability, what Wilson identifies as the 'public voice' (1997, p. 218), and it can be impractical to diverge to follow the train of thought of a single group member.

Surveys have numerous important uses in education and form an important aspect of education research. For guidance on designing effective survey studies see Oppenheim (1992). Their limitations, however, are well documented. The views of teachers, learners, parents, etc., are extremely important in their own right, but they are just that, views. Surveys do not constitute objective data about the success of a policy or the consequences of an institutional change. This disparity is well illustrated by a study on implementation of the national literacy strategy (Fisher, 2002). Teacher attitudes towards the literacy hour were assessed by questionnaire and interview, and their implementation of it was assessed by observations. No relationship emerged between teacher attitudes and their classroom behaviour. This is not to suggest that it was not useful to assess teacher attitudes, merely to underline the limited inferences we can draw from such assessments.

Case studies

The feature of the case study is the detailed analysis of a single case; this may involve a single learner or a class or an institution, but will be focused on a particular set of circumstances. We may, for example, be concerned with how a particular child responded to educational therapy (Chapter 7) or the organisational stress engendered by the merging of two colleges (Chapter 9). Data vary widely according to the nature of the study, but are typically gathered by a range of means, including questionnaires, observations and interviews.

Some cases trace change in an individual learner or institution following a targeted intervention strategy. These studies can be thought of as experimental, in that the effect of an independent variable is being observed. For example, we might track symptom reduction in a child undergoing educational therapy. Such case studies are sometimes called $n = 1$ experiments. An example is shown in Figure 10.1.

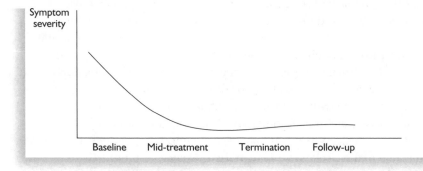

Figure 10.1 **Symptom reduction in a case of educational therapy**

Case studies provide rich data to help understand a situation, and often provide the only available data for understanding the effect of independent variables. This is particularly true where a situation is highly unusual or cannot be replicated for ethical reasons. For example, a refugee child traumatised by the political murder of a parent will have a complex emotional response requiring in-depth analysis, but this situation is sufficiently unusual to allow gathering a large sample size and is self-evidently impossible to replicate artificially.

The limitations of case studies are obvious and well documented. Essentially they are one-offs and it is impossible to know how far results can be generalised to other individuals or institutions. Take the above hypothetical case of educational therapy. It is very likely that while tracking one case might reveal the pattern of symptom reduction shown in Figure 10.1, another apparently similar case might not show any symptom reduction at all. Case studies do not allow the assessment of sufficient variables to understand why this variance in outcome might take place.

Action research

Action research in education research represents not so much a distinctive methodology as an *ethos*. Action researchers are less concerned with generating generalisable results than understanding their own practice in the specific context in which they work. Kemmis offers the following definition: 'Action research is a form of self-reflective enquiry undertaken by participants in social (including educational) situations in order to improve the rationality and justice of (a) their own social or educational practices, (b) their understanding of these practices, and (c) the situations in which the practices are carried out' (1993, p. 177).

Social psychologist Kurt Lewin, who first used the term 'action research' (Lewin, 1946), laid the foundations for the ethos on which current action research is founded, predicated on three principles. First, action research involves collaboration leading to the achievement of joint aspirations; in education the collaboration is most commonly between teachers and learners. This is in marked contrast to the distance maintained by most academic researchers and their participants. Second, in contrast to the ideological neutrality of traditional science, action researchers are committed to democratic principles and see the research process as an expression of democracy and a contributor to democracy. Thus, through participation in action research, learners are exerting power over their situation. Third, to action researchers, the twin ideals of social change and improved professional practice are indivisible. In other words, as the individual's understanding of their own educational practice improves, so does the social justice attached to their relationship with their learners. Table 10.4 summarises the contrast between action research and traditional scientific research.

Table 10.4 **Comparison of action research and academic research**

Principle	Action research	Academic research
Researcher–participant relationship	Collaborative	Formal
Ideological orientation	Social justice	Neutral
Aim of research	Improved practice or social change	Improved understanding

The research methods employed by action researchers are as varied as those of 'academic' research. Action research may, for example, involve experimentation with a new pedagogical technique, student surveys, content analysis of lessons or observation of interactions. Some methods are more closely associated with sociological rather than psychological research, including ethnographic and account methods. However, the process of action research is characterised by a distinctive cycle of planning, action, observing and reflecting. Thus, an issue is identified, an educational practice is implemented and/or scrutinised and its impact is assessed in collaboration with those affected by it. Cohen and Manion (1994) identify five benefits of conducting action research:

- It can help remedy classroom problems and improve practice.
- It constitutes professional development for the individuals involved, improving their awareness of their practice and their analytical abilities.
- It injects innovation into systems characterised by staid and stale practices.
- It improves the normally poor relationship between teachers and researchers.
- Although usually lacking to some extent in rigour, action research is preferable to the more subjective and impressionistic approaches by which teachers usually monitor and develop their practice.

There can be considerable benefit for the teacher in carrying out action research. A more complex question concerns its benefits for the wider educational community. In any balanced consideration of the virtues of action research, we have to remember its purpose; the primary idea behind action research is to benefit the practitioner-researcher and their charges, and only secondarily to inform the wider community of researchers and teachers. So it is perhaps unfair to criticise action research studies on the basis of their generalisability to other contexts, their obvious limitation. Moreover, it could be argued that all research based in the real educational environment is conducted in a specific context and that academic researchers who assume generalisability are simply naive. In one sense, action researchers are simply more aware than some academics concerning the wider applicability of their findings.

A less talked of but potentially more serious issue with action research concerns the ability of untrained practitioners to conduct research effectively. The lack of awareness of the seriousness of this problem was well expressed in the comment 'surely bad research is better than no research' (anon., personal communication). Actually 'bad research' may be considerably more harmful than no research, because it can produce misleading findings and lead to practitioners following unsound practices. Consequently, there is a strong case for collaboration between teachers wishing to conduct action research and trained researchers. However, an additional problem concerning action research is that in attempting to emulate researchers, teachers devalue their core skills and strengthen the status differences between practising teachers and education academics. This may lead to a paternalistic relationship between practitioners and researchers and inadvertently contribute to the low status of teachers. There is thus a counter-argument against collaboration and potentially against action research itself. This problem can only be overcome if quality training in research methodology is made available to teachers, so they become able to determine their own research agenda and plan and conduct research in their own right.

Reflection point

Consider where you stand on the question of action research. Is it only useful to the teacher-researcher and their learners? How does it compare with traditional scientific research?

Multiple studies: review and meta-analysis

Besides research papers describing individual studies, the education litera-ture contains review papers that aim to provide an overview of a research field, often drawing conclusions pointed to by the bulk of studies. Some research reviews are relatively informal. Typically these papers finish with a tentative conclusion about what the bulk of studies point towards and identify directions for future research. However, two formal review methods are worth looking at in more detail.

Systematic review

As the name suggests, systematic reviews are rather more systematic than informal reviews. Whereas informal reviews may aim to provide a general overview of the state of play in a field of research, systematic reviews tend to have one or more specific aims. For example, the aims of a recent systematic review by Dunlop (2004) were to identify the most commonly used and most effective interventions in teacher stress. Systematic reviews come into their own when there has been a large volume of research into an area but methodologies and results are inconsistent, making overall conclusions difficult to reach.

The first stage to conducting a systematic review is to define the area that is being researched and to gather together as many studies as possible that seem relevant to that issue. Typically this is done using manual searches (going through the journals in a university library), electronic searches using keyword searches of databases such as ERIC and PsycINFO, and perhaps by consulting experts in the particular field. This stage can generate several hundred studies; the Dunlop study initially identified over 1000 references. The next task is to cut down the number of studies being examined to a manageable number of directly relevant studies.

First, studies that have corresponding key words but actually a different focus are discarded. Then more rigorous criteria may be applied to eliminate studies that are relevant to the research question but whose methods are not up to the highest standards. In some reviews this is made impossible by the general poor quality of research in a field. Where there is a substantial body of quality research, choosing the criteria on which to eliminate studies is fraught with difficulty. By deciding that a particular approach to researching a problem is not appropriate, an influential research team or tradition can be taken out of the reckoning and the overall conclusions skewed; this is clearly open to bias. Finally, at least in principle, a small number of studies are left that focus precisely on the issue being examined and have been carried out to the highest standards. Looking at their findings, it is possible to come to a conclusion about what the research in this field shows.

Meta-analysis

If systematic review is a qualitative method for arriving at overall conclusions from large numbers of studies, meta-analysis is its quantitative equivalent. A large proportion of education research involves small samples studied in a particular context, which may or may not generalise more widely. Meta-analysis involves combining the results of a number of smaller studies, weighting each for sample size, and arriving at an overall figure. For example, we might have 20 small-scale studies concerned with the effectiveness of cognitive acceleration in boosting the results of public examinations. Combining these results has several benefits. First, we end up with a large sample size encompassing a good range of contexts. Second, the statistical method of meta-analysis expresses findings as an *effect size*. This allows us to see just how powerful are the benefits of cognitive acceleration. Effect size is expressed in standard deviations and plotted on a normal distribution curve (Figure 10.2).

In Figure 10.2 meta-analysis shows a shift of one standard deviation. An intervention like cognitive acceleration, with an effect size of one standard deviation, would move a child on average from the second percentile (i.e. the bottom 2% of the population) to the thirty-fourth percentile, putting them in the top two-thirds of the population.

Glass and Smith, who developed the technique, carried out the first meta-analysis in education in the 1970s, investigating the relationship between

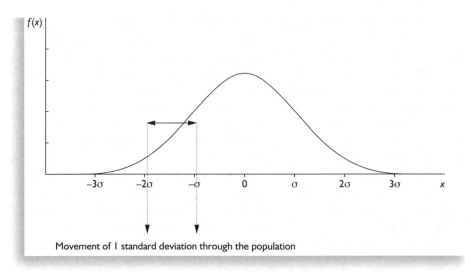

Movement of 1 standard deviation through the population

Figure 10.2 **An effect size of one standard deviation**

class sizes and learning (Glass and Smith, 1978). Some 725 small studies were found and included in the meta-analysis, giving a total sample of almost 900 000. A clear association between class size and learning emerged. A further advantage of meta-analysis is the ability to filter the studies input to the equation so as to isolate particular conditions. For example, Glass and Smith were able to look at the class size–learning relationship in different subjects and age groups. Interestingly, age and subject did not affect the findings – class size mattered regardless.

Discussion of review methods

Systematic review and meta-analysis have been tremendous steps forward in understanding the factors affecting educational outcome and the success of various interventions; small-scale studies are no longer limited by their context and become part of a greater whole. However, there are important limitations to the technique. First, the validity of the results depends on the quality of the data input. As computer programmers say: garbage in, garbage out. Combining the results of methodologically poor studies may simply compound the problems of each. Moreover, there is a serious risk of bias in the selection of studies, meaning that a reviewer or meta-analyst can consciously or unconsciously influence findings by favouring one research tradition over another.

Criticisms and limitations of education research

It is an unfortunate but undeniable fact that education research often has little credibility with practitioners. Setting aside the more abstract debates concerning the epistemology and ideology of education research, there are two major practical limitations, quality and relevance.

The quality issue

Although there is no single agreed criterion for what constitutes 'quality research', there is widespread concern over the quality of some education research, as opposed to research in educational psychology. A. Hargreaves (1997) compared the research base underlying education with that of medicine and concluded that it was seriously lacking in rigour. In one influential review, Tooley and Darby (1998) report that of a random selection of published studies, only one-third met the majority of their quality criteria, which were rigorous sampling and triangulation, use of primary sources and the avoidance of bias. Few quantitative studies in education employ multivariate designs, and many qualitative studies do not follow published research protocols. In their interviews with funding bodies, Hillage *et al.* found widespread criticism. As one respondent put it, 'We get endless research outlines that are, quite frankly, rubbish. Some are very good, but generally the volume has gone up while the average quality has fallen' (1998, p. 25). Hillage *et al.* summarise the concerns over research quality in four categories:

- *Duplication and replication*: an overabundance of duplication, with different research teams 'reinventing the wheel', and a corresponding lack of replication, whereby ideas are retested in different contexts using different methodologies.
- *Quality assurance procedures*: lack of agreed protocols for the conduct of particular methods and of mentoring for inexperienced researchers.
- *Peer review*: lack of accountability for reviewers leading to inadequate peer input, mismatch in area of expertise between reviewer and reviewed, and a conservative bias against more radical and innovative ideas.
- *Methodological rigour and researcher skills*: lack of research expertise in teacher-trainers, who conduct most education research, leading to research with small unrepresentative samples, poor experimental control and oversimple analysis, both quantitative and qualitative.

The relevance issue

Although teachers are concerned with the rigour of education research (e.g. quickly spotting context-specificity in published studies), a more common objection from practitioners concerns the *relevance* of much published research to their everyday practice. Only a minority of published studies are directly concerned with teaching or learning. It can be a formidable task for the teacher to go to the literature and locate a study into precisely the issue they want, based within their subject, conducted on learners of the age group they teach and using a sample with a similar demographic profile. Arguably, education research has collectively failed to provide what the teacher needs unless such studies are available.

Educational psychology research raises different issues. Some studies, such as those testing the psychometric properties of assessment tools, are of little or no interest to teachers, but a large proportion of studies deal with issues like motivation (22% of articles published in the *British Journal of Educational Psychology* in 2003), emotional factors in learning (13%) and learning styles (10%), which are of direct interest. The problem for teachers tends to be the *accessibility* of educational psychology research. Studies are most commonly multivariate quantitative designs that are anything but user-friendly to the uninitiated. Educational psychology is further characterised by the use of highly technical terms and the assumption of a degree of familiarity with a different set of theories than those typically expounded in initial teacher training.

Reflection point

Reflect on your own experiences of using education research. Where do you stand on the issues of quality and relevance?

Conclusions and personal reflections

For the past 100 years there has been research into education, but the field is still characterised by some important tensions: between proponents of policy-related research and proponents of blue skies research, between qualitative traditions and quantitative traditions, and between those whose background lies in psychology and sociology. Although these divisions can engender bad feeling on occasion, actually it is healthy for an academic discipline to be influenced by a range of perspectives. Without support for blue skies research the field risks becoming utilitarian; on the other hand, a preponderance of esoteric research too far removed from the concerns of practitioners could lead to the divorce of research and practice and ultimately diminish its importance. The tradition of psychological research in education has brought with it sophisticated designs that can illuminate subtle relationships between variables; these are most highly developed in educational psychology. The contribution of sociology is seen in the appreciation of social context and ideological implications of research.

Although education research can offer a variety of benefits, it has attracted a variety of critiques. These range from its lack of rigour compared with other academic disciplines to its lack of relevance and accessibility to teachers. In many cases these concerns are justified, but there is little doubt that research can inform practice, as (I hope!) is evidenced by the research cited throughout this book. A related problem concerns the role of the teacher in research. Conducting action research has often been suggested as a means of bridging the gap between research and practice. While action research has undoubted benefits for institutions and individual practitioners, I would challenge its role in bridge-building on the basis that all too often action research simply means inferior research by untrained researchers. As well as generating misleading findings, poor-quality teacher research encourages a paternalistic relationship between 'real' researchers and teachers in which the teachers try and fail to emulate the researchers, confirming their status.

Self-assessment questions

1. Discuss the purpose of education research with reference to the engineering model and the place of blue skies research.

2. What is knowledge? Consider how alternative views on the nature of knowledge can inform research.

3. Critically discuss the benefits of action research. How does it compare with mainstream academic research?

4. What criticisms have been levelled at education research, and how justified are they? Illustrate your answer with examples drawn from other chapters.

5. Critically compare the research agenda of education and educational psychology. Refer to research topics and research methods, and compare their relative quality and relevance to practice.

Further reading

•••••• Anon. (2003) In praise of educational research. A special issue of *British Educational Research Journal*, 29(5).

•••••• Cohen, L. and Manion, L. (1994) *Research Methods in Education*. Routledge, London.

•••••• Hammersley, M. (ed.) (1993) *Educational Research: Current Issues*. Paul Chapman, London.

•••••• Hayes, N. (2000) *Doing Psychological Research*. Open University Press, Milton Keynes, Bucks.

•••••• Hillage, J., Pearson, R., Anderson, A. and Tamkin, P. (1998) *Excellence in Research in Schools*. HMSO, Norwich.

References

Abrams, M. and Ellis, A. (1996) Rational emotive behaviour therapy in the treatment of stress. In: *Stress Management And Counselling* (ed. Palmer, S. and Dryden, W.). Cassell, London.

Adams, E. (2001) A proposed causal model of teacher stress. *Journal of Vocational Education and Training*, 53, 223–246.

Adey, P. and Shayer, M. (1994) *Really Raising Standards: Cognitive Intervention and Academic Achievement*. Routledge, London.

Adey, P. and Shayer, A. (2002) *Learning Intelligence*. Open University Press, Milton Keynes, Bucks.

Admiraal, W. F., Korthagen, F. A. J. and Wubbels, T. (2000) Effects of student teachers' coping behaviour. *British Journal of Educational Psychology*, 70, 33–52.

Ainsworth, M. D. S., Blehar, M. C., Waters, E. and Wall, E. (1978) *Patterns of Attachment*. Lawrence Erlbaum, Hillsdale NJ.

Albee, G. W. (2000) Commentary on prevention and counselling psychology. *The Counselling Psychologist*, 28, 845–853.

Allinson, J. and Hayes, C. (1996) The cognitive style index: a measure of intuition-analysis for organisational research. *Journal of Management Studies*, 33, 119–135.

Allport, D. A. (1980) Attention and performance. In: *Cognitive Psychology: New Directions* (ed. Claxton, G.). Routledge, London.

Aluja, A. and Blanch, A. (2002) The children depression inventory as a predictor of social and scholastic competence. *European Journal of Psychological Assessment*, 18, 259–274.

Alvarez, A. (1992) *Live Company*. Routledge, London.

Alvidrez, J. and Weinstein, R. S. (1999) Early teacher perceptions and later student academic achievement. *Journal of Educational Psychology*, 91, 731–746.

Anderson, J. R. (1995) *Learning and Memory: An Integrated Approach*. John Wiley, Chichester, W. Sussex.

Anderson, V. L., Levinson, E. M., Barker, W. and Kiewra, K. R. (1999) The effects of meditation on teacher perceived occupational stress, state and trait anxiety and burnout. *School Psychology Quarterly*, 14, 3–25.

Andreani, O. D. (1995) Knowledge and intrinsic motivation. *European Journal for High Ability*, 6, 220–225.

AQA (2000) GCE Psychology Specification A. AQA, Guildford, Surrey.

Aronson, J., Fried, C. B. and Good, C. (2002) Reducing the effects of stereotype threat on African American college students by shaping theories of intelligence. *Journal of Experimental Social Psychology*, 38, 113–125.

Atkinson, L., Niccols, A., Paglia, A., Coolbear, J., Parker, K. C. H., Poulton, L., Guger, S. and Sitarenios, G. (2000) A meta-analysis of time between maternal sensitivity and attachment assessments: implications for internal working models in infancy/toddlerhood. *Journal of Social and Personal Relationships*, 17, 791–810.

Bacete, F. J. G. and Remirez, J. R. (2001) Family and personal correlates of academic achievement. *Psychological Reports*, 88, 533–547.

Baharudin, R. and Luster, T. (1998) Factors related to the quality of home environment and children's achievement. *Journal of Family Issues*, 19, 375–403.

Bain, J., Mills, C., Ballantyne, R. and Packer, J. (2002) Developing reflection of practice through journal writing: impacts of variations in the focus and level of feedback. *Teachers and Teaching: Theory and Practice*, 8, 176–196.

Baldry, A. C. and Farrington, D. P. (2004) Evaluation of an intervention programme for the reduction of bullying and victimisation in schools. *Aggressive Behaviour*, 30, 1–15.

Bandura, A. (1986) *Social Foundations of Thought and Action*. Prentice Hall, Englewood Cliffs NJ.

Bandura, M. and Dweck, C. S. (1981) The relationship of conceptions of intelligence and achievement goals to achievement-related cognition, affect and behaviour. Unpublished manuscript, Harvard University, Cambridge MA.

Barber, P. (2002) Critical analysis of psychological research: rationale and design for a proposed course for the undergraduate psychology curriculum. *Psychology Learning and Teaching*, **2**(2), 95–101.

Barnett, W. S. (1998) Long-term cognitive and academic effects of early childhood education of children in poverty. *Preventative Medicine*, **27**, 204–207.

Barrett, M. and Trevitt, J. (1991) *Attachment Behaviour and the School Child: An Introduction to Educational Therapy*. Routledge, London.

Bassey, M. (1995) *Creating Education through Research*. BERA, Edinburgh.

Becta (2003) ICT research. www.becta.org.uk/research.

Beishuizen, J. J., Hof, E., van Putten, C. M., Bouwmeester, S. and Asscher, J. (2001) Students' and teachers' cognitions about good teachers. *British Journal of Educational Psychology*, **71**, 185–201.

Benmansour, N. (1998) Job satisfaction, stress and coping strategies among Moroccan high school teachers. *Mediterranean Journal of Educational Studies*, **3**, 12–33.

Bhargava, A. (2002) Gender bias in computer software programmes: a checklist for teachers. *Information Technology in Childhood Education Annual*, **14**, 205–218.

Bibou-Nakou, I., Stogiannidou, A. and Kiosseoglou, G. (1999) The relation between teacher burnout and teachers' attributions and practices regarding school behaviour problems. *School Psychology International*, **20**, 209–217.

Binet, A. and Simon, T. (1905) Methodes nouvelles pour le diagnostic du niveau intellectuel des anormoux. *L'Annee Psychologique*, **11**, 191–244.

Bion, W. R. (1962) The psycho-analytic study of thinking. *Proceedings of the 22nd International Psychoanalytic Congress*, pp. 306–310.

Björkvist, K., Osterman, K. and Kaukiainen, A. (1992) The development of direct and indirect aggressive strategies in males and females. In: *Of Mice and Women: Aspects of Female Aggression* (ed. Bjorkvist, K. and Niemala, P.). Academic Press, San Diego CA.

Blackmore, J. (1996) Doing emotional labour in the education market place: stories from the field of women in management. *Discourse: Studies in the Cultural Politics of Education*, **17**, 337–349.

Blagg, N., Ballinger, M. and Gardner, R. (1988) *Somerset Thinking Skills Course*. Simon & Schuster, Hemel Hempstead, Herts.

Blatchford, P. (1996) Pupils' views on school and work from 7–16 years. *Research Papers in Education*, **11**, 263–288.

Blatchford, P. and Sumpner, C. (1998) What do we know about break time? Results from a national survey of break time and lunch time in primary and secondary schools. *British Educational Research Journal*, **24**, 79–94.

Bloom, B. S. (ed.) (1956) *Taxonomy of Educational Objectives: The Classification of Educational Goals*, Handbook I, *Cognitive Domain*. McKay, New York.

Bond, L., Carlin, J. B., Thomas, L., Rubin, K. and Patton, G. (2001) Does bullying cause emotional problems? A prospective study of young teenagers. *British Medical Journal*, **323**, 480–484.

Borich, G. D. and Tombari, M. L. (1997) *Educational Psychology: A Contemporary Approach*. Longman, New York.

Bornas, X. and Llabres, J. (2001) Helping students build knowledge: what computers should do. *Information Technology in Childhood Education Annual*, **13**, 267–280.

Bowlby, J. (1969) *Attachment and Loss*, Vol. I. Pimlico, London.

Bradmetz, J. (1999) Precursors of formal thought: a longitudinal study. *British Journal of Developmental Psychology*, **17**, 61–81.

Brosnan, M. J. (1999) A new methodology, an old story? Gender differences in the 'draw a computer' test. *European Journal of Psychology of Education*, **14**, 375–385.

Brouwers, A. and Tomic, W. (2000) A longitudinal study of teacher burnout and perceived self-efficacy in classroom management. *Teaching and Teacher Education*, **16**, 239–253.

Brown, A. L. and Palincsar, A. S. (1989) Guided co-operative learning and individual knowledge acquisition. In: *Knowing, Learning and Instruction: Essays in Honour of Robert Glaser* (ed. Resnick, L. B.). Lawrence Erlbaum, Hillsdale NJ, pp. 393–451.

Bruntlett, S. (2001) Making and using multimedia: a critical examination of the learning opportunities. In: *Issues in Teaching Using ICT* (ed. Leask, M.). Routledge Falmer, London.

Burman, E. (1994) *Deconstructing Developmental Psychology*. Routledge, London.

Butler, S. (2001) College websites, intranets, on-line learning. *Virtual Learning Environments*, no. 31.

Cahill, L. T., Kaminer, R. K. and Johnson, P. G. (1999) Developmental, cognitive and behavioural sequelae of child abuse. *Child and Adolescent Clinics of North America*, **8**, 827–843.

Cains, R. A. and Brown, C. R. (1998) Newly qualified teachers: a comparative analysis of the perceptions held by BEd and PGCE trained primary teachers of the level and frequency of stress experienced during the first year of teaching. *Educational Psychology*, **18**, 97–110.

Capel, S. A. (1997) Changes in students' anxieties and concerns after their first and second teaching practices. *Educational Research*, **39**, 211–228.

Carlyle, D. and Woods, P. (2002) *Emotions of Teacher Stress*. Trentham Books, Stoke-on-Trent, Staffs.

Carrey, N. J., Butter, H. J., Persinger, M. A. and Bialik, R. J. (1996) Physiological and cognitive correlates of child abuse. *Journal of the American Academy of Child and Adolescent Psychiatry*, **34**, 1067–1075.

Cassidy, S. and Eachus, P. (2002) Developing the computer user self-efficacy (CUSE) scale: investigating the relationship between computer self-efficacy, gender and experience with computers. *Journal of Educational Computing*, **26**, 133–153.

Catalano, R. F., Berglund, L., Ryan, A. M., Lonczak, H. S. and Olson, J. J. (2002) Positive youth development in the United States: research findings on evaluations of positive youth development programmes. *Prevention and Treatment* **5**, article 15.

Cernovsky, Z. Z. (1997) A critical look at intelligence research. In: *Critical Psychology: An Introduction* (ed. Fox, D. and Prilleltensky, L.). Sage, London.

Chaiken, A., Sigler, E. and Derlega, V. (1974) Non-verbal mediators of teacher expectancy effects. *Journal of Personality and Social Psychology*, **30**, 144–149.

Chan, D. W. (2001) Assessing giftedness of Chinese secondary students in Hong Kong: a multiple intelligences perspective. *High Ability Studies*, **12**, 215–234.

Chen, P. (2002) Exploring the accuracy and predictability of the self-efficacy beliefs of seventh-grade mathematics students. *Learning and Individual Differences*, **141**, 77–90.

Childress, M. D. and Overbaugh, R. C. (2001) The relationship between learning style and achievement in a one-way video, two-way audio preservice teacher education computer literacy course. *International Journal of Educational Telecommunications*, **7**, 57–71.

Chorney, L. A. (1998) Self-defeating beliefs and stress in teachers. *Dissertation Abstracts International*, **58**, 2820.

Christison, M. A. (1999) Multiple intelligences: theory and practice in adult ESL. *ERIC Digest*.

Churach, D. and Fisher, D. (2001) Science students surf the web: effects on constructivist classroom environments. *Journal of Computers in Mathematics and Science Teaching*, **20**, 221–247.

Church, M. (2000) Understanding genius. *The Psychologist*, **13**, 445–446.

Cifuentes, L. and Murphy, K. L. (2000) Promoting multicultural understanding and positive self-concept through a distance learning community: cultural connections. *Educational Technology: Research and Development*, **48**, 69–83.

Clarke, C. (2004) Secretary of State for Education. Available at www.becta.org.uk/corporate/index.cfm. Accessed 9 February 2004.

Coalter, M. (2002) *An Educated Approach to Stress*. City of York Council.

Cohen, L. and Manion, L. (1994) *Research Methods in Education*. Routledge, London.

Coie, J. D. and Dodge, K. A. (1983) Continuities and changes in children's social status: a five-year longitudinal study. *Merrill-Palmer Quarterly*, **29**, 261–282.

Coie, J. D. and Dodge, K. A. (1988) Multiple sources of data on social behaviour and social status in the school: a cross-age comparison. *Child Development*, **59**, 815–829.

Coie, J. D., Dodge, K. A. and Coppotelli, H. (1982) Dimensions and types of social status: a cross-age perspective. *Developmental Psychology*, **18**, 557–570.

Cole, M. (1996) *Cultural Psychology: A Once and Future Discipline*. Harvard University Press, Cambridge MA.

Conner, D. B. and Cross, D. R. (2003) Longitudinal analysis of the presence, efficacy and stability of maternal scaffolding during informal problem-solving interactions. *British Journal of Developmental Psychology*, **21**, 315–334.

Conyne, R. K. (1991) Gains in primary prevention: implications for the counselling profession. *Journal of Counselling and Development*, **69**, 277–279.

Cooper, C. (1999) *Intelligence and Abilities*. Routledge, London.

Cooper, C. L., Cooper, R. D. and Eaker, L. H. (1988) *Living with Stress*. Penguin, Harmondsworth.

Copeland-Mitchell, J., Denham, S. A. and DeMulder, E. K. (1997) Q-sort assessment of child–teacher attachment relationships and social competence in the preschool. *Early Education and Development*, **8**, 27–39.

Coren, A. (1997) *A Psychodynamic Approach to Education*. Sheldon, London.

Cornwell, B. (2001) Will awareness of their own intelligence profiles help my students become more independent learners. In: *Multiple intelligences in practice* (ed. Kallenbach, S. and Viens, J.). NCSALL occasional paper.

Cote, J. E. and Levine, C. G. (2000) Attitude vs aptitude: is intelligence or motivation more important for positive higher-educational outcomes? *Journal of Adolescence Research*, **15**, 58–80.

Cox, T. (1978) *Stress*. Macmillan, Basingstoke, Hants.

Craik, F. I. M. and Lockhart, R. S. (1972) Levels of processing: a framework for memory research. *Journal of Verbal Learning and Verbal Behaviour*, **11**, 671–684.

Craske, M. L. (1988) Learned helplessness, self-worth motivation and attribution retraining for primary school children. *British Journal of Educational Psychology*, **58**, 152–164.

Crook, C. (1994) *Computers and the Collaborative Experience of Learning*. Routledge, London.

Cuban, L. (1993) Computers meet classroom: classroom wins. *Teachers College Record*, **95**, 185–210.

Dal Vesco, A., Mattos, D., Beninca, C. and Tarasconi, C. (1998) Correlation between, WISC and school performance in public and private schools. *Psicologia: Reflexao e Critica*, **11**, 481–495.

Daniels, K. (1996) Why aren't managers concerned about occupational stress? *Work and Stress*, **10**, 352–366.

Davydov, V. V. (1995) The influence of L. S. Vygotsky on education theory, research and practice. *Educational Researcher*, **24**, 12–21.

Dawes, L. (2000) First connections: teachers and the National Grid for learning. *Computers and Education*, **33**, 235–252.

Dawes, L. (2001) What stops teachers using new technology? In: *Issues in Teaching Using ICT* (ed. Leask, M.). Routledge Falmer, London.

Day, J. D. and Cordon, L. A. (1993) Static and dynamic measures of ability: an experimental comparison. *Journal of Educational Psychology*, **85**, 75–82.

Deci, E. L., Vallerand, R. J., Pelletier, L. G. and Ryan, R. M. (1991) Motivation and education: the self determination perspective. *Educational Psychologist*, **26**, 325–346.

De Landsheere, G. (1988) History of education research. In: *Educational Research, Methodology and Measurement: An International Handbook* (ed. Keeves, J. P.). Pergamon, Oxford.

DfEE (2000) *Don't Suffer in Silence*. DfEE, London.

Doherty, K. and Anderson, I. (1998) Talking about rape. *The Psychologist*, **11**, 583–587.

Donaldson, M. (1978) *Children's Minds*. Fontana, London.

Donegan, M. (2002) TELENET project, summary report. ACE Centre, www.ace-centre. org.uk.

Duff (1997) A note on the reliability and validity of a 30-item version of Entwistle and Tait's Revised Approaches to Studying Inventory. *British Journal of Education Psychology*, **67**, 529–541.

Dufresne, R., Mestre, J., Hart, D. M. and Rath, K. A. (2002) The effect of web-based homework on test performance in large enrolment introductory physics courses. *Journal of Computers in Mathematics and Science Teaching*, **21**, 229–251.

Duncan, R. D. (1999) Maltreatment by parents and peers: the relationship between child abuse, bully victimisation and psychological distress. *Child Maltreatment*, **4**, 45–55.

Dunlop, C. (2004) Report of the Healthy Working Lives Research Group. Paper presented at the Improving Employee Effectiveness in the Public Sector Conference, University of Stirling, September 2004.

Dunn, J. and Munn, P. (1985) Becoming a family member: family conflict and the development of social understanding in the first year. *Child Development*, **50**, 306–318.

Dupeyrat, C. and Marine, C. (2001) Implicit theories of intelligence, achievement goals and learning strategy use. *Psychologische Beitrage*, **43**, 34–52.

Durlak, J. and Wells, A. (1997) Primary prevention mental health programmes for children and adolescents: a meta-analytic review. *American Journal of Community Psychology*, **25**, 115–152.

Dussault, M., Deaudelin, C., Royer, N. and Loiselle, J. (1999) Professional isolation and occupational stress in teachers. *Psychological Reports*, **84**, 943–946.

Dweck, C. S. (1991) *Self-theories and Goals: Their Role in Motivation, Personality and Development*. Nebraska Symposium on Motivation 38, University of Nebraska.

Dweck, C. S. (2000) *Self-theories: Their Role in Motivation, Personality and Development*. Psychology Press, Philadelphia PA.

Dweck, C. S., Chiu, C. and Hong, Y. (1995) Implicit theories and their role in judgments and reactions: a world from two perspectives. *Psychological Inquiry*, **6**, 267–285.

Edexcel (2000) *Edexcel Advanced Subsidiary GCE in Psychology*. Edexcel, London.

Engler, B. (1999) *Personality Theories: An Introduction*. Houghton-Mifflin, Boston.

Entwistle, N. J. and Tait, H. (1994) *The Revised Approaches to Studying Inventory*. University of Edinburgh, Edinburgh.

Entwistle, N. J., Hanley, M. and Hounsell, M. (1979) Identifying distinctive approaches to studying. *Higher Education*, **8**, 365–380.

Entwistle, N. J., Hounsell, D., Macaulay, C., Situnayke, G. and Tait, H. (1989) *The Performance of Electrical Engineering Students in Scottish Higher Education*. Final report to the Scottish Education Department. University of Edinburgh, Edinburgh.

Erwin, P. (1998) *Friendships in Childhood and Adolescence*. Routledge, London.

Facione, N. C. and Facione, P. A. (1997) *Critical Thinking Assessment and Nursing Education Programs: An Aggregate Data Analysis*. California Academic Press, Millbrae CA.

Facione, P. A. (1995) The disposition toward critical thinking. *Journal of General Education*, **44**, 1–25.

Faria, L. (1998) Personal conceptions of intelligence, attributions and school achievement: development of a comprehensive model of inter-relations during adolescence. *Psicologia: Revista da Associacao Psicologia*, **12**, 101–113.

Faria, L. and Fontaine, A. M. (1997) Adolescents' person conceptions of intelligence: the development of a new scale and some exploratory evidence. *European Journal of Psychology of Education*, **12**, 51–62.

Felder, R. (1993) Reaching the second tier: learning and teaching styles in college science education. *Journal of College Science Teaching*, **23**, 286–290.

Felder, R. and Henriques, E. R. (1995) Learning and teaching styles in foreign and second language education. *Foreign Language Annals*, **28**, 21–31.

Felder, R. M. and Silverman, L. K. (1988) Learning and teaching styles in engineering education. *Engineering Education*, **78**, 674–681.

Fenstermacher, G. D. and Soltis, J. F. (1992) *Approaches to Teaching*. Teachers' College Press, New York.

Feuerstein, R. and Rand, Y. (1977) *Studies in Cognitive Modifiability. Instrumental Enrichment: Redevelopment of Cognitive Functions of Retarded Early Adolescents*. HWCRI, Jerusalem.

Feuerstein, R., Rand, Y., Hoffman, M. B. and Miller, R. (1980) *Instrumental Enrichment: An Intervention for Cognitive Modifiability*. University Park Press, Baltimore MD.

Fisher, R. (1995) *Teaching Children to Think*. Nelson Thornes, Cheltenham, Glos.

Fisher, R. (2001) The Queen's Beacon School thinking skills project. Summary paper for the TTA/DfEE Teacher Research Conference, March 2001.

Fisher, R. (2002) *Inside the Literacy Hour*. Routledge Falmer, London.

Fisher, R. (2003) *Teaching Thinking*. Continuum, London.

Flavell, J. H. (1985) *Cognitive Development*. Prentice Hall, Englewood Cliffs NJ.

Flavell, J. H. (1999) Cognitive development: children's knowledge about the mind. *Annual Review of Psychology*, **50**, 21–45.

Fodor, J. (1983) Modularity of mind. In: *Cultural Psychology: A Once and Future Discipline* (ed. Cole, M.). Harvard University Press, Cambridge MA.

Foot, H., Morgan, M. and Shute, R. (1990) *Children Helping Children*. John Wiley, Chichester, W. Sussex.

Ford, N. and Chen, S. Y. (2000) Individual differences, hypermedia navigation and learning: an empirical study. *Journal of Educational Multimedia and Hypermedia*, **9**, 281–311.

Foster, P. (1997) How should we judge the usefulness of educational research? *Times Educational Supplement*, 21 November.

Fowler, W. (1990) Early stimulation and the development of verbal talents. In: *Encouraging the Development of Exceptional Abilities and Talents* (ed. Howe, M. J. A.). British Psychology Society, Leicester.

Freud, S. (1914) *The Psychopathology of Everyday Life*. Hogarth Press, London.

Friedman, I. A. (2000) Burnout in teachers: shattered dreams of impeccable professional performance. *Journal of Clinical Psychology*, **56**, 595–606.

Furst-Bowe, J. A. (1997) Comparison of student reactions in traditional and videoconferencing courses in training and development. *International Journal of Instructional Media*, **24**, 197–206.

Gagne, F. and StPere, F. (2002) When IQ is controlled, does motivation still predict achievement? *Intelligence*, **30**, 71–100.

Galton, F. (1884) *Record of Family Faculties*. Macmillan, London.

Galton, M. and Williamson, J. (1992) *Groupwork in the Primary School*. Routledge, London.

Garber, H. L. (1988) *The Milwaukee Project: Preventing Mental Retardation in Children at Risk*. American Association of Mental Retardation, Washington DC.

Garcia, P. A. (2002) Online assistants in children's hypermedia software. *Information Technology in Childhood Education Annual*, **14**, 103–121.

Gardner, H. (1983) *Frames of Mind*. Harper Collins, New York.

Gardner, H. (1993) *Frames of Mind*, 2nd edn. Harper Collins, New York.

Gardner, H. (1997) *Building a Bridge to Knowledge for Every Child*. Edutopia, www.glef.org.

Gardner, H. (1999) *Intelligence Reframed: Multiple Intelligences for the 21st Century*. Basic Books, New York.

Gardner, H. (2002) Interview with Steen Nepper Larsen, 30 January 2002, www.pz.harvard.edu/ PIs/HG.htm.

Gardner, H. (2003) Multiple intelligences after twenty years. Invited address to the American Psychological Association.

Gaskill, P. J. and Murphy, P. K. (2004) Effects of a memory strategy on second-graders' performance and self-efficacy. *Contemporary Educational Psychology*, **29**, 27–49.

Gilbert, J. (1999) But where is the teacher? Cost-effective distance learning made possible. *Learning and Teaching with Technology*, **27**, 42–44.

Gillies, R. M. (2003) The behaviours, interactions and perceptions of junior high school students during small group learning. *Journal of Educational Psychology*, **95**, 137–147.

Glass, G. V. and Smith, M. L. (1978) *Meta-analysis of Research on the Relationship between Class Size and Achievement*. Far West Laboratory, San Francisco.

Goleman, D. (1996) *Emotional Intelligence*. Bloomsbury, London.

Good, T. L. and Brophy, J. E. (1991) *Looking in Classrooms*. Harper & Row, New York.

Gorey, K. M. (2001) Early childhood education: a meta-analytic affirmation of the short- and long-term benefits of educational opportunity. *School Psychology Quarterly*, **16**, 9–30.

Goswami, U. (1998) *Cognition in Children*. Psychology Press, Hove, W. Sussex.

Gregorc, A. R. (1982) Style delineator. MA, Gabriel Systems.

Greene, R. W., Abidin, R. R. and Kmetz, C. (1997) The index of teaching stress: a measure of teacher–student compatibility. *Journal of School Psychology*, **35**, 239–259.

Greenhalgh, P. (1994) *Emotional Growth and Learning*. Routledge, London.

Griffith, J., Steptoe, A. and Cropley, M. (1999) An investigation of coping strategies associated with job stress in teachers. *British Journal of Educational Psychology*, **69**, 517–531.

Grigorenko, E. L. and Carter, A. S. (1996) Co-twin, peer and mother–child relationships and IQ in a Russian adolescent twin sample. *Journal of Russian and East European Psychology*, **34**, 59–87.

Grigorenko, E. L., Jarvin, L. and Sternberg, R. J. (2002) School-based tests of the triarchic theory of intelligence: three settings, three samples, three syllabi. *Contemporary Educational Psychology*, **27**, 167–208.

Gross, R. (2000) *Psychology: The Science of Mind and Behaviour*. Hodder & Stoughton, London.

Hall, E., Hall, C. and Abaci, R. (1997) The effects of human relations training on reported teacher stress, pupil control ideology and locus of control. *British Journal of Educational Psychology*, **67**, 483–496.

Hallinan, P. and Danaher, P. (1994) The effect of contracted grades on self-efficacy and motivation in teacher education courses. *Educational Research*, **36**(1), 75–82.

Handy, J. (1995) Rethinking stress: seeing the collective. In: *Managing Stress: Emotion and Power at Work* (ed. Newton, T.). Sage, London.

Hargreaves, A. (1997) The four stages of professionalism and professional learning. *Journal of the Australian College of Education*, **23**, 86–114.

Hargreaves, D. H. (1996) Teaching as a research-based profession: possibilities and prospects. TTA annual lecture.

Harris, C. A. (1999) The relationship between principal leadership styles and teacher stress in low socio-economic urban elementary schools as perceived by teachers. *Dissertation Abstracts International*, **60**, 1911.

Hart, B. and Risley, T. (1995) *Meaningful Differences in Everyday Parenting and Intellectual Development in Young Children*. Brooks, Baltimore MD.

Hartup, W. (1992) Friendships and their developmental significance. In: *Childhood Social Development: Contemporary Perspectives* (ed. McGurk, H.). Lawrence Erlbaum, Hove, W. Sussex.

Hayes, N. (1998) *Foundations of Psychology*. Nelson, London.

Hayes, N. (2000) *Doing Psychological Research*. Open University Press, Milton Keynes, Bucks.

Henson, K. T. and Eller, B. F. (1999) *Educational Psychology for Effective Teaching*. Wadsworth, Belmont CA.

Hepburn, A. and Brown, S. D. (2002) Teacher stress and the management of accountability. *Human Relations*, **54**, 691–715.

Hillage, J., Pearson, R., Anderson, A. and Tamkin, P. (1998) *Excellence in Research in Schools*. HMSO, Norwich.

Hoel, H., Rayner, C. and Cooper, C. L. (1999) Workplace bullying. In: *International Review of Industrial and Organisational Psychology* (ed. Cooper, C. L. and Robertson, I. T.). John Wiley, Chichester, W. Sussex.

Honey, P. and Mumford, A. (1992) *The Manual of Learning Styles*, revised edition. Peter Honey, Maidenhead, Berks.

Hong, Y., Chiu, C., Dweck, C. and Lin, D. (1998) A test of implicit theories and self confidence as predictors to achievement challenges. Unpublished manuscript, Harvard University, Cambridge MA.

Horppu, R. and Ikonen-Varila, M. (2001) Are attachment styles general interpersonal orientations? Applicants' perceptions and emotions in interaction with evaluators in a college entrance examination. *Journal of Social and Personal Relationships*, **18**, 131–148.

Howe, C., Tolmie, A. and Rodgers, A. (1996) The acquisition of conceptual knowledge in science by primary school children: group interaction and the understanding of motion down an incline. In: *Critical Readings on Piaget* (ed. Smith, L.). Routledge, London.

Howe, M. J. A. (1988) Hot house children. *The Psychologist*, **1**, 356–358.

Howe, M. J. A. (1998) Can IQ change? *The Psychologist*, **11**, 69–72.

Howes, C. (1997) Teacher sensitivity, children's attachment and play with peers. *Early Education and Development*, **8**, 41–49.

HSE (2002) Occupational stress statistics information sheet. HSE Books, Sudbury, Suffolk.

HSE (2003) *Tackling Stress*. HSE Books, Sudbury, Suffolk.

Hsueh, W. C. (1998) A cross-cultural comparison of gifted children's theories of intelligence, goal orientation and responses to challenge. *Dissertation Abstracts International*, 58, 3416.

Hudson, L. (1966) *Contrary Imaginations*. Methuen, London.

Hughes, M. (1975) Egocentrism in preschool children. PhD thesis, Edinburgh University.

Ireson, J. and Hallam, S. (2001) *Ability Grouping in Education*. Paul Chapman, London.

Iszatt, J. and Colmer, E. (1996) Responding to a tragedy: consultation in school. In: *The Reflective Professional in Education* (ed. Jennings, C. and Kennedy, E.). Jessica Kingsley, London.

Jacob, A. V., Loureiro, S. R., Marturano, E. M. Linhares, M. B. M. and Machado, V. L. S. (1999) Affective behaviour and academic achievement. *Psicologia: Teoria a Pequisa*, 15, 153–162.

Jarvis, M. (2002) Teacher stress: a critical review of recent findings and suggestions for future research directions. *Stress News*, 14, 12–16.

Jarvis, M. (2003) Can social representations theory explain negative responses from teachers to CBT-based stress management training? A case analysis. *Stress News*, 15, 5–8.

Jarvis, M. (2004a) *Psychodynamic Psychology: Classical Theory and Contemporary Research*. Thomson Learning, London.

Jarvis, M. (2004b) A modern conceptual framework for understanding and managing teacher stress. Paper delivered at the Improving Employee Effectiveness in the Public Sector Conference, Stirling University, September 2004.

Jeffrey, B. and Woods, P. (1998) *Testing Teachers: The Effect of School Inspections on Primary Teachers*. Falmer Press, London.

Jennings, C. (1996) Training the reflective professional: the practice of supervision. In: *The Reflective Professional in Education* (ed. Jennings, C. and Kennedy, E.). Cassell, London.

Jennings, C. and Kennedy, E. (1996) *The Reflective Professional in Education*. Jessica Kingsley, London.

Jesson, D. (2000) Further evidence on comparative GCSE performance between selective and non-selective schools and LEAs. Paper presented at the NUT Secondary Education Conference, March 2000.

JISC (2003) Managing the future with MLEs. Joint Information Systems Committee, www.nilta.org.uk/NILTA/docs/ILT/man_future_mle.pdf.

Johnson-Pynn, J. S. and Nisbet, V. S. (2002) Preschoolers effectively tutor novice classmates in a block construction task. *Child Study Journal*, 32, 241–255.

Jules, V. and Kutnick, P. (1997) Student perceptions of a good teacher: the gender perspective. *British Journal of Educational Psychology*, 67, 497–511.

Kalu, D. (2002) Containers and containment. *Psychodynamic Practice: Individuals, Groups and Organisations*, 8, 359–373.

Kamin, L. J. (1995) Lies, damned lies and statistics. In: *The Bell Curve Debate: History, Documents, Opinions* (ed. Jaccoby, R. and Glauberman, L. B.). Times Books, New York.

Karatzias, A., Power, K. G. and Swanson, V. (2001) Bullying and victimisation in Scottish secondary schools: same or separate entities? *Aggressive Behaviour*, 28, 45–61.

Karin, N. G., Albreksten, G. and Qvarnstrom, U. (2001) Psychosomatic symptoms among victims of school bullying. *Journal of Health Psychology*, 6, 365–377.

Karmiloff-Smith, A. (1996) *Beyond Modularity*. MIT Press, Cambridge MA.

Kemmis, S. (1993) Action research. In: *Educational Research: Current Issues* (ed. Hammersley, M.). Paul Chapman, London.

Kerns, K. A. (1994) A longitudinal examination of links between mother–infant attachment and children's friendships. *Journal of Personality and Social Relationships*, 11, 379–381.

Kerns, K. A. and Stevens, A. C. (1996) Parent–child attachment in late adolescence. *Journal of Youth and Adolescence*, 25, 323–342.

Kerry, T. and Wilding, M. (2004) *Effective Classroom Teacher*. Longman, London.

Kinnunen, U. and Leskinen, E. (1989) Teacher stress during a school year: covariance and mean structure analyses. *Journal of Occupational Psychology*, 62, 111–122.

Kitayama, S. and Markus, H. R. (1992) Construal of self as cultured frame: implications for internationalising psychology. Paper presented at the Symposium on Internationalisation and Higher Education, Ann Arbor MI.

Kitzinger, J. (1994) The methodology of focus groups: the importance of interaction between research participants. *Sociology of Health and Illness*, 16, 103–121.

Klein, M. (1945) The Oedipus complex in the light of early anxieties. *International Journal of Psychoanalysis*, 26, 1.

Klein, M. (1959) Our adult world and its roots in infancy. *Human Relations*, 12, 291–303.

Kornhaber, M. L. (2001) Howard Gardner. In: *Fifty Modern Thinkers in Education* (ed. Palmer, J. A.). Routledge, London.

Koulomzin, M., Beebe, B., Anderson, S., Jaffe, J., Feldstein, S. and Crown, C. (2002) Infant gaze, head, face and self-touch at 4 months differentiate secure vs avoidant attachment at 1 year: a microanalytic approach. *Attachment and Human Development*, 4, 3–24.

Kozulin, A. (1998) *Psychological Tools: A Sociocultural Approach to Education*. Harvard University Press, London.

Kramarski, B. and Mevarech, Z. R. (1997) Cognitive-metacognitive training within a problem-solving based LOGO environment. *British Journal of Educational Psychology*, 67, 425–446.

Kumpulainen, K., Raesaenen, E. and Puura, K. (2001) Psychiatric disorders and the use of mental health service among children involved in bullying. *Aggressive Behaviour*, 27, 102–110.

Kutnick, P. and Jules, V. (1993) Pupils' perceptions of a good teacher: a developmental perspective from Trinidad and Tobago. *British Journal of Educational Psychology*, 63, 217–235.

Kutnick, P. and Manson, I. (2000) Enabling children to learn in groups. In: *The Psychology of Teaching and Learning in the Primary School* (ed. Whitebread, D.). Routledge Falmer, London.

Kyriacou, C. (1995) An evaluation of teacher appraisal in schools within one education authority. *School Organisation*, 15, 109–116.

Kyriacou, C. (2000) *Stress-Busting for Teachers*. Nelson Thornes, Cheltenham, Glos.

Kyriacou, C. (2001) Teacher stress: directions for future research. *Educational Review*, 53, 28–35.

Kyriacou, C. and Pratt, J. (1985) Teacher stress and psychoneurotic symptoms. *British Journal of Educational Psychology*, 55, 61–64.

Kyriacou, C. and Sutcliffe, J. (1978) A model of teacher stress. *Educational Studies*, 4, 1–6.

La Freniere, P. J. and Sroufe, L. A. (1985) Profiles of peer competence in the preschool: interrelations between measures, influence of social ecology and relation to attachment theory. *Developmental Psychology*, 21, 56–69.

Lane, D. J. (1998) Cognitive and clinical implications of sexual victimisation on boys. *Dissertation Abstracts International*, 59, 3064.

Langlois, J. H., Ritter, J. M., Casey, R. J. and Sawin, D. B. (1995) Infant attractiveness predicts maternal behaviours and attitudes. *Developmental Psychology*, 31, 464–472.

Larkin, M. (2002) Using scaffolding instruction to optimize learning. *ERIC Digest*.

Lazar, L., Darlington, R., Murray, H., Royce, J. and Snippet, A. (1982) Lasting effects of early education: a report for the consortium for longitudinal studies. *Monographs of the Society for Research in Child Development*, 47, 2–3.

Lazarus, R. S. and Folkman, S. (1984) Coping and adaptation. In: *The Handbook of Behavioural Medicine* (ed. Gentry, W. D.). Guilford, New York.

Leafe, D. (2001) Intranets: developing a learning community. In: *Issues in Teaching Using ICT* (ed. Leask, M.). Routledge Falmer, London.

Leary, M. R., Kowalski, R. M., Smith, L. and Phillips, S. (2003) Teasing, rejection and violence: case studies of the school shootings. *Aggressive Behaviour*, 29, 202–214.

Lee, D. and Gavine, D. (2003) Goal-setting and self-assessment in year 7 students. *Educational Research*, 45, 49–59.

Leondari, A. and Gialamas, V. (2002) Implicit theories. Goal orientations and perceived competence: impact on students' achievement behaviour. *Psychology in the Schools*, 39, 279–291.

Levy, S., Stroessner, S. and Dweck, C. (1998) Stereotype formation and endorsement: the role of implicit theories. *Journal of Personality and Social Psychology*, 74, 1421–1436.

Lewin, K. (1946) Action research and minority problems. *Journal of Social Issues*, 2, 34–46.

Lewis, A. (1992) Group child interviews as a research tool. *British Educational Research Journal*, 18, 413–421.

Lewis, J. D. and Knight, H. V. (2000) Self-concept in gifted youth: an investigation employing the Piers–Harris subscales. *Gifted Child Quarterly*, 44, 45–53.

Lewis, R. (1999) Teachers coping with the stress of classroom discipline. *Social Psychology of Education*, 3, 155–171.

Lipman, M. (1974) *Harry Stottlemeier's Discovery*. Institute for the Advancement of Philosophy for Children, Montclair State University, Montclair NJ.

Lipman, M. (1982) Philosophy for children. *Thinking*, 3, 35–44.

Loo, R. (1999) Issues in factor-analysing ipsative measures: the Learning Styles Inventory (LSI-1985) example. *Journal of Business and Psychology*, 14, 149–154.

Looker, O. and Gregson, T. (1996) The biological basis of stress management. In: *Stress Management and Counselling* (ed. Palmer, S. and Dryden, W.). Cassell, London.

Lopes, J., Cruz, C. and Rutherford, R. B. (2002) The relationship of peer perceptions to student achievement and teacher ratings of 5th and 6th grade students. *Education and Treatment of Children*, 25, 476–495.

Lou, Y., Abrami, P. C. and d'Apollonia, S. (2001) Small group and individual learning with technology: a meta-analysis. *Review of Educational Research*, 71, 449–521.

Lou, Y., Abrami, P. C., Spence, J. C., Poulsen, C., Chambers, B. and d'Appolonia, S. (1996) Within-class grouping: a meta-analysis. *Review of Educational Research*, 66, 423–458.

Lyotard, J. F. (1984) *The Postmodern Condition: A Report on Knowledge*. Manchester University Press, Manchester.

MacFadden, R. J., Maiter, S. and Dumbrill, G. C. (2002) High tech and high touch: the human face of online education. *Journal of Technology in Human Services*, 20, 283–300.

Main, M. and Solomon, J. (1986) Discovery of a disorganised disoriented attachment pattern. In: *Affective Development in Infancy* (ed. Main, M. and Solomon, J.). Ablex, Norwood NJ.

Male, D. and May, D. (1998) Stress and health, workload and burnout in learning support coordinators in colleges of further education. *Support for Learning*, 13, 134–138.

Marshall, S. P. (1990) What students learn and remember from word instruction. Paper presented at the Annual Meeting of the American Educational Research Association, Boston.

Marstrander, A. (1996) A Norwegian perspective on educational therapy. In: *Educational Therapy in Clinic and Classroom* (ed. Barrett, M. and Varma, V.). Whurr, London.

Maslach, C. and Schaufeli, W. B. (1993) Historical and conceptual development of burnout. In: *Professional Burnout: Recent Developments in Theory and Research* (ed. Maslach, C., Schaufeli, W. B. and Marek, T.). Taylor & Francis, Washington DC.

Maslow, A. (1954) *Motivation and Personality*. Harper & Row, New York.

Maslow, A. (1970) *Motivation and Personality*, 2nd edn. Harper & Row, New York.

Mautner, T. (1998) *Dictionary of Philosophy*. Penguin, Harmondsworth.

McCune, V. and Entwistle, N. (2000) The deep approach to learning: analytic abstraction and idiosyncratic development. Paper presented at the Innovations in Higher Education Conference, Helsinki.

McGarrigle, J. and Donaldson, M. (1974) Conservation accidents. *Cognition*, 3, 341–350.

McGuinness, C. (1999) *From Thinking Skills to Thinking Classrooms*. DfEE, London.

McGuinness, C. (2000) ACTS (Activating Children's Thinking Skills): a methodology for enhancing children's thinking skills. Paper presented at the ESRC TLRP First Programme Conference, Leicester University, November 2000.

McGuinness, C., Curry, C., Greer, B., Daly, P. and Salters, M. (1997) *Final Report on the ACTS Project. Phase 2: Belfast*. Northern Ireland Council for Curriculum, Examinations and Assessment.

McIntyre, D. (2000) The nature of classroom teaching expertise. In: *The Psychology of Teaching and Learning in the Primary School* (ed. Whitebread, D.). Routledge Falmer, London.

Menesini, E., Codesca, E., Benelli, B. and Cowie, H. (2003) Enhancing children's responsibility to take action against bullying: evaluation of a befriending intervention in Italian middle schools. *Aggressive Behaviour*, 29, 10–14.

Mercer, N. (2000) *Words and Minds: How We Use Language to Think Together*. Routledge, London.

Millar, J. and Jagger, N. (2001) *Women in ITEC: Courses and Careers*. Department for Education and Skills, Department for Employment, The Women's Unit, London, p. 156.

Miller, D. I., Verhoek-Miller, N., Ceminsky, J. and Nugent, C. (2000) Bullying in a school environment and its relationship with student satisfaction, performance and coping reactions. *Psychology: A Journal of Human Behaviour*, 37, 15–19.

Miller, L., Wood, T. A., Halligan, J., Keller, L., Hutchinson-Pike, C., Kornbrot, D. and deLotz, J. (2000) Saying 'welcome' is not enough: women, information systems and equity in work. *Career Development International*, 5, 379–389.

Morton, L. L., Vesco, R., Williams, N. H. and Awender, M. A. (1997) Student teacher anxieties related to class management, pedagogy, evaluation and staff relations. *British Journal of Educational Psychology*, 67, 69–89.

Mucherach, W. M. (2003) The influence of technology on the classroom climate of social studies classrooms: a multidimensional approach. *Learning Environments Research*, 6, 37–57.

Mueller, C. M. and Dweck, C. S. (1997) Implicit theories of intelligence: malleability beliefs, definitions and judgments of intelligence. Unpublished manuscript, Harvard University, Cambridge MA.

Mueller, C. M. and Dweck, C. S. (1998) Praise for intelligence can undermine children's motivation and performance. *Journal of Personality and Social Psychology*, 75, 33–52.

Myron-Wilson, P. and Smith, P. K. (1998) Attachment relationships and influences on bullying. *Proceedings of the British Psychological Society*, 6(2), 89–90.

Nash, P. (2004) The teacher support network. Paper presented at the Improving Employee Effectiveness in the Public Sector Conference, University of Stirling, September 2004.

Nath, L. R. and Ross, S. M. (2001) The influence of a peer-tutoring training model for implementing co-operative groupings with elementary students. *Educational Technology Research and Development*, 49, 41–56.

National Learning Network (2004) Learning Technologies. Available at www.ccm.ac.uk/ltech/ilt/default.asp. Accessed 9 February 2004.

Natvig, G. K., Albreksten, G. and Qvarnstrom, U. (2001) School related stress experience as a risk factor for bullying behaviour. *Journal of Youth and Adolescence*, **30**, 561–575.

Naylor, P. and Cowie, H. (1999) The effectiveness of peer support systems in challenging school bullying: the perspectives and experiences of teachers and pupils. *Journal of Adolescence*, **22**, 467–479.

Neihart, M. (1999) The impact of giftedness on psychological well-being: what does the empirical literature say? *Roeper Review*, **22**, 10–17.

Newton, T. (1995) *Managing Stress: Emotion and Power at Work*. Sage, London.

Nias, J. (1996) Thinking about feeling: the emotions in teaching. *Cambridge Journal of Education*, **26**, 293–306.

Nichols, J. D. (1996) Cooperative learning: a motivational tool to enhance student persistence, self-regulation and efforts to please teachers and parents. *Educational Research and Evaluation*, **2**, 246–260.

Nisbett, J. and Shucksmith, J. (1986) *Learning Strategies*. Routledge & Kegan Paul, London.

Nisbett, R. E. (1993) *Rules for Reasoning*. Lawrence Erlbaum, Hillsdale NJ.

NUT (1990) *Health and Safety: Teachers, Stress and Schools*. National Union of Teachers, London.

NUT (2000) *Proceedings of the Annual Conference*. National Union of Teachers, London.

O'Connell, P., Pepler, D. and Craig, W. (1999) Peer involvement in bullying: insights and challenges for intervention. *Journal of Adolescence*, **22**, 437–452.

OCR (2000) *Advanced Subsidiary GCE Psychology*. OCR, Cambridge.

Oliver, C. and Candappa, M. (2003) *Tackling Bullying: Listening to the Views of Children and Young People*. DfES, London.

Olweus, D. (1991) Bully/victim problems among schoolchildren: basic facts and effects of a school based intervention programme. In: *The Development and Treatment of Childhood Aggression* (ed. Pepler, D. and Rubin, K.). Lawrence Erlbaum, Hillsdale NJ.

Olweus, D. (1993) Victimisation by peers: antecedents and long-term outcomes. In: *Social Withdrawal, Inhibition and Shyness in Childhood* (ed. Rubin, K. and Asendorf, J. B.). Lawrence Erlbaum, Hillsdale NJ.

Olweus, D. (2001) *Olweus Core Programme against Bullying and Antisocial Behaviour: A Teacher Handbook*. Research Centre for Health Promotion, University of Bergen, Norway.

O'Moore, M. and Kirkham, C. (2001) Self-esteem and its relationship to bullying behaviour. *Aggressive Behaviour*, **27**, 269–283.

Oppenheim, A. N. (1992) *Questionnaire Design, Interviewing and Attitude Measurement*. Pinter, London.

Paivio, A. (1971) Styles and strategies of learning. *British Journal of Educational Psychology*, **46**, 128–148.

Palmer, S. (1996) The multimodal approach: theory, assessment, techniques and interventions. In: *Stress Management and Counselling* (ed. Palmer, S. and Dryden, W.). Cassell, London.

Palmer, S. (2001) Stress management: a masterclass. *Stress News*, **13**(1).

Papert, S. (1980) *Mindstorms: Children, Computers and Powerful Ideas*. Basic Books, New York.

Papert, S. (1996) *The Connected Family: Bridging the Digital Generation Gap*. Longstreet Press, Atlanta GA.

Pask, G. (1976) Style and strategies of learning. *British Journal of Educational Psychology*, **51**, 128–148.

Passey, D. (1999) Anytime anywhere learning (AAL) project evaluation. Implementation summary, Lancaster University.

Paul, R. (1993) *Critical Thinking: How to Prepare Students for a Rapidly Changing World.* Foundation for Critical Thinking, Rohnert Park CA.

Pellegrini, A. D. and Blatchford, P. (2000) *The Child at School: Interactions with Peers and Teachers.* Edward Arnold, London.

Pellegrini, A. D. and Melhuish, E. C. (1998) Friendship, individual differences and children's literacy. *Proceedings of the British Psychological Society*, 6, 90.

Perrine, R. M. (1999) Please see me: students' reactions to professors' request as a function of attachment and perceived support. *Journal of Experimental Education*, 68, 60–72.

Piaget, J. (1970) *Science of Education and the Psychology of the Child.* Orion, New York.

Piaget, J. and Inhelder, B. (1956) *The Child's Conception of Space.* Routledge & Kegan Paul, London.

Pietsche, J., Walker, R. and Chapman, E. (2003) The relationship among self-concept, self-efficacy, and performance in mathematics during secondary school. *Journal of Educational Psychology*, 95, 589–603.

Pifarre, M. and Sanuy, J. (2002) Peer problem solving: incidence of computer mediation in interaction and learning processes. *Infancia y Aprendziaje*, 25, 209–225.

Pines, A. M. (2000) Treating career burnout: a psychodynamic-existential perspective. *Journal of Clinical Psychology*, 56, 1–10.

Pines, A. M. (2002) Teacher burnout: a psychodynamic perspective. *Teachers and Teaching: Theory and Practice*, 8, 121–140.

Pithers, B. (2000) Field dependence – field independence and vocational teachers. Paper presented at the International Post-compulsory Education and Training Conference, Gold Coast, Queensland, December 2000.

Pithers, R. T. and Soden, R. (1998) Scottish and Australian teacher stress and strain: a comparative study. *British Journal of Educational Psychology*, 68, 269–279.

Postman, N. and Weingartner, C. (1971) *Teaching as a Subversive Activity.* Harmondsworth, Penguin.

Price, S. and Jones, R. A. (2001) Reflections on anti-bullying peer counselling in a comprehensive school. *Educational Psychology in Practice*, 17, 35–40.

Prior, S. M. and Welling, K. A. (2001) 'Read in your head.' A Vygotskian analysis of the transition from oral to silent reading. *Reading Psychology*, 22, 1–15.

Rafferty, F. (1997) Pension rules battle goes to court. *Times Educational Supplement*, 10 January, p. 3.

Ramey, C. T., Campbell, F. A. and Ramey, S S. L. (1999) Early intervention: successful pathways to improving intellectual development. *Developmental Neuropsychology*, 16, 385–392.

Ramirez, C. and Avila, A. G. (2002) Influence of teachers' causal attributions on students' academic achievements. *Psicothema*, 14, 444–449.

Rapport, M. D., Denney, C. B., Chung, K. M. and Hustace, K. (2001) Internalising behaviour problems and scholastic achievement in children: cognitive and behavioural pathways as mediators of outcome. *Journal of Clinical Child Psychology*, 30, 536–551.

Reid, D. J. and Johnson, M. (1999) Improving teaching in higher education: student and teacher perspectives. *Educational Studies*, 25, 269–281.

Rehbein, L., Hinostroza, E., Ripoll, M. and Alister, I. (2002) Students' learning through hypermedia. *Perceptual and Motor Skills*, 95, 795–805.

Reynolds, M. (1997) Learning styles: a critique. *Management Learning*, 28(2), 115–133.

Reznick, J. S., Corley, R. and Robinson, J. (1997) A longitudinal study of intelligence in the second year. *Monographs of the Society for Research in Child Development*, 62, 1–154.

Rice, J. M. (1913) *Scientific Management in Education.* Hinds, Noble and Eldredge, New York.

Richardson, K. (1991) *Understanding Intelligence.* Open University Press, Milton Keynes, Bucks.

Riding, R. J. (1991) *Cognitive Styles Analysis*. Learning and Training Technology, Birmingham.

Riding, R. J. and Burton, D. (1998) Cognitive style, gender and conduct behaviour in secondary school pupils. *Research in Education*, 60, 1–22.

Riding, R. J. and Cheema, I. (1991) Cognitive styles: an overview and integration. *Educational Psychology*, 11, 193–215.

Riding, R. J. and Craig, O. (1997) Cognitive style and problem behaviour in boys referred to residential special schools. Unpublished study cited in Riding, R. and Rayner, S., 1998, *Cognitive Styles and Learning Strategies*. David Fulton, London.

Riding, R. J. and Pearson, F. (1994) The relationship between cognitive style and intelligence. *Educational Psychology*, 14, 413–425.

Riding, R. J. and Rayner, S. (1998) *Cognitive Styles and Learning Strategies*. David Fulton, London.

Riding, R. J. and Read, G. (1996) Cognitive style and pupil learning preferences. *Educational Psychology*, 16, 81–106.

Riding, R. J. and Watts, M. (1997) The effect of cognitive style on the preferred format of instructional material. *Educational Psychology*, 17, 179–183.

Riding, R. J. and Wheeler, H. (1995) Occupational stress and cognitive style in nurses. *British Journal of Nursing*, 4, 160–168.

Riding, R. J., Burton, D., Rees, G. and Sharratt, M. (1995) Cognitive style and personality in 12-year-old children. *British Journal of Educational Psychology*, 65, 113–124.

Rimiene, R. (2002) Assessing and developing students' critical thinking *Psychology Learning and Teaching*, 2, 17–22.

Risi, S., Gerhardstein, R. and Kistner, J. (2003) Children's classroom peer relationships and subsequent educational outcomes. *Journal of Clinical Child and Adolescent Psychology*, 32, 351–361.

Roazzi, A. and Bryant, P. (1998) The effect of symmetrical and asymmetrical social interaction on children as logical inference. *British Journal of Developmental Psychology*, 16, 175–181.

Rocka, R. (2001) How does knowledge of multiple intelligence theory broaden a multi-sensory approach to the teaching of writing? In: *Multiple Intelligences in Practice* (ed. Viens, J. and Kallenbach, S.). NCSALL occasional paper.

Rogers, C. (1961) *On Becoming a Person: A Therapist's View of Psychotherapy*. Houghton-Mifflin, Boston.

Rohrbeck, C. A., Ginsbury-Block, M. D., Fantuzzo, J. W. and Miller, T. R. (2003) Peer-assisted learning interventions with elementary school students: a meta-analytic review. *Journal of Educational Psychology*, 95, 240–257.

Rosenthal, R. and Jacobson, L. (1968) *Pygmalion in the Classroom: Teacher Expectations and Pupils' Intellectual Development*. Holt, Rinehart and Winston, New York.

Rushton, J. P. (1988) Race differences in behaviour: a review and evolutionary analysis. *Personality and Individual Differences*, 9, 1009–1024.

Rust, J. and Golombok, S. (1999) *Modern Psychometrics*. Routledge, London.

Sadler-Smith, E. (2001) A reply to Reynolds's critique of learning style. *Management Learning*, 32, 291–304.

Salo, K. (1995) Teacher stress processes: how can they be explained? *Scandinavian Journal of Educational Research*, 39, 205–222.

Salovey, P. and Mayer, J. D. (1990) Emotional intelligence. *Imagination, Cognition, and Personality*, 9, 185–211.

Saracho, O. N. (1991) Students' preference for field-dependence-independence teacher characteristics. *Educational Psychology*, 11, 323–332.

Schaufeli, W. B. (1998) Burnout and lack of reciprocity among teachers. Paper presented at a symposium on teacher burnout at the Annual Meeting of the American Psychological Association, San Francisco, August 1998.

Scheerens, J. (1992) *Effective Schooling: Research, Theory and Practice*. Cassell, London.

Schon, D. A. (1983) *The Reflective Professional: How Professionals Think in Action*. Avebury, Aldershot, Hants.

Schon, D. A. (1987) *Educating the Reflective Practitioner*. Jossey Bass Wiley, San Francisco.

Schunk, D. H. (1991) Self-efficacy and academic motivation. *Educational Psychologist*, **26**, 207–232.

Schwartz, D. and Gorman, A. H. (2003) Community violence exposure and children's academic functioning. *Journal of Educational Psychology*, **95**, 163–173.

Schwartz, R. and Parks, S. (1994) *Infusing the Teaching of Critical and Creative Thinking into Content Instruction: A Lesson Design Handbook for the Elementary Grades*. Critical Thinking Press and Software, Pacific Grove CA.

Seitz, V. (1990) Intervention programmes for impoverished children: a comparison of educational and family support models. *Annals of Child Development*, **7**, 73–103.

Selinger, M. (2001a) The role of the teacher: teacherless classrooms? In: *Issues in Teaching Using ICT* (ed. Leask, M.). Routledge Falmer, London.

Selinger, M. (2001b) Setting authentic tasks using the internet in schools. In: *Issues in Teaching Using ICT* (ed. Leask, M.). Routledge Falmer, London.

Selwyn, N., Dawes, L. and Mercer, L. (2000) Promoting Mr Chips: the construction of the teacher/computer relationship in educational advertising. *Journal of Teaching and Teacher Education*, **16**(6).

Sharron, H. and Coulter, M. (1994) *Changing Children's Minds*. Imaginative Minds, Birmingham.

Shayer, M. (1999) *GCSE 1999: Added Value from Schools Adopting the CASE Intervention*. Centre for the Advancement of Learning, London.

Shields, A. and Cicchetti, D. (2001) Parental maltreatment and emotional dysregulation as risk factors for bullying and victimisation in middle childhood. *Journal of Clinical Child Psychology*, **30**, 349–363.

Shultz, N. R. and Moore, D. (1989) Further reflections on loneliness research. In: *Loneliness: Theory, Research and Applications* (ed. Hojat, M. and Crandall, R.). Sage, London.

Siegler, R. S. and Crowley, K. (1996) The microgenetic method: a direct means for studying cognitive development. In: *Critical Readings on Piaget* (ed. Smith, L.). Routledge, London.

Sigel, I. E. (1987) Early childhood education: developmental enhancement or developmental acceleration? In: *Early Schooling: The National Debate* (ed. Kagan, S. L.). Yale University Press, New Haven CT.

Simon, E. (2002) An experiment using electronic books in the classroom. *Journal of Computers in Mathematics and Science Teaching*, **21**, 53–66.

Sinason, V. (1992) *Mental Handicap and the Human Condition: New Approaches from the Tavistock*. Free Association Books, London.

Smith, P. K. and Sharpe, S. (1994) The problem of school bullying. In: *School Bullying* (ed. Smith, P. K. and Sharpe, S.). Routledge, London.

Smith, P. K., Cowie, H. and Blades, M. (1998) *Understanding Children's Development*. Blackwell, Oxford.

Smith, S. M. and Woody, P. C. (2000) Interactive effect of multimedia instruction and learning styles. *Teaching of Psychology*, **27**, 220–223.

Snowman, J. and Biehler, R. (2000) *Psychology Applied to Teaching*. Houghton-Mifflin, Boston.

Snyder, R. F. (2000) The relationship between learning styles/multiple intelligences and academic achievement of high-school students. *High School Journal*, **83**, 11–20.

Solomon, B. A. and Felder, R. (1996) *Index of Learning Styles*. North Carolina State University, Raleigh NC.

Spender, D. (1980) *Man Made Language*. Routledge & Kegan Paul, London.

Stern, W. (1912) *Differentielle Psychologie*. J. A. Barth, Leipzig.

Sternberg, R. J. (1985) *Beyond IQ: A Triarchic Theory of Human Intelligence*. Cambridge University Press, New York.

Sternberg, R. J. (1988) *The Triarchic Mind*. Viking, New York.

Sternberg, R. J. (1997) What does it mean to be smart? *Educational Leadership*, **54**, 20–24.

Sternberg, R. J. (1999) A comparison of three models for teaching psychology. *Psychology Teaching Review*, **8**, 37–43.

Sternberg, R. J. and Clinkenbeard, P. R. (1995) A triarchic model for identifying, teaching and assessing gifted children. *Roeper Review*, **17**, 255–260.

Sternberg, R. J. and Horvath, J. A. (1995) A prototype view of expert teaching. *Educational Researcher*, **24**, 9–17.

Sternberg, R. J., Torff, B. and Grigorenko, E. L. (1998) Teaching triarchically improves school achievement. *Journal of Educational Psychology*, **90**, 1–11.

Sternberg, R. J., Grigorenko, E. L. and Bundy, D. A. (2001) The predictive value of IQ. *Merrill-Palmer Quarterly*, **47**, 1–41.

Stevenson, H. W., Lee, S., Chen, C., Stigler, J., Hsu, C. C. and Kitamura, S. (1990) Contexts of achievement: a study of American, Chinese and Japanese children. *Monographs of the Society for Research in Child Development*, **55**, 1–2.

Sturman, L. (2002) *A Survey of Quality of Working Life Amongst Teachers*. NFER, Slough, Berks.

Subbotsky, E. (2000) Causal reasoning and behaviour in children and adults in a technologically advanced society: are we still prepared to believe in animism? In: *Children's Reasoning and the Mind* (ed. Mitchell, P. and Riggs, K. J.). Taylor & Francis, Hove, W. Sussex.

Subhi, T. (1999) The impact of LOGO on gifted children's achievement and creativity. *Journal of Computer-Assisted Learning*, **15**, 98–108.

Sutherland, S. (1997) *Teacher Education and Training: A Study*. National Committee of Inquiry into Higher Education.

Svensson, A. K. (2000) Computers in school: socially isolating or a tool to promote collaboration. *Journal of Educational Computing Research*, **22**, 437–453.

Taggart, A. (2004) *ILT in Hampshire, England – Past, Present and Future. How Has ILT in Hampshire Developed and Can It Be Improved for Future Learners?* Liverpool University.

Teacher Support Network (2001) *Teacher Support Line User-Satisfaction Survey: Spring 2001, Self-selecting Responses to Effectiveness of Service*. Teacher Support Network, London.

Teacher Support Network (2004) *Teacher Support Line: Four Years On*. Teacher Support Network, London.

Terman, L. M. (1916) *The Measurement of Intelligence*. Houghton-Mifflin, Boston.

Tharp, R. and Gallimore, R. (1991) A theory of teaching as assisted performance. In: *Learning to Think* (ed. Light, P., Sheldon, S. and Littleton, K.). Routledge, London.

Tobin, J. J., Wu, J. Y. D. and Davidson, D. H. (1989) Komatsudani: a Japanese preschool. In: *Cultural Worlds of Early Childhood* (ed. Woodhead, M., Faulkner, D. and Littleton, K.). Routledge, London.

Tooley, J. and Darby, D. (1998) *Educational Research: A Critique*. Ofsted, London.

Topping, K. (1998) Promoting social competence. www.dundee.ac.uk/psychology/prosoc.html.

Training Press Releases (2001) www.trainingpressreleases.com/newsstory.asp?NewsID=108. Accessed 9 February 2004.

Travers, C. and Cooper, C. (1997) Stress in teaching. In: *Directions in Educational Psychology* (ed. Shorrocks-Taylor, D.). Whurr, London.

Triona, L. M. and Klahr, D. (2003) Point and click or heft and grab: comparing the influence of physical and virtual instructional materials on elementary schools' ability to design experiments. *Cognition and Instruction*, **21**, 149–173.

Troman, G. and Woods, P. (2001) *Primary Teachers' Stress*. Routledge Falmer, New York.

Trowell, J., Jennings, C. and Burrell, S. (1996) Child sexual abuse: can we bear it? In: *The Reflective Professional in Education* (ed. Jennings, C. and Kennedy, E.). Jessica Kingsley, London.

Troy, M. and Sroufe, L. A. (1987) Victimisation among preschoolers: role of attachment relationship history. *Journal of the Academy of Child and Adolescent Psychiatry*, **26**, 166–172.

Tudge, J. R. H., Winterhoff, P. A. and Hogan, D. M. (1996) The cognitive consequences of collaborative problem-solving with and without feedback. *Child Development*, **67**, 2892–2909.

Tyler, C. (1999) Beyond the content – videoconferencing. *Speaking English*, **32**, 15–27.

Tytherleigh, M. (2003) HEFCE-funded study investigating occupational stress in higher education institutions. *Education Safety News*, July 2003.

Usher, R., Bryant, I. and Johnston, R. (1997) *Adult Education and the Postmodern Challenge*: *Learning Beyond the Limits*. Routledge, London.

van Braak, J. (2001) Individual characteristics influencing teachers' class use of computers. *Journal of Educational Computing Research*, **25**, 141–157.

van Dick, R., Wagner, U., Petzel, T., Lenke, S. and Sommer, G. (1999) Occupational stress and social support: first results of a study among schoolteachers. *Psychologie in Erziehung und Unterricht*, **46**, 55–64.

van Ijzendoorn, M. H. (1995) Adult attachment representations, parental responsiveness and infant attachment: a meta-analysis on the predictive validity of the Adult Attachment Interview. *Psychological Bulletin*, **117**, 387–403.

van Ijzendoorn, M. H. and Kroonenberg, P. M. (1988) Cross-cultural patterns of attachment: a meta-analysis of the strange situation. *Child Development*, **59**, 147–156.

van Zwanenberg, N., Wilkinson, L. J. and Anderson, A. (2000) Felder and Silverman's index of learning styles and Honey and Mumford's Learning Styles Questionnaire: how do they compare and do they predict academic performance? *Educational Psychology*, **20**, 365–380.

Vondra, J. I., Shaw, D. S., Swearingen, L., Cohen, M. and Owens, E. B. (1999) Early relationship quality from home to school: a longitudinal study. *Early Education and Development*, **10**, 163–190.

von Glasersfeld, E. (1996) Learning and adaptation in the theory of constructivism. In: *Critical Readings on Piaget* (ed. Smith, L.). Routledge, London.

Weare, K. and Gray, G. (2003) *What Works in Developing Children's Emotional and Social Competence and Well-being?* DfEE, London.

Wechsler, D. (1939) *The Measurement of Adult Intelligence*. Williams & Wilkins, Baltimore MD.

Weiner, B. (1992) *Human Motivation: Metaphors, Theories and Research*. Sage, Thousand Oaks CA.

Weinstein, F. E. and van Mater Stone, G. (1996) Learning strategies and learning to learn. In: *International Encyclopedia of Developmental and Instructional Psychology* (ed. De Corte, E. and Weinert, F. E.). Pergamon, New York, pp. 419–423.

Weller, L. D. and Hartley, S. H. (1994) Total quality management and school restructuring: Georgia's approach to educational reform. *Quality Assurance in Education*, **2**, 18–25.

Wells, G. (1994) Learning and teaching scientific concepts: Vygotsky's ideas revisited. Paper presented at the Vygotsky and Human Sciences Conference, Moscow, September 1994.

Wells, G. (1999) *Dialogic Enquiry: Towards a Sociocultural Practice and Theory of Education*. Cambridge University Press, Cambridge.

Wells, J., Barlow, J. and Stewart-Brown, S. (2003) A systematic review of universal approaches to mental health promotion in schools. *Health Education*, Vol. 4..

Wertsch, J. V. (1991) *Voices of the Mind: A Sociocultural Approach to Mediated Action*. Harvard University Press, Cambridge MA.

Wertsch, J. V. and Tulviste, P. (1996) L. S. Vygotsky and contemporary psychology. In: *Learning Relationships in the Classroom* (ed. Woodhead, M., Faulkner, D. and Littleton, K.). Routledge, London.

Wilberg, S. (2002) Preschooler's cognitive representations of their homeland. *British Journal of Developmental Psychology*, **20**, 157–170.

Wilson, V. (1997) Focus groups: a useful qualitative method for educational research? *British Educational Research Journal*, **23**, 209–224.

Wilson, V. (2000) *Educational Forum on Teaching Thinking Skills*. Scottish Executive Education Department, Edinburgh.

Witkin, H. A. (1964) Origins of cognitive style. In: *Cognition: Theory, Research, Promise* (ed. Scheerer, C.). Harper & Row, New York.

Witkin, H. A., Dyk, R. B., Faterson, H. F., Goodenough, D. R. and Karp, S. A. (1962) *Psychological Differentiation*. John Wiley, New York.

Wittenberg, I., Henry, G. and Osborne, E. (1983) *The Emotional Experience of Learning and Teaching*. Routledge, London.

Wong, E. H., Wiest, D. J. and Cusick, L. B. (2002) Perceptions of autonomy support, parent attachment, competence and self-worth as predictors of motivational orientation and academic achievement: an examination of sixth and ninth grade regular education students. *Adolescence*, **37**, 255–266.

Wood, D. (1991) *How Children Think and Learn*. Blackwell, Oxford.

Wood, D. (1998) *How Children Think and Learn*, 2nd edn. Blackwell, Oxford.

Wood, D., Bruner, J. C. and Ross, G. (1976) The role of tutoring in problem solving. *Journal of Child Psychology and Psychiatry*, **17**, 89–100.

Woodhead, C. (1999) The rise and fall of the reflective practitioner. Ofsted chief inspector's annual lecture.

Zeichner, K. and Tabachnick, B. (2001) Reflections on reflective teaching. In: *Teacher Development: Exploring Our Own Practice* (ed. Solar, J., Craft, A. and Burgess, H.). Paul Chapman, London.

Zeidner, M. and Schleyer, E. J. (1999) The big-fish-little-pond effect for academic self-concept, test anxiety and school grades in gifted children. *Contemporary Educational Psychology*, **24**, 305–329.

Zettergren, P. (2003) School adjustment in adolescence for previously rejected, average and popular children. *British Journal of Educational Psychology*, **73**, 207–221.

Zhang, F. and Hazan, C. (2002) Working models of attachment and perception processes. *Personal Relationships*, **9**, 225–235.

Zigler, E. and Seitz, B. (1982) Measure for measure? *American Psychologist*, **35**, 9.

Index

Page reference in italics indicate boxes, figures or tables

ability 43, 68
  as a social construct 6
  cognitive 50
  see also intelligence; IQ
ability grouping 64–5, *65*
  research into 65–6
accommodation, learning and 20
achievement
  celebrating 132
  IQ and 49–50
  and learning styles 86
  multiple intelligences and 56
action research 216–18, *217*
active learners 81, 85
ACTS (activating children's thinking skills) 110
  effectiveness of 111
  infusion 110
  metacognitive strategies 111
adaptation, learning and 20
agency 19, 23
Ainsworth, Mary
  and attachment theory 143–4
animism 22, 24
applicability of learning styles 76
appraisals and teacher stress 197
artefacts (tools), psychological and technical 28, 30
ASI (Approaches to Studying Inventory) 88, 91
assimilation, learning and 20
ASSIST (Approaches and Study Skills Inventory for Students) 89–90, *89*, *90*, 91, *91*
attachment theory 142
attachment types 143–4
  and bullying 152
  and emotional trauma and learning 147
  compared to Kleinian psychoanalysis 144–5
  internal working models 142–3
  sensitive responsiveness 144
  social constructivists and 6
attractiveness and sociometric status 152
attribution theory 124–7, *124*, *125*, *126*
autism 37

banding (ability grouping) 65, *65*
Bandura, Albert
  self-efficacy theory 127–9

BAS (British Ability Scales) 49
behavioural systems 142
behaviourism 5
BFLPE (big fish little pond effect) 66–7
binocular vision 6, 14
Bion, Winifred
  ideas on relationships and learning 142
Bloom's taxonomy of thinking skills 97–8, *97*
Bowlby, John
  attachment theory 142–3
bridging, thinking skills and 104
British Ability Scales (BAS) 49
bullying 154
  anti-bullying strategies 156–7
  assessing 154, *155*
  effects of 154–5
  factors affecting 156
  those most likely to be bullies and victims 152–3
burnout 183–6
  psychodynamic factors 190
  self-efficacy and 189
  see also stress

case studies 215–16
causal inferences 124, *125*, 126
causality 124–5
CCDTI (California Critical Thinking Dispositions Inventory) 114–15, *114*
centration 21
child abuse 146–7
class inclusion and cognitive development 22, 24
class system and concept of intelligence 44
cognitive ability 50
  see also intelligence
cognitive acceleration 111–12
  effectiveness of 113, *113*
  subject-specific programmes 112
  three-act model 112–13, *112*
cognitive development theory 4, 18–19, 38–9
  and ILT 172–3
  modular approach 36–8
  Piagetian theory 18–23
    applying to education 24–6
    current status of 23–4

discussion of contribution of 26–7
Vygotskian theory 27
    culture, mediation and tools 27–8
    current status of 29–30
    implications for education 32–6
    later developments in social
        constructionist theory 30–2
    role of language 29
    social interaction and ZPD 28
    see also intelligence; thinking skills
cognitive psychology 3–4, 9–10
    and motivation 124
        attribution theory 124–7
        goal orientation theory 130–2
        self-efficacy 127–9
    and reflective practice 9
cognitive restructuring in stress
        management 198–9
cognitive styles 73, 74, 77, *77*
    field dependence 77–80
    see also learning styles
Cognitive Styles Analysis (CSA) 83, 84, 85,
        85–6, 86
community of enquiry 108
componential intelligence 57
concrete operational stage of
        development 21, *21*, 23, 24
conservation, cognitive development
        and 22, 24
constructivism
    approach to learning 18
    Piagetian theory 19–27
    view of ILT 172–3
    Vygotskian theory 27–36
containment and thinking 142
contextual intelligence 57–8
contingency and scaffolding 31
control, locus of 124, *124*, 125, *125*
controllability and causality 125, *125*
cooperative learning 34–5, *35*
coping strategies for teacher stress 190,
        191–2, *191*, 197–8
correlational research 212–13
counselling
    educational therapy 149–50
    teacher stress management 199–200
craft-knowledge
    reflectivity and 14–15
    and teaching 8
creative thinking 58, 99–100
critical psychology 6–7
    and intelligence research 44
critical thinking 99
    development in higher education
        114–15
    philosophy for children and 107, *107*
    triarchic theory and 58

cross-lagging in research 213
CSA (Cognitive Styles Analysis) 83, 84, 85,
        85–6, 86
culture
    and child's development 27–8, 30
    culture of achievement 129
    importance of firm cultural
        foundation 103
    variation in understandings of
        'intelligence' 45
current affairs, thinking about 109, *109*
curriculum
    multiple intelligences and curriculum
        development 54–5
    National Curriculum and Piaget's
        theory 24–5

decentring 24, 25
Deci, Edward
    self-determination theory 122
deep learning 87, *87*, 90, 91
defensive unthinking 11
depersonalisation, stress and 184
depressive position 141
DIAS (Direct and Indirect Aggression
        Scales) 154, *155*
discipline, classroom
    and stress 188
discovery learning 26, 27
disequilibrium, sensation of 20
domain-general and domain-specific
        theories of cognitive
        development 36–8
Dweck, Carol
    goal orientation theory 130–2
    research into intelligence beliefs 45–7,
        46

e-learning 165, 169
education
    applying field independence to 78–9
    applying multiple intelligences to
        53–6, *54*, *55*
    applying Piaget's ideas to 24–6
    applying triarchic theory to 58
    implications of social constructivist
        theory for 32–6
education research 204–5, 222–3
    aims and purpose 206–7, *207*
    criticisms and limitations of 220–1
        quality issue 221
        relevance issue 221–2
    epistemological foundations 207–8
    historical context 205–6
    into relationships and education 145–9
    major research methods 209, *210*
        action research 216–18, *217*

case studies 215–16
correlation 212–13
experiment 210–12
surveys 213–15
multiple studies 218
discussion of review methods 220
meta-analysis 219–20, *220*
systematic review 218–19
qualitative versus quantitative
methods 208–9
educational therapy 5, 149–50, *150*
EFT (Embedded Figures Test) 78, *78*
egocentric speech 29
egocentrism 22, 25, *25*
emotional factors 4–5, 138–40, 161
emotional intelligence 158
development programmes 158,
160–1
emotional competencies 158, *159*
learning and relationships 140
attachment theory 142–4
Kleinian psychoanalysis 140–2
theories compared 144–5
peer relationships 150–1
bullying 154–7
sociometric status 151–4
research into relationships and
education 144
educational therapy 149–50
family relationships 145–7
teacher relationships 147–9
teacher response to theory and
research 13
emotional intelligence 158
development programmes 158, 160
effectiveness of programmes 160–1
taxonomy of emotional competences
158, *159*
engineering model of education
research 206, 207
entity beliefs 47, 130–1, 132
environment and intelligence
development 60–2
epistemology 207–8
equilibrium, state of 20
ethnic groups
bullying and 154
stereotyping abilities of 133–4
eugenics movement 44–5
evaluation apprehension and teacher
stress 188
evaluation as a thinking skill 99
executive model of the teacher 7
expectations and motivation 132–4
experiential intelligence 57
experimental research 210–12
extrinsic motives 119

family relationships 145–6
child abuse 146–7
levels of support 146
and teacher relationships 148–9
Felder, R. & Silverman, L.
ILS (Index of Learning Styles) 80–2, *82*,
84–5, *85*, 86
Fenstermacher, G.D. & Soltis, J.F
classification of teachers 7–8
Feuerstein, Reuven 102
instrumental enrichment 102–6
field dependence and field
independence 77–8, *77*
applying field independence to
education 78–9
discussion of 79–80
EFT (Embedded Figures Test) 78, *78*
and ILT use 175–6
Fisher, Robert
and philosophy for children 107–9
thinking process cues 98, *98*
focus groups 213, 214–15
Fodor, Jerry
modular theory 37
formal operational stage of development
21, 23, 24, 28
Fowler, W.
accelerated language development
programme 64
France, teacher stress in 186–7
friendships 153
benefits of 153–4

Galton, Francis
and eugenics movement 44
Gardner, Howard *51*
multiple intelligences theory 51–6, *52*
gender
and cognitive style 78
and ILT use 176
as a social construct 6
general intelligence 50
genes and intelligence 60–2
giftedness 66, *67*
BFLPE (big fish little pond effect)
66–7
psychological well-being of gifted
children 67–8
global learners 81
goals
goal orientation theory 130–2, *130*
self-efficacy and 129, *129*
see also motivation
group work 34–5, *35*

Harry Stottlemeier's Discovery (Lipman)
107

Hawthorne effect and education
   experiments 211–12
Headstart project, USA 62–3
helplessness-oriented learners 130
hermeneutic approach 208
heuristics 12, 32
   and evaluation of learning styles 76,
      85–6
   value of learning strategies 91
   value of reflectivity 9
higher education, thinking skills in
   114–15
Honey, P. & Mumford, A.
   Learning Style Questionnaire 83–4, *83*,
      84–5, *84*, 85, 212, *212*
hothousing 63–4
humanistic psychology 5, 119
   Maslow's hierarchy of needs 120–2,
      120
   self-determination theory 122–3, *123*
hypermedia 166–7, 168
   learning style and use of 176

ICT (information and communication
      technology) 164
   basic terminology 165–8
   factors affecting uptake 169–71, *170*
   see also ILT
ideology and teaching models 7
IDZs (intermental development zones)
      32
ILS (Index of Learning Styles) 80–2, *82*,
      84–5, *84*, 85, 86
ILT (information and learning
      technology) 165, 176–7
   benefits of
      constructivist view 172–3
      social constructivist view 173–5
   delivery methods 165–8
   effectiveness in enhancing learning
      168–9
   factors affecting uptake 169–72
   individual differences in use 175–6
Implicit Theories of Intelligence Scale
      45–7, *46*
incremental beliefs 47, 130–1, 132
Index of Learning Styles (ILS) 80–2, *82*,
      84–5, *84*, 85, 86
infusion approach to thinking skills
      development 110
insight 5
inspection systems and teacher stress
      193, *193*
instrumental enrichment 102–3
   cultural deprivation and 103
   effectiveness of 106
   instruments of enrichment 104–6, *105*

mediation 103–4
   and structured mediation 104
intelligence 4, 13, 43, 68
   and academic ability 43
   beliefs about 45–7, *46*
   cultural variation in understanding of
      45, 99
   developing
      ability grouping 64–6, *64*
      giftedness 66–8, *67*
      hothousing 63–4
      nature-nurture debate 60–2
      preschool intervention 62–3
   emotional 158–61
   general intelligence 50
   multiple intelligences 50–6
   as a social construct 6, 44–5
   triarchic theory of 57–60, 98
   see also IQ
interactive whiteboards 167–8
intermental development zones (IDZs) 32
internal working models 142–3
internet and education 168–9, 172
interpretative approach 208
interviews, research 213, 214
intranets 165–6, 173–4
intrinsic motives 118
introjection 141
intuitive learners 81
IQ (intelligence quotient) 43
   child abuse and 146–7
   and class 44
   evidence for possibility of increasing
      61, *61*
   gifted children 66, *67*
   and performance 49–50
   tests and testing 43, 47–9, *48*, *49*, 52,
      205
      field independents and 79
      Sternberg's triarchic theory and 59

Jacobson, L. & Rosenthal, R.
   study into 'Pygmalion effect' 132–3,
      133

Karmiloff-Smith, A.
   progressive modularisation 37–8
Klein, Melanie
   ideas concerning relationships 140–2,
      145–6
knowledge
   'in action' 9
   on intermental and intramental
      planes 28
   metacognitive 101, *102*
Kyriacou, Chris
   model of teacher stress 194, *195*

language
    and cognitive development 29, 30
    Fowler accelerated language
        development programme 64
    literate 153
leadership styles and teacher stress
        192–3
learning
    cognitive development 18, 38–9
        modular approach 36–8
        Piagetian theory 18–27
        Vygotskian theory 27–36
    definitions of 2–3
    psychological paradigms and 3–7
learning (mastery) goals 130–1, *130*
learning strategies 73, 74, 86–7
    assessing learning strategy 88–90, *89,
        90*
    deep and shallow learning 87–8
    developing strategic learning 91–2
    evaluation of learning strategies
        approach 91
    knowledge of 101, *102*
    strategic learners 88, *88*
Learning Style Questionnaire (LSQ) 83–4,
        83, 84–5, *84, 85*, 212, *212*
learning styles 4, 72–3, 74, 92–3
    classification systems
        evaluating 75–6
        multidimensional 80–4, *80*
        multidimensional compared 84–6
        multidimensional discussed 86
    and ILT 175–6
    see also cognitive styles; learning
        strategies
Lewin, Kurt
    and action research 216
liberationist model of the teacher 7
Lipman, Matthew
    and philosophy for children 106–7
literate language 153
locus of control 124, *124*, 125, *125*
Logo programming language 172–3
'lone scientists' children as 20, 26
LSQ (Learning Style Questionnaire) 83–4,
        83, 84–5, *84, 85*, 212, *212*

MA (mental age) 48
managed learning environments (MLEs)
        166, *167*
Maslow's hierarchy of needs 120–2, *120*
mastery goals 130–1, *130*
MBTI (Myers-Briggs type indicator) 81
mediation
    and culture and development 27–8
    and instrumental enrichment 103–4
mental age (MA) 48

Mercer, N.
    Talk lessons programme 33
meta-analysis of research 219–20, *220*
metacognition 101, *102*
    metacognitive strategies and ACTS 111
MIs *see* multiple intelligences
MLEs (managed learning environments)
        166, *167*
MLEs (mediated learning experiences)
        103
modular theory 37–8
    Gardener's multiple intelligences
        51–6, *52*
motivation 23, 118, 134
    agency 19, 23
    cognitive approaches to 124
        attribution theory 124–7
        goal orientation theory 130–2
        self-efficacy 127–9
    and depth of learning 87
    effects of expectations 47, 132–4,
        133
    group work and 35
    humanistic tradition and 119
        Maslow's hierarchy of needs 120–2,
            120
        self-determination theory 122–3,
            123
    intrinsic and extrinsic motives 118–19
    significance of 119
multimedia 56, 166
multiple intelligences (MIs) 50
    applying to education 53–6, *54*
    assessing 52, *53*
    Gardner's theory 51, *52*
    Gardner's theory discussed 56
    and ILT use 175–6
    relationship with achievement 56
multiple regression (correlation) 213
multisensory learning 55–6, *55*
Mumford, A. & Honey, P.
    Learning Style Questionnaire 83–4, *83,
        84*–5, *84, 85*, 212, *212*
Myers-Briggs type indicator (MBTI) 81

National Curriculum
    and Piaget's stages of development
        24–5
natural experiments 211
nature-nurture debate and intelligence
        development 60–2
needs
    Maslow's hierarchy of needs 120–2,
        120
    self-determination theory and 122
NQTs (newly qualified teachers) and
        stress 197

NUT (National Union of Teachers)
    action plan for teacher stress 195–6,
        196

Olweus anti-bullying programme 157,
        157
Operation Headstart, USA 62–3
operations (rules) 20–1

Papert, Seymour
    on ILT 172
paradigms 3
paranoid-schizoid position 141
parataxic distortion 141
partial correlation 212–13
Participant Roles Scale 153
peer relationships 150–1
    bullying 154
        anti-bullying strategies 156–7
        assessing 154
        effects of 154–5
        factors affecting 156
    and cognitive development
        computer-aided tasks 174–5
        group work 34–5
        peer tutoring 36
    sociometric status and 151, *151*
        and educational achievement 153–4
        factors affecting 152–3
performance goals 130–1, *130*
    see also achievement
personal knowledge 101, *102*
personality
    and teacher stress 189–92
    teacher's personal characteristics
        13–14
    and teaching models 7
perturbation, sensation of 20
Pettijohn's locus of control scale 124,
        124
phantasy 140
philosophy for children 106–7
    discussion and community of enquiry
        107–8
    effectiveness of 110
    stories for thinking 108–9
    thinking about current affairs 109
physical attractiveness and sociometric
        status 152
Piaget, Jean 18–19, *19*
    applying his ideas to education 24–6
    challenges to his theory 36–8
    current status of his ideas 23–4
    discussion of his contributions 26–7
    his theory of learning 18–23
positivism 9–10, 208
postmodernism 5, 10, 208

practice
    reflective 8–11
    relationship with theory 11–12
pre-experiments 210
preoperational stage of development 21,
        21–2, *21*, 23–4
    challenged 23–4
    and language 29
preschool intervention programmes
        62–3
problem-solving 26
progressive modularisation approach
        37–8
psychodynamic psychology 4–5
    attachment theory 142–4
    Kleinian psychoanalysis 140–2
    theories compared 144–5
psychological tools 28, 30
psychology 3
    see also cognitive psychology;
        humanistic psychology;
        psychodynamic psychology;
        social contructionism
psychometric tests 75
    assessing thinking skills 114–15
    of learning strategy 91
    of learning style classifications 75–6,
        84–5, 85–6
'Pygmalion effect', studies into 132–4,
        133

qualitative and quantitative methods of
        research 208–9
quasi-experiments 211
questionnaires, research 213, 214

RASI (revised Approaches to Studying
        Inventory) 88, *89*, 91
Raven's progressive matrices 44
REBT (rational emotive behaviour
        therapy) 199
reciprocal teaching 34
reflective learners 81, 85
reflective practice 8
    recent work on 10–11
    reflectivity and craft-knowledge 14–15
    Schon's approach 8–10
    and theory, research and practice
        11–12
regression to the mean 212
relationships 139, 140
    educational therapy 149–50, *150*
    family relationships 145–7
    peer relationships 150–1
        bullying 154–7
    sociometric status and 151–4
    psychodynamic theories 140

attachment theory 142–4
  Kleinian psychoanalysis 140–2
  theories compared 144–5
teacher relationships 147–9
research 12, 204–5, 222–3
  aims and purpose 206–7, 207
  criticisms and limitations of 220–1
    quality issue 221
    relevance issue 221–2
  epistemological foundations 207–8
  historical context 205–6
  into relationships and education
      145–9
  major research methods 209, 210
    action research 216–18, 217
    case studies 215–16
    correlation 212–13
    experiment 210–12
    surveys 213–15
  multiple studies 218
    discussion of review methods
        220
    meta-analysis 219–20, 220
    systematic review 218–19
  personal responses to 12–13
  qualitative versus quantitative
      methods 208–9
Rice, J.M.
  education research 206
Riding, Richard
  model of learning styles 82–3
role overload and stress 188
Rosenthal, R. & Jacobson, L.
    study into 'Pygmalion effect' 132–3,
        133

scaffolding 30–2
educational software and 174
schemas 20, 23
Schon, D.A.
  model of professional expertise
      8–10
selection (ability grouping) 65, 65
self knowledge 101, 102
self-actualisation 120, 121, 122
self-awareness 11
self-determination theory 121–2, 122
self-efficacy 127–9, 129
  and teacher stress 189
self-esteem 121–2, 127
sensitive responsiveness 144
sensorimotor stage of development 21,
    21
sensory learners 81
sequential learners 81
setting (ability grouping) 65, 65
shallow (surface) learning 87, 90, 91

Silverman, L. & Felder, R.
  ILS (Index of Learning Styles) 80–2, 82,
      84–5, 84, 85, 86
social constructionism 5–7, 10, 12
  and cognitive development 19
    challenge to 36–8
    developments after Vygotsky 30–2
    implications for education 32–6
    Vygotsky's theory 27–30
  and concept of intelligence 44–5
  and reflective practice 9
  view of ILT 173–5
social interaction
  and development of language 29
  and learning 20, 27, 29–30
  and zone of proximal development 28
social releasers 142
social skills and sociometric status 152
sociometric status 151, 151
  and educational achievement 153–4
  factors affecting 152–3
Socrates (Greek philosopher) 107
software
  gender bias in 176
  interaction with 174
  Papert's criticism's of 172
Soltis, J.F & Fenstermacher, G.D.
  classification of teachers 7–8
speech, egocentric and internalised 29,
    30
splitting 141
stability and causality 125, 125
Stanford-Binet IQ test 47–8
stereotyping
  of abilities of ethnic groups 133–4
  and entity and incremental beliefs 132
Sternberg, Robert 57
  triarchic theory of intelligence 57–60,
      98
stories for thinking 108–9
strategies see learning strategies
strategy knowledge 101, 102
streaming (ability grouping) 65, 65
stress 180–1, 200–1
  burnout 183–5
  causal factors 186–7
    individual differences 189–92
    intrinsic to teaching 187–9
    systemic factors 192–3
    transactional picture 194, 195
  common symptoms 184
  defensive unthinking and 11
  defining teacher stress 182–3
  legal context 181–2
  managing 194–5
    cognitive interventions 198–9
    combined interventions 200

counselling services 199–200
    individual interventions 197–8
    organisational interventions 195–7
    measuring teacher stress 183, *185*
Surestart project, UK 63
surface learning 87, 90, 91
survey research 213–15
systematic review of research 218–19,
        220

Tabachnick, B. & Zeichner, K.
    classification of reflective practice
        10–11, *10*
Talk lessons programme 33, *34*
targets
    goal orientation theory 130–2, *130*
    self-efficacy and 129, *129*
    see also motivation
task knowledge 101, *102*
Teacher Support Network 199, 200
teachers and teaching 7
    craft-knowledge 8
        reflectivity and 14–15
    definitions of teaching 3
    Fenstermacher and Soltis'
        classification of teachers 7–8
    and ICT 170–1
    personal characteristics of teachers
        13–14
    personal responses to theory and
        research 12–13
    pupil-teacher relationships 147–9
    teacher as reflective professional 8–12
    teacher stress 180–1, 200–1
        burnout 183–6
        causal factors 186–94, *195*
        defining 182–3
        legal context 181–2
        managing 194–200
        measuring 183, *185*
        symptoms *184*
    teachers as source of attributions
        126–7
    see also education
technical rationality 9
technical tools 28
theory 12
    personal responses to 12–13
    relationship with practice 11–12
    see also research
therapist model of the teacher 7
thinking skills 4, 96–9
    creative thinking 99–100
    critical thinking 99
    current work on developing 100–1,
        102, 115

development programmes 102
    ACTS (activating children's thinking
        skills) 110–11
    cognitive acceleration 111–13
    instrumental enrichment 102–6
    philosophy for children 106–10
    in higher education 114–15
    Piaget and 26
    see also cognitive development
        theory; cognitive styles
tools, psychological and technical 28,
        30
TQM (total quality management) 197
transference and relationships 5, 141
triadic dialogue 33
triarchic theory of intelligence 57–8
    applying to education 58
    discussion of 59–60
    effectiveness of triarchic teaching
        59
    and IQ testing 59
true experiments 210–11
twin studies 61

uncertainty and scaffolding 31

verbal learners 81, 85
videoconferencing 167, 169
visual learners 81, 85, 175
VLEs (virtual learning environments)
        166, *167*
Vygotsky, Lev 19, 26
    application of his theory to education
        32–6
    challenge to his theory 36–8
    current status of his theory 29–30
    developments from his theory 30–2
    his theory on cognitive development
        27–9

Wechsler IQ test 48, *48, 49*
Weiner, Bernard
    attribution theory 124–7
whiteboards, interactive 167
whole-class interactive teaching 32–3,
        168
Williams syndrome 37
workload and teacher stress 187–8

Zeichner, K. & Tabachnick, B.
    classification of reflective practice
        10–11, *10*
zone of proximal development (ZPD) 28,
        29, 30–1, *31*
    educational software and 174
    theoretical alternative to 32